Praise for *The Retire Sooner Method*

"I retired sooner, and I encourage you to give yourself the same option. Wes Moss' book can help you on this journey. *The Retire Sooner Method* is like discovering the 'latte factor' of your entire retirement life—small, intentional moves that quietly add up to years of freedom you didn't know you could afford."

—**DAVID BACH**, 10x *New York Times* best-selling author, including *The Automatic Millionaire* and *The Latte Factor*

"Wes and I both see money for what it is—a tool, not the end goal. This book is the retire-sooner version of *rich living on less*, presenting practical, research-backed steps to get your financial life dialed in so you can spend more time and energy on the 'super activities' that actually make life feel full."

—**JOEL LARSGAARD**, cofounder and cohost, *How To Money* podcast

"In *The Retire Sooner Method*, Wes Moss lets you capitalize on his years of experience. You can feel his expertise deftly breaking down practical ways to not only have more money but build a life you're actually excited to wake up to."

—**JOE SAUL-SEHY**, creator and cohost, *Stacking Benjamins* and *Stacking Adventures* podcasts

"Living large for the long haul means stretching every dollar without feeling deprived. What I appreciate here is how this book combines smart money moves with concrete ideas for building a life you actually love living in retirement."

—**CLARK HOWARD**, 3x *New York Times* best-selling author; nationally syndicated radio host, *The Clark Howard Show*; and host, *The Clark Howard Podcast*

"Most retirement books read like they were written by robots for other robots. Wes actually studied happy human beings. If you're cynical about Wall Street, politicians, and the whole circus—but still want a shot at a free and interesting life after work—this is the rare book that talks to you like an adult."

—**ERIC VON HAESSLER**, award-winning radio host and creator, *The Von Haessler Doctrine*

THE RETIRE SOONER METHOD

THE RETIRE SOONER METHOD

The 5 Secrets Behind America's Happiest (and Unhappiest) Retirees

WES MOSS

Kiplinger
BOOKS

Kiplinger Books
New York, New York
www.kiplinger.com

Distributed by Greenleaf Book Group

For ordering information or special discounts for bulk purchases, please contact Greenleaf Book Group at PO Box 91869, Austin, TX 78709, 512.891.6100.

Design and composition by Greenleaf Book Group
Cover design by Porchlight
Graphics for the 2025 Money and Happiness in America study illustrated by Porchlight
Figure 8.4 data from DALBAR's *2025 Quantitative Analysis of Investor Behavior (QAIB) Report*. Used with permission.

Publisher's Cataloging-in-Publication data is available.

Print ISBN: 978-1-969190-02-5

eBook ISBN: 978-1-969190-03-2

To offset the number of trees consumed in the printing of our books, Greenleaf donates a portion of the proceeds from each printing to the Arbor Day Foundation. Greenleaf Book Group has replaced over 50,000 trees since 2007.

Printed in the United States of America on acid-free paper

26 27 28 29 30 31 32 33 10 9 8 7 6 5 4 3 2 1

I dedicate this book to my wife and four boys,
my partners at CIA, and my family and friends:
all that truly matters in this world.

CONTENTS

INTRODUCTION: Your Roadmap to Yes 1

PART ONE: THE RETIRE SOONER METHOD 7

1: The Happy Retiree Basics 9

2: Secret #1: The Money Green Zones 25

3: Secret #2: Super Activities, aka Hobbies on Steroids 47

4: Secret #3: Get a Life! (i.e., a Community) 69

5: Secret #4: Mapping Out Your Future 89

6: Secret #5: The Happy Retiree Superpower 113

PART TWO: MONEY MATTERS 131

7: Wilting Dollars and Shrinking Dreams: The Truth About Inflation 133

8: The Five Pillars of Income Investing: An Antidote to Wilting Dollars 149

CONCLUSION: Time to Say Yes 193

APPENDIX A: Research and Data Descriptions 199

APPENDIX B: Planning Tools and Frameworks 211

ACKNOWLEDGMENTS 217

NOTES 221

INDEX 227

ABOUT THE AUTHOR 235

INTRODUCTION

Your Roadmap to Yes

I'm an American. That means I get on a wild roadway every day, just like you.

I used to fire up Waze to find the fastest route through traffic, until I got annoyed by the purple line—too distracting. So I switched over to Google Maps, which kept flipping upside down on me. Plus it talks too much. The last thing I want to do while driving my boys to a lacrosse game is fiddle around with my phone to put the directions lady on silent. Lately I've been using Apple Maps, which is okay so far, but I'm still waiting for the ghost of Steve Jobs to call me out on a wrong turn.

All these apps are basically the same. We enter our destination—maybe it's our kids' school, maybe it's work, maybe it's home—and our phone spits out a couple of routes. For our purposes, we'll say those routes are all around thirty minutes.

Of course, if you live in Atlanta, like I do—or really any big city in America—thirty can easily turn into thirty-two, then thirty-five. For all the advancements of tech and AI, the app doesn't understand how bad traffic is ahead of us.

So when we see that fabled "thirty minutes," our brains throw down the psychological gauntlet. We're determined to beat the map app. Because in my mind, when I see thirty minutes, I inevitably think, *I can do it in twenty-eight.*

I maintain this isn't just about my need for speed. It's something we inherently do as humans. We want to get things done sooner. We want to get there a little faster. And if we time the stoplights just right, we might shave off a couple of minutes—the first victory of our day.

At first, two minutes may not sound like a big deal. But two minutes on a thirty-minute trip isn't nothing. When you divide two by thirty, it comes out to a little over .06; in other words, 6 percent.

Here's where it gets interesting. Let's say you're planning to retire at sixty-five, when Medicare kicks in and you start collecting Social Security. What if you "shaved two minutes" off your trip? Apply that same 6 percent to those sixty-five years and you get a little over four years. **That means you could retire at sixty-one—*and get four years of your life back.***

Imagine what you could do with those four years. What trips would you take? What activities would you engage in? What kind of impact—physically, mentally, emotionally—would it have on your life?

Imagine what you could do with even just *one* year. How would you feel waking up every morning with the knowledge that your day is yours to do with what you will?

I've been studying retirees for nearly two decades. Along the way, I've discovered dozens of lifestyle and financial habits that tip the scales toward a happy retirement. It's become my passion and my purpose, sparking multiple national research studies, books, radio shows, and hundreds of insightful messages from readers and listeners. A few years back, we launched the *Retire Sooner* podcast, founded on a simple mission: to help at least one million Americans of any age retire sooner, creating a million years of extra joy and freedom. The podcast grew into the Retire Sooner Method: the title of the book you're reading right now.

Like any method worth its salt, this one needed to be stress-tested with fresh data. Honestly, I didn't anticipate any big surprises when our team began the 2025 "Money and Happiness in America" study. The core tenets of our approach—both the financial principles and lifestyle habits—have stayed constant. After all this time, I thought I knew the game.

But the data revealed something so fundamental, so deceptively simple, it reframed everything: **Simply getting to retirement raises happiness levels by more than 20 percent.** Just being able to say "Yes, I'm retired" is already a massive happiness boost.

So how do you become what I like to call the "happiest retiree on the block"?

To answer that, let me tell you where this whole idea came from.

HOW IT ALL BEGAN

When my first book, *You Can Retire Sooner Than You Think*, came out more than a decade ago, my goal was simple: to share the habits of happy retirees with a wider audience. It was also the first time I introduced the idea of the "happiest retiree on the block," which had become a guiding principle behind the book. But I've never told the origin story of how that came to be.

When my wife, Lynne, and I were sleep-deprived new parents hungry for guidance, there was a popular book called *The Happiest Baby on the Block*. The idea was to offer a systematic approach to keeping your baby happy based on observation and research, not guesswork. A restaurant server told us about it one night. The next morning, I was listening to the radio while brushing my teeth and someone did a book review. I thought, *Wow, this book is everywhere.*

Then a light bulb went off. If someone could write a book on what makes babies happy, why couldn't I write a book about what makes retirees happy? What about the happiest *retiree* on the block?

That's right. The concept of the "HROB" was born right there at my bathroom sink.

If you really think about the definition of *happiness*, it's a tough one. Philosophers and psychologists have spent centuries trying to figure this out. Is it about "hedonistic" happiness—pleasure, comfort, and the absence of pain? Or is it about "eudaemonic" happiness—the deeper fulfillment that comes from purpose, connection, and meaning?

Hedonistic sounds a little like a wild weekend in Las Vegas to me—not something most retirees are looking for. (Though if you're the exception to the rule, more power to you; just don't forget the Advil.) For the purposes of this book, we'll be talking about happiness of the eudaemonic strain. We're not measuring how someone feels in a particular moment but rather their overall sense of well-being in life.

Aristotle figured this out over two thousand years ago, in ancient Greece, when he wrote about eudaemonia. For Aristotle, happiness wasn't an amazing trip or a feast or a massive villa; it was the lifelong pursuit of living with purpose and intention. It's something that reveals itself over the course of time through steady effort and growth.

In the Retire Sooner Method, happiness is Aristotle-approved: It comes from purpose, connection, curiosity, and using your gifts in ways that matter. The happiest retirees I know aren't chasing constant pleasure. They're building lives that feel engaged, rich, and aligned with who they really are. They have deep, steady satisfaction that comes from having people they love, work or activities they care about, and enough financial breathing room to spend their years doing what engages and inspires them.

Unhappiness, on the other hand, shows up when life drifts away from meaning and control. It's the slow erosion that happens when purpose fades, connections shrink, or days feel empty instead of intentional. Unhappy retirees aren't necessarily in pain—they're unanchored. Their time isn't directed toward activities that grow them or allow them to contribute to others, and that absence of purpose leaves room for worry, rumination, and restlessness. In the Retire Sooner Method, unhappiness is less about hardship or financial insecurity and more about disconnection from the values, people, and activities that make life worth living.

My goal is to keep you out of the unhappy camp with the UROBs (*un*happiest retirees on the block) and get you to a happy retirement sooner than you might have thought possible.

Since my first book came out, I've been hearing from more and more people who say things like, "I'm sixty and I'd like to retire," or "I'm fifty-eight and I'm thinking about retirement," or "I'm fifty, and I know this sounds crazy . . . but my wife and I want to know if we can make it work."

It doesn't sound crazy to me at all. That's the whole reason I do what I do: to help people shave those one, two, even five minutes—aka years—off the journey. All of my books are part of a broader movement in America to figure out how to retire sooner than conventional wisdom says you can.

For our 2025 study, I went back to the drawing board to see if I could learn even more. Boy, did I ever. We surveyed over twelve hundred Americans aged fifty and up across every region of the country, exploring how everything from finances and friendships to purpose and sleep shapes happiness in retirement. The 2025 Money and Happiness in America study revealed five deceptively simple "secrets" that became the foundation for everything you'll read in this book.

HOW TO READ THIS BOOK

Good news: You don't have to read this book cover to cover. If you already have your finances dialed in and want to focus on purpose and connection, you might skip to Chapters 3 and 4. If you're solid on lifestyle but need help with investment strategy, consider going straight to Chapters 7 and 8. The appendix includes and summarizes the key research behind each figure in the book, giving a simple explanation of what every chart or illustration is meant to show—perfect for those who would rather skip right to the data than read my commentary.

But however you choose to engage with this book, know this: The happiest retirees aren't lucky. Before they enjoy that 20 percent happiness boost from saying yes to retirement, they've faithfully followed the Retire Sooner Method. In the pages that follow, you'll find that method, complete with the best routes, real-life examples, and research-backed shortcuts to get you there sooner. If the method were a cake, think of these five secrets as five ingredients—and we're giving you the recipe. I've even included a recipe card on page 198.

You're on the road to "yes" already; you picked up this book.

So let's stop talking about it and start driving. Your destination is up ahead. Why not get there sooner than you think?

PART ONE

THE RETIRE SOONER METHOD

CHAPTER 1

The Happy Retiree Basics

The world has changed dramatically since I first started studying happy retirees.

We've had three presidents, lived through a global pandemic, endured inflation levels not seen since the 1970s, and watched the economy swing from boom to near-bust and back again. Supply chains have collapsed and been rebuilt, and with the Great Resignation, the very nature of work has transformed. My wife and I had our fourth son; a fervent pickleball craze swept the nation; Tom Brady retired, then unretired, then retired again.

Yet through all this turmoil—economic, political, cultural, and the amount of carpooling in my family—**the core financial and lifestyle principles of happy retirees have stood strong.**

Our 2025 Money and Happiness in America study—the first national study of its kind—showed that the overarching principles we first introduced in *You Can Retire Sooner Than You Think* have held true for over a decade. It also revealed new insights and surprising secrets from real-life retirees who have been able to retire sooner and happier, Americans who've discovered **five secrets that unlock a 96 percent chance of happiness.**

Now, you might wonder: why exactly five? Our research identified more than twenty-five factors that influence retirement satisfaction—everything from health habits to housing decisions to what kind of core pursuits people choose. You could certainly pick seven factors, or ten, or for the overachievers, try to tackle all twenty-five. But when we analyzed our findings to distill the most efficient combination that mathematically produces the highest probability of happiness, by nailing the fewest of the habits, these five secrets rose to the top:

- **Secret #1: Hit the Money Green Zones.** Build a nest egg of $1 million or more in liquid investable assets, observing the 4+ percent rule of thumb for withdrawals. You should also have multiple income sources and a mortgage payoff within sight.
- **Secret #2: Boost your core pursuits.** You know those meaningful activities and "hobbies on steroids" that bring joy and purpose to your life? Spend five-plus *more* hours a week doing them—and seek out new adventures to enrich your days.
- **Secret #3: Build a community.** Cultivate four or more close friendships through consistent socialization and genuine connection. Plot twist: Weave those friends into your core pursuits, combining Secrets #2 and #3 for the ultimate happiness hack.
- **Secret #4: Map out your future.** Create a written financial plan or life map. Both are strategic tools that transform anxiety into confidence. This doesn't have to be laborious—it can even be fun!
- **Secret #5: Harness the Happy Retiree Superpower.** Prioritize quality sleep as the foundation that makes everything else

possible. Aim for a solid seven to eight hours, so you feel rested and restored.

If you could focus on only five things to maximize your chances of a happy retirement, these would be the ones. Think of it as the minimum effective dose.

When we boiled the secrets down to five, we didn't tear down the house of our original research from 2014. But we did renovate with brand new data, shoring up and expanding the old research. Now the happy house is sparkling and up to date, with an island in the kitchen. Who doesn't love a kitchen island?

This book is not me sharing my personal thoughts and feelings about how much money you'll need to be able to retire or how many core pursuits you should have. It's less about my opinion on what works and more about what the research shows. As described earlier, the data for our Money and Happiness in America study comes from a comprehensive study of twelve hundred Americans across all fifty states—carefully mapped to US Census proportions to ensure accurate representation—done in partnership with CGK Research. These were people aged fifty-plus, both approaching retirement and in retirement; in other words, people just like you.

In the pages that follow, we'll roll up our sleeves and dig into the juicy data. But first, let's acknowledge the challenge.

THE REALITY CHECK: WHERE MOST AMERICANS STAND

According to the Federal Reserve's Survey of Consumer Finances, the median net worth for Americans aged fifty-five to sixty-four—those approaching or in early retirement—stands at just $364,270. That's everything: home equity, retirement accounts, brokerage accounts, bank accounts, the works.[1]

The 2025 Money and Happiness in America study shows that Americans who want to land in the happy retiree zone should target the $1 million range or more in liquid, investable assets. When you see that gap between $364,270 and $1 million—a whopping $635,000—it's no wonder 55 percent of older Americans report being anxious about their financial future.[2]

But people are also anxious because they're getting bad intel. On a recent episode of the *Afford Anything* podcast, Suze Orman said, "Two million is nothing. It's nothing. It's pennies in today's world, to tell you the truth." Then she dropped the real bomb: that $10 million is the bare minimum. She asserted that you need "$20 (million), $30 (million), $50 (million) or $100 million" to retire early.[3]

But the numbers we've uncovered in our latest research paint a different story—a far more manageable and attainable story for a much greater percentage of Americans. Of course, that's assuming you're not island-hopping on your private jet between your homes in Manhattan and Malibu every month.

I'm here to give you hope that you don't need to be Jeff Bezos's cousin in order to have a magically fulfilling retirement. You don't have to be wealthy enough to encase yourself in bubble wrap and attend the Met Gala with the Kardashians. The secret isn't having tens of millions—it's achieving the freedom to choose how you spend your days.

The good news is that our research has uncovered much more attainable financial levels, which I believe anyone in the US can reach with enough time and discipline, as well as lifestyle habits, behaviors, and checkpoints—and this can ultimately lead to a very happy retirement. This, in a nutshell, is the Retire Sooner Method.

It all starts with a small but mighty three-letter word.

THE POWER OF YES

In America, the word *retirement* often carries negative baggage. There's this underlying assumption that once you're retired, you're leaving the world of productivity, socialization, and meaning—that you're somehow stepping off the grand stage of life. This flawed notion stubbornly persists: Retirement means you're being put out to pasture, at your kitchen table online shopping for a deal on the new swivel glide La-Z-Boy rather than finally being free to pursue what matters most to you.

FIGURE 1.1. Happiness Levels of Americans Who Are Retired vs. Non-Retired[4]

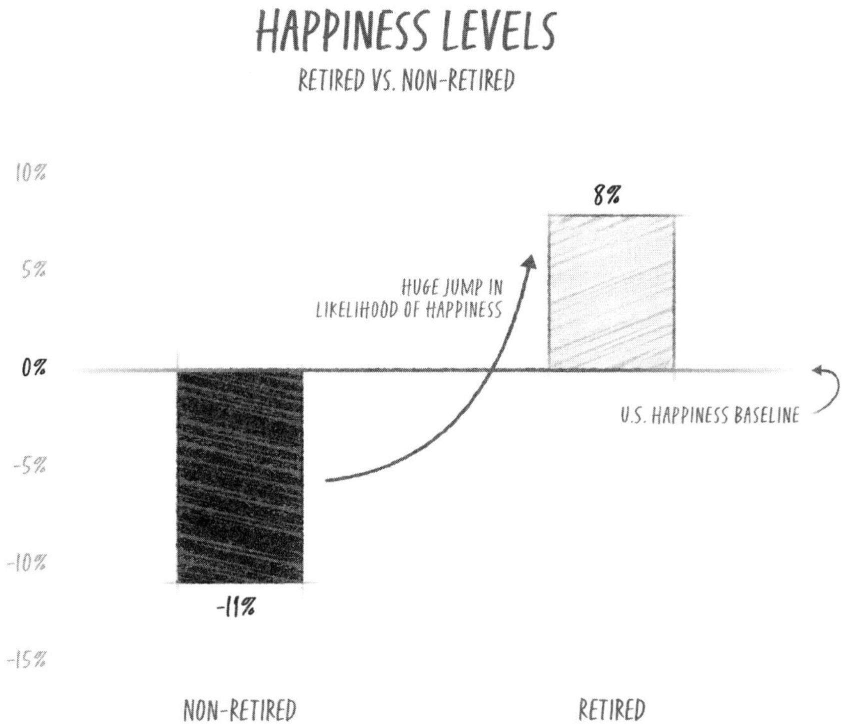

For anyone checking the math: Because retirees score 8 percent above the happiness baseline (80 percent) and non-retirees score 11 percent below it (66 percent), comparing those two numbers—80 divided by 66—shows that retirees are about 21 percent more likely to land in the happy camp.

Other cultures handle this transition differently. In Japan, for instance, their concept of retirement focuses on leaving "formal" jobs—like an athlete retiring from professional sports—while emphasizing the shift toward deeper life meaning in what comes next. They even have a word, *ikigai*, which roughly translates to "life's purpose" or "reason for being." It's seen as moving into a more purposeful, non-work-related phase of life rather than an ending.

I think it's time to pour a little ikigai into our morning coffee, don't you?

In our study, we defined retirement as "being in a financial position where you have the freedom to choose whether or not to work full-time." One of our most powerful findings is shown in Figure 1.1: **Americans who could simply answer yes to the question "Are you retired?" are 8 percent above the US happiness baseline, while the non-retired group is 11 percent below the baseline. When you crunch the numbers, that means the retired group is 21 percent more likely to land in the happy camp than the non-retired group.** That's a huge difference and a massive jump, simply based on your work status.

Retirement isn't necessarily about work—many retirees in our study still did part-time work or had a "side hustle" they enjoyed. But the act of crossing that threshold—from "I have to work" to "I choose to work"—delivers an immediate, measurable boost.

This chart shows that something magical happens from a happiness perspective from simply getting into the retired camp.

Boom. It's as easy as Amish apple pie.

A WORD ABOUT THE CHARTS IN THIS BOOK

We're slicing and dicing the data to uncover financial and lifestyle habits that nudge Americans toward one group or another, happy versus unhappy. In each case, we'll explain how we're looking at the data from a visual perspective. For many of the charts in this book, we'll be looking at reported happiness relative to what we call the "US happiness baseline."

For example, if a chart is looking at two categories—married and unmarried, retired and non-retired, etc.—we are often looking at each group's reported happiness levels relative to what we found to be the US happiness baseline. In our study, the US happiness baseline was 74 percent of Americans. If 84 percent of a particular group landed in the happy group, this would be well above baseline. Conversely, if only 60 percent of a group reported being happy, they would be well below the US happiness baseline.

Figure 1.1 shows how happiness levels change between those who report being unretired and those who report being retired. The non-retired group is 11 percent below the baseline here, and the retired group is 8 percent above the baseline. Mathematically, this means there is a 21 percent jump in happiness levels from the non-retired group to the retired group.

Remember: If the numbers plunge below the baseline with a particular behavior or asset point, it doesn't mean you can't still be happy; it just gives you all the more impetus to take action now to move yourself into the happy group.

When I talk to retirees, especially happy ones, what I often hear sounds more like ikigai than the pressure cooker version of "life purpose" you'll find here in America. It's about living with meaning, not just achieving something meaningful. Happy retirees aren't trying to start the next Amazon or save all the unhoused lemurs in Africa. They're walking their grandkids to school, volunteering twice a week, planting tomatoes, or playing in a community jazz band.

That's real purpose. That's the American version of ikigai.

America is full of happy people. As we've seen, 74 percent of our research's total population falls into the somewhat happy or very happy group. Unfortunately, that means more than one in four Americans still fall into the unhappy or neutral group.

Our goal is to change that. Being able to jump wholeheartedly into the activities you love has a huge impact on how you feel about your life—and which happiness level you put yourself into. The minute you are in the position to say no to work and yes to retirement, your overall state of being improves.

So how do you reach that position? It's not like you can instantly close this book and triumphantly declare, "I'm retiring right now!" Retiring sooner and happier requires planning, foresight, and a deeper understanding of what you'll need. It all starts with a solid financial base. Let's nail that down so we can get to the fun stuff later.

THE THREE MONEY AND HAPPINESS ZONES

In my first book, I wrote that the happiest retirees generally have at least half a million in liquid assets. But times have changed. The numbers have grown since we first crunched them fifteen years ago, just like my family has grown from three boys to four. New son, new numbers.

Our 2025 study revealed a clear pattern when it comes to money and happiness in retirement. We found three distinct zones, so we assigned them three distinct colors: Red, Yellow, and Green. You'll see the whole range in Figure 1.2.

The Red Zone is under $100,000 in assets—where, as you might expect from a Red Zone, happiness levels fall dramatically below the baseline. The Yellow Zone spans $100,000 to just under $1 million—where happiness stabilizes around the national average. The Green Zone starts at $1 million in investable assets, which is where we see a significant jump in overall happiness levels. This isn't just about having more money; it's about the psychological impact of financial security. **When you know you won't run out of money, happiness levels soar.**

FIGURE 1.2. Happiness Levels by Investable Assets

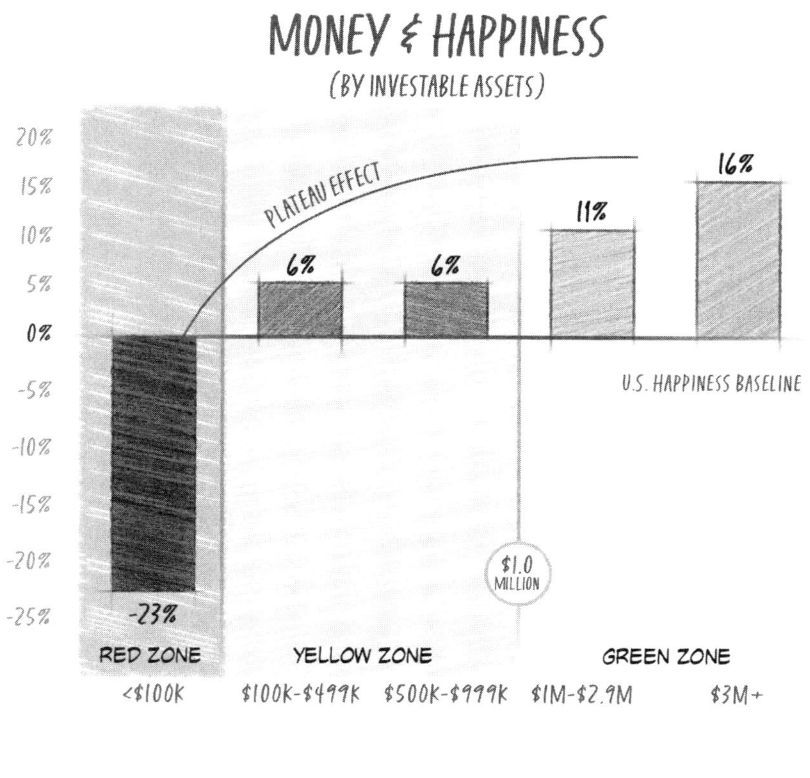

We'll delve more deeply into the three zones—and how to get to the million-dollar magic—in Chapter 2.

Since your smartphone is probably sitting next to you: if you want to see an even better version of this black-and-white chart, use the QR code below to unlock all the charts in this book in vivid color.

WWW.YOURWEALTH.COM/RETIRESOONERMETHOD

MONEY AND HAPPINESS

This is a critically important chart. I also don't want to make too much of the exact dollar amount in each category. But directionally, we see a clear relationship here. It's unmistakable: We want to get out of the Red Zone as soon as possible. The Yellow Zone isn't Port Sulphur, Louisiana—it's not a bad place to vacation. But the thriving metropolis Green Zone is where we aspire to be.

BEYOND THE MONEY: THE LIFESTYLE HABITS THAT MATTER

Whether these financial numbers seem easily achievable or like you'll have to stretch your dollars more than Spandex or constrict spending more than SPANX, the point isn't to discourage you; it's to show empirically where happiness inflection points exist.

And here's the crucial insight: While money matters enormously—it's the backbone of Secret #1—we'll spend significant time in this book talking about the lifestyle choices that can lead to a happy retirement. Secrets #2 and #3 of the Retire Sooner Method are all about core pursuits and socialization.

FIGURE 1.3. Average Number of Core Pursuits

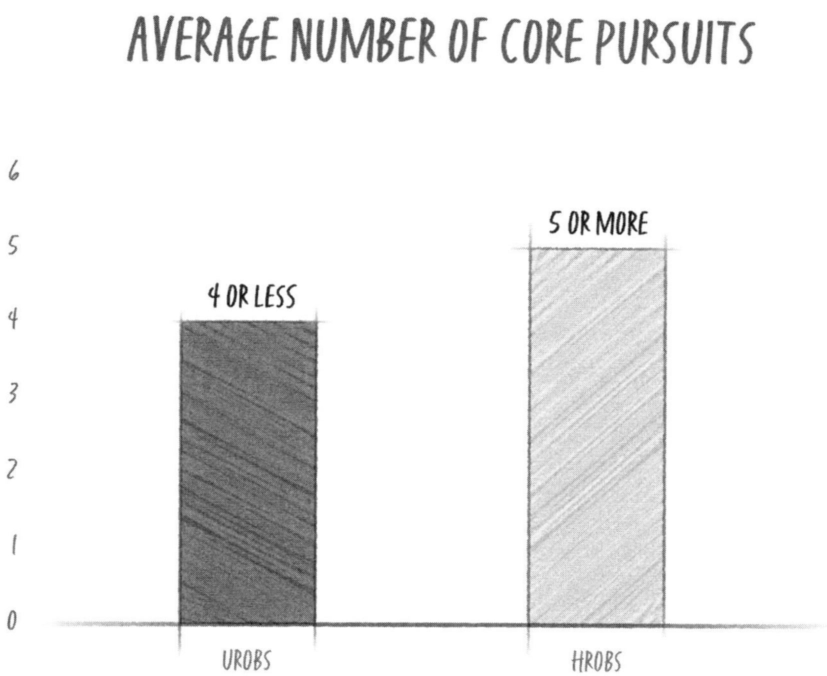

Happy retirees distinguish themselves through specific, measurable habits:

- **They have more core pursuits:** Figure 1.3 says it all: Happy retirees average five or more core pursuits (what I call "hobbies on steroids"), while unhappy retirees typically have four or fewer. These might include hiking, biking, pickleball, golf, fishing, gardening, painting, playing music, skiing, sailing, yoga, exercise groups, or any activity you love.

- **They spend more time on what matters:** Happy retirees spend nearly six more hours per week on their core pursuits—activities that bring them joy and purpose. They mentor, teach, volunteer at animal rescues, help out at their church, spearhead community improvement programs, and spend time with family. That's over 280 additional hours per year of meaningful engagement.
- **They prioritize adventure:** Happy retirees have nearly two adventure-related pursuits versus just one for unhappy retirees—they love traveling in the US or abroad, RVing, exploring new destinations, backpacking, mountain biking, caving, kayaking, hot-air ballooning, skydiving, scuba diving, paddleboarding, bird-watching, and horseback riding. Most striking: A hefty 57 percent of unhappy retirees have zero adventure-related core pursuits.
- **They exercise just fifteen minutes more:** Happy retirees spend an average of one hour per day on health and fitness, while unhappy retirees average just forty-five minutes. Staying active could encompass anything from vigorous gardening or a neighborhood walking group to a high-intensity interval training (HIIT) boot camp or a Pilates class that makes you glow (as my Southern grandmother would say, "Horses perspire, men sweat, but ladies glow"). That extra fifteen minutes per day creates a measurable happiness difference.
- **They're more social than unhappy retirees:** Happy retirees have 1.5 social core pursuits versus just 1.0 for unhappy retirees—that means 50 percent more social engagement. As shown earlier, you can pair socialization with core pursuits to get more bang for your buck—walking groups, exercise classes, community volunteering, etc. Any group activity counts. You could host a family gathering, create a dinner club, or kick off a weekly game of poker or pinochle. Who knows? Maybe you'll find a new identity in retirement as the local card shark.

FAILING TO PLAN IS PLANNING TO FAIL

One of the most striking predictors of retirement happiness isn't how much money you have—it's whether you have a plan for how to use it. When our research showed that happy retirees are twice as likely to have a formal written financial plan compared to unhappy retirees, we knew we'd found the fourth secret of the Retire Sooner Method.

This isn't just correlation; it's causation. **Having a plan makes retirees 2.5 times more likely to be confident about their financial decisions and 3.2 times more likely to be satisfied with their current financial situation.** It's like having a GPS for your finances—the kind with a lovely British accent—instead of just wandering around and hoping you don't get lost.

THE SECRET SUPERPOWER OF HAPPY RETIREES

Leonardo da Vinci said it best: "A well-spent day brings happy sleep." Call me Renaissance man if you will, but this guy was correlating sleep and happiness centuries before I was.

Here's the most unexpected finding from our research: **Sleep is the superpower of happy retirees.** It's the unsung hero, slipping quietly into fifth place under the hum of a white noise machine. Look at Figure 1.4. A full 69 percent of HROBs (happiest retirees on the block) report getting enough sleep each night, compared to only 38 percent of UROBs (unhappiest retirees on the block).

I recently saw a LinkedIn post with the headline "My 5 to 9 before my 9 to 5!" This guy gets up at four thirty a.m. every day, goes to the gym, deadlifts, runs five miles, takes a cold plunge, meditates, journals—all before work. If you're stuck on a similar hamster wheel, rest assured that schedule is out the window once you've retired. You can put that guy's five-to-nine where the sun don't shine.

FIGURE 1.4. The Percentage of HROBS vs. UROBs Who Say Yes to "I Get Enough Sleep"

Happy retirees have discovered that sleep isn't lazy—it's essential. Think of it as washing your brain overnight. Better sleep leads to better focus, better health, better relationships, and, yes, better financial decisions. Sometimes the most productive thing you can do is *stop* doing and hit the hay.

THE RECIPE FOR HAPPINESS

I'm going to shoot straight with you. All these lifestyle habits and financial benchmarks—asset levels, core pursuits, social connections, planning, sleep patterns—none of them is a silver bullet. There's no single golden ticket to guaranteed happiness in retirement.

Some of you may be thinking, *Wes, there are so many important factors you looked at in your research—what about all the other combinations?* You're absolutely right. While the five secrets we're focusing on in this book create a 96 percent probability of happiness, many other combinations reach 94 or 95 percent. This just happens to be the result from an econometric exercise in backing into the five most powerful factors when put together. If you could choose only five, these would lead to the highest probability of the outcome we're all looking for.

Here's the thing: I think it's an extraordinary concept to model behavior after people who are already living lives we'd like to emulate—which is exactly what we're doing here. You can look at it Secret by Secret, or as the killer combo at the core of the Retire Sooner Method, because if you implement these five alone, I would be shocked if you don't end up a happy retiree.

Ready to get into it? Each of the following chapters takes you deep into one of these five secrets, starting with Secret #1: the Money Green Zones, and going all the way to Chapter 6, which covers the superpower of getting enough sleep. When you combine these financial and lifestyle principles in the right proportions, something remarkable happens.

That's exactly what the following chapters will show you. Each one focuses on a core truth we know works—not because *I* think it should but because the data spells it out. Together, this combination of all five secrets forms a method that delivers what we've found to be a 96 percent happy retiree success rate.

Chapter 2 dives deep into the financial strategies for a happy retirement—how to build a solid foundation that gets you into the Green Zone and keeps you there.

Chapter 3 explores your core pursuits—the "hobbies on steroids" that give your retirement days meaning and your years purpose.

Chapter 4 lays out why having close friends isn't just nice but essential for long-term happiness.

Chapter 5 shows you how to create your written financial plan and retirement life map—the roadmap that transforms financial anxiety into confidence and joy.

Chapter 6 reveals the surprising importance of sleep: the secret superpower of the happy retiree.

Chapter 7 digs into the truth about inflation and how to protect your dollars from wilting.

Chapter 8 is the investment chapter, where the rubber meets the road. You'll find enough numbers to choke an HP 12c calculator—but the five pillars of income investing can help you create sustainable, worry-free income for decades.

Full disclosure: Chapters 1–7 are less about my opinion and more what the numbers tell us—a clear, practical method drawn from the data and research. In Chapter 8, I'll give you my educated opinion on income investing (hint: I love it). While I strongly believe in the core principles of income investing, I'll be the first to acknowledge there are endless ways to invest. For our purposes, we'll focus on the five pillars, which my team and I have relied on as foundations for constructing portfolios aimed at weathering storms while providing the steady cash flow retirees need.

By the time you finish this book, you'll know the five secrets at the heart of the Retire Sooner Method—which has helped thousands of Americans retire happily—and have a clear, actionable plan for how to retire sooner yourself.

CHAPTER 2

Secret #1: The Money Green Zones

$1 Million or More in Investable Assets

When I first met Ricky and Claudia, they were worried.[1]

They were sixty-three and sixty-two, respectively, and had spent their entire careers in the medical device industry. They worked hard and had been diligently saving for decades. Ricky and Claudia were active and healthy, happily child-free. As financial podcast listeners—and listeners of the *Retire Sooner* podcast—they dreamed of doing exactly what our podcast discusses: retire sooner.

And yet.

"We've been reading all these retirement articles," Claudia explained, opening a dog-eared yellow folder. She splayed the articles on the table, each marked with brightly colored tabs.

"One says we need $3 million in assets. Another says $4.5 million. And this one . . ." She picked up the third document warily and held it away from her body, as if it might bite. "This one tells us we need multi-millions if we don't want to end up eating cat food in our golden years!"

I couldn't help but chuckle. The $10–$50 million retirement target has scared more Americans than the housing bubble, dot-com crash, and cryptocurrency roller coaster combined.

"We've done the math," Ricky said. "At this rate, I'll be working until I'm eighty-five, which would be impressive considering nobody in my family has lived past eighty-two."

"Listen," I said, "before we let the Retirement Grim Reaper kill your retirement dreams, let's see what you've got."

Claudia gently pushed their financials toward me. "In your first book, back in 2015, you discussed how some happy retirees reported having $500,000," she said quietly. "But I guess I'm scared that times have changed, and we won't have enough."

"Good memory, Claudia. That was a long time ago, and inflation has had a big impact on where those numbers stand today."

"Oh boy, have we ever felt inflation," Ricky said. "We're thinking about buying chickens just to combat the price of eggs!"

I smiled. "Like with any good financial plan, let's just start fresh."

As Claudia walked me through their financial situation, it didn't take long to understand she and Ricky were going to be a lot happier walking out of my office than they were coming in. Our 2025 study showed that the happiest retirees have a nest egg of a million dollars or more—and they had $1.25 million. They'd also lived in their house for three decades and paid off their mortgage the previous year.

"Okay," I said, pulling out my favorite gadget: a reMarkable tablet, a digital notebook that provides a realistic pen-on-paper feel. "Let's figure out if you can hit $100,000 in household income. That's the threshold where we see happiness levels really jump in retirement."

They leaned forward, full of anticipation.

"Can we?" Claudia asked.

"Let's find out."

I started mapping out their income sources, walking them through each one as I scribbled numbers on my screen:

- **Social Security:** Ricky would collect $3,000 monthly from Social Security, with Claudia set to receive $1,400. That's $52,800 a year.
- **Pension:** Ricky, God bless him, had a small but mighty pension—that would provide an additional $1,300 a month. That's $15,600 a year.
- **Liquid investable retirement assets:** Their largest assets were their retirement accounts: $250,000 in Claudia's IRA; $500,000 in Ricky's. Assuming a 4 percent annual rate of withdrawal—more on that shortly—they'd have another $30,000 a year.
- **After-tax retirement investments:** Their overall after-tax assets (brokerage accounts with dividend-paying stocks, ETFs, and mutual funds) totaled about $500,000. This could provide another $20,000 per year, assuming a 4 percent annual rate of withdrawal.

Once I had those numbers, determining their monthly retirement income was simple:

$68,400 in annual income from their first two sources

+ **$30,000** from their IRAs and

+ **$20,000** from their after-tax accounts

= **$118,400 a year**

That's a lot of income, given their spending needs. It should persist and even outpace inflation—which we'll talk about later—through the full duration of their retirement.

"Here's the research," I said. "Happy retirees are much less likely to worry about running out of money versus unhappy retirees. With all of these income sources and your projected spending needs, you shouldn't have to worry about running out of money, either."

Their posture visibly relaxed. Ricky looked like he might pass out from relief, and Claudia looked proud. I could tell they were beginning to see the future was brighter than they'd imagined—with or without a flock of hens.

"Let me ask you something else," I went on. "What do you two love doing most?"

"We love taking our RV on weekend trips," Ricky said. "Though we've been thinking about longer journeys once we retire. Maybe do the great American road trip and hit all sixty-three national parks."

"I teach pottery at the community center," Claudia said, "and I'd love to turn our garage into a home studio. Oh, and my monthly Texas Hold'em game with the ladies is sacred—I try not to miss it. I won $560 last month. Is *that* a retirement income source?"

She shot me a wry grin. I grinned back.

"I like where your head's at, Claudia." She was really starting to get it. Of course, she knew she couldn't rely on poker income—but she didn't need to. They had plenty of other income sources that were slightly more predictable.

"We're also pretty involved at First Presbyterian," Ricky added. "We'd love to contribute to our church community more once we stop working."

"None of those sound like multimillionaire-dollar activities to me," I said. "As my kids would say, you've got your core pursuits 'locked in.' I believe you are going to have more than enough money to fund your purpose—and to kick off your retirement sooner than you thought."

One year later, Ricky was able to say yes to retirement and cut that first slice of cake. Claudia had her cake—and ate it, too—six months later. Ricky now leads monthly RV day trips to neighboring attractions like Stone Mountain for other church members. Claudia turned their garage into a studio and expanded her pottery teaching to three classes per week. Her Thursday night Texas Hold'em group has grown from four to six players (I guess inflation even applies to poker). She and

Ricky have even added something new to their purpose portfolio: hosting an annual Thanksgiving feast for church members who don't have family nearby.

Let's talk turkey: Ricky and Claudia aren't ten-millionaires who have a private island and seats on Blue Origin's next trip to Mars. They wouldn't want to be! They're the textbook example of how it's possible to retire comfortably and live fulfilling lives with the $1.25 million they so carefully saved in their working years.

And they didn't need that wacky $10 million they heard about from the scare-mongering money gurus. Because guess what: Ricky and Claudia are some of the happiest retirees I know.

WHY ARE AMERICANS SO SCARED?

In defense of the talking heads pushing the retirement terror campaign, they're not speaking in a vacuum. Rather, they're tapping into a very real anxiety gripping Americans across the country.

Look, I get it. When you're constantly bombarded with messages about how expensive everything is, how the stock market is volatile, and how inflation is eating away at your purchasing power, it's easy to think you need to invent the next AI company simply to not outlive your money.

In our 2025 research study, anxiety about the economic future ranked as the number one challenge when people were contemplating retirement. Take a look at Figure 2.1.

Unpredictable economic conditions ranked first; declining health came in second. Both of these are scary: Unpredictable conditions are, by nature, hard to predict and plan for, and no matter how much yoga you do or kale you eat, your health can still change in a heartbeat.

What I found interesting was that nearly half of all Americans are worried about the vague and elusive "running out of money." Not about

FIGURE 2.1. Americans' Reported Biggest Challenges When Contemplating Retirement

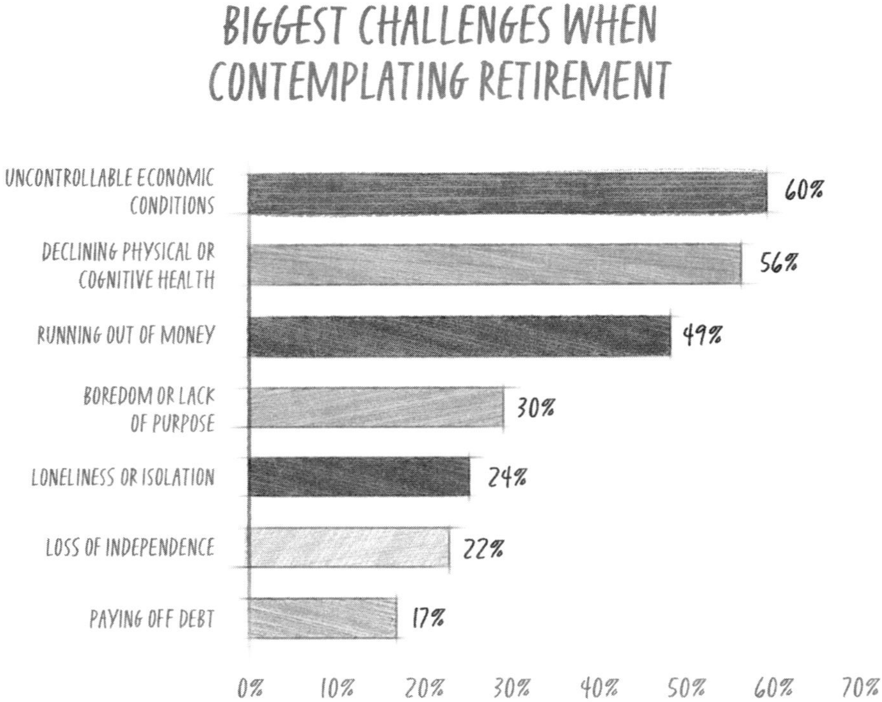

market volatility or inflation specifically—but losing sleep over the fear of running out.

Here's the really fascinating part: This fear of running out of money persists even at high levels of savings. Among those with $500,000–$999,999 in assets, 45 percent still have this as a top worry. Even 39 percent of the $1–$2.9 million group are concerned about running out of money. And believe it or not, 24 percent of those with $3 million or more still worry about running out of money! That's like having a full tank of gas and worrying you won't make it across town.

As you can see in Figure 2.2, the fear of running out of money is ever-present for a large number of Americans. But I think those numbers should be a lot lower. There are ways to mitigate and reduce this

FIGURE 2.2. Percentage of Americans (by Investable Assets) Who Rank Fear of Running Out of Money as a Top Financial Concern

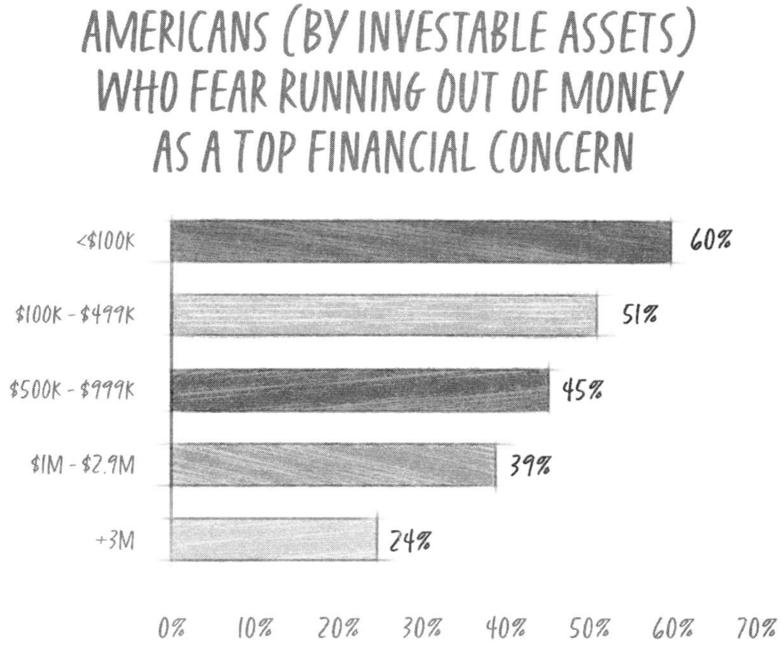

pervasive fear, and wouldn't you know it, they're the same financial strategies we'll be sharing in this book.

HOW TO GET INTO THE GREEN ZONE

There are four core components of Secret #1 of the Retire Sooner Method that will help get you to the Green Zone:

- $1 million or more in liquid investable assets (your nest egg)
- Multiple income sources that add up to $100,000 or more
- Mortgage payoff within sight (nine years or fewer)
- The 4+ percent rule of thumb (the biggest antidote to running out of money)

Financial planning is also essential—so essential that having a written financial plan is its own secret in Chapter 5.

These four components are the elixirs for the fear of running out of money. And here's another telling statistic: Our data shows that unhappy retirees are twice as likely to have this worry than happy retirees.

ZOOMING IN ON THE THREE MONEY AND HAPPINESS ZONES

You've seen the Money and Happiness graphic in the first chapter, but it's a chart so nice I've included it twice. The three money and happiness zones were one of the most powerful findings from our research—and a transformative roadmap for your financial future.

FIGURE 2.3. Happiness Levels by Investable Assets

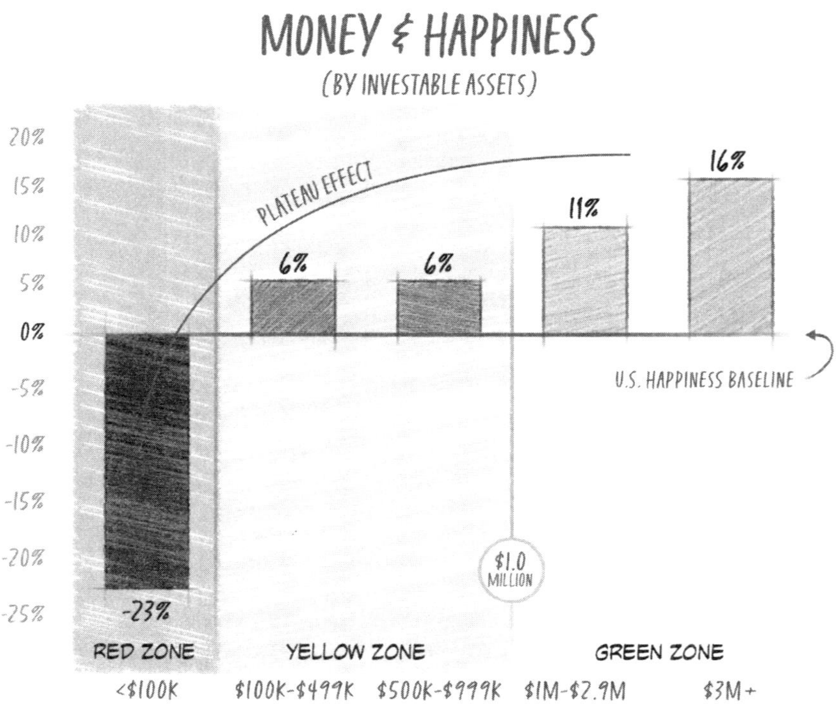

This chart is specifically about liquid investable assets, which include anything you can get your hands on and spend relatively quickly: cash, CDs, investment accounts, brokerage accounts, Roth IRAs, regular IRAs, 401(k)s, 403(b)s, stocks, bonds, mutual funds, etc. Real estate doesn't go in this category because, by definition, it's illiquid—you can't pay for groceries with your home equity. Real estate absolutely counts toward your overall net worth, but for our purposes, we're talking about money you can access readily when you need it, even while it's producing income and growth for you throughout retirement. You might call it your nest egg.

As a reminder, if you want to see the Green Zone in actual green, all the full-color versions of these charts are available at the QR code.

WWW.YOURWEALTH.COM/RETIRESOONERMETHOD

In Figure 2.3, you can see that happiness relative to savings/liquid investment assets levels jumps significantly from the Red to the Yellow Zone, where it begins to level off. Getting to a million dollars in savings lands you in the Green Zone, where people report happiness levels markedly higher than the baseline average.

Here's a little more detail on the three zones.

THE RED ZONE: UNDER $100,000 IN ASSETS

Americans with less than $100,000 in investable assets report happiness levels that fall dramatically below the baseline. This makes intuitive sense—when you're worried about basic financial security, it's difficult to feel content or optimistic about the future. This is the financial equivalent of checking your bank balance before ordering an appetizer and realizing you can't afford the breadbasket.

THE YELLOW ZONE: $100,000–$999,999 IN ASSETS

Once Americans cross into six-figure territory, happiness levels stabilize just above the baseline. Whether you have $100,000 or $500,000 or $800,000, the happiness levels remain relatively similar within this range. You've achieved basic security, but you haven't yet reached the comfort zone. You've graduated to the "I can order a steak without panic" level, but you're still nervous about adding the turtle cheesecake.

THE GREEN ZONE: $1 MILLION AND ABOVE

Here's where the magic happens. **Once Americans crest the $1 million mark in investable assets, we see a significant jump in overall happiness.** Happiness levels continue to rise once you reach the $3+ million category, before leveling off. This is "order whatever you want" territory. Finally, you can say, "I'll have the surf and turf" without breaking into a cold sweat.

This isn't just about money for money's sake. What we're really measuring is the psychological impact of financial security. When you're confident you won't run out of money, when you can handle unexpected expenses, when you can be generous with family and causes you care about—that's when happiness levels seem to take flight.

More money does correlate with greater happiness but begins to wane at a certain point. I think of this as the money and happiness plateau effect. Once you hit the Green Zone, the data shows—and I've seen this play out in real life—you enter what I call "diminishing marginal returns" when it comes to happiness per new dollars. The happiness gains start to slow, meaning that each additional dollar past a certain point produces less new happiness than the one before it.

This threshold might be different for everyone. Since there's no perfect or agreed-upon inflection point among economists and researchers, I think it's fruitless to try to nail an exact number when the switch flips. I find it more helpful and more accurate to look at this as the zone we want to reach, and from my research, that zone starts at a million dollars.

The plateau effect reinforces a concept we'll return to throughout this book: the power of "enough." In the early stages of wealth accumulation, there are dramatic jumps in happiness as financial security gets added. Moving through the Red Zone into the Yellow Zone creates measurable relief. Breaking into the Green Zone brings another significant boost. But once we reach a certain threshold—that point where we have enough to do the things we want to do and care for our families—we start seeing diminishing marginal returns per new dollar when it comes to happiness.

This doesn't mean you should stop accumulating wealth once you hit $1 million. Far from it. There's nothing wrong with continuing your journey through the Green Zone, building assets and security. But understanding the plateau effect liberates you from the tyranny of "more." Yes, having $5 million or $10 million for retirement is wonderful and fine, but you don't need $5 or $10 million to be happy. The research shows that once you've crossed into the Green Zone, additional millions produce relatively modest happiness gains compared to that initial leap from Red to Yellow to Green.

This is why Suze Orman's multimillion-dollar, sky-high retirement targets are so damaging. They ignore the plateau effect entirely, suggesting that happiness scales linearly with wealth—that somehow $10 million makes you twice as happy as $5 million. At these levels, that's not how it works. You're already in the Green Zone.

In all my years working with retirees, I've yet to meet someone who said, "My life became dramatically better when I went from $3 million to $4 million" or "$5 million to $10 million." When a retiree realizes they're not going to outlive their nest egg, it significantly reduces financial stress and liberates them to explore more pathways to joy and fulfillment. But beyond that security threshold, the happiness gains level off.

Think about Ricky and Claudia. If they had burned the midnight oil at their jobs for another ten or twenty years to build a $5 million nest egg instead of $1.25 million, not only would their RV have gathered dust—they wouldn't have experienced the massive spike in day-to-day happiness that comes from simply being retired. Sometimes the best investment isn't more money; it's more time to enjoy the money you already have. Just saying yes can be powerful.

INCOME: YOUR RETIREMENT CASH FLOW ENGINE

The same Red, Yellow, and Green Zone pattern holds true for household income—and this chart tells a compelling story about what retirees actually need to live happily.

Figure 2.4 shows that Americans earning less than $50,000 annually find themselves in the happiness Red Zone—21 percent below the baseline. This makes intuitive sense: When you're stretching every dollar just to cover basic expenses, it's hard to feel secure about the future. You're living paycheck to paycheck, retirement or not.

Those earning $50,000–$99,999 land in the Yellow Zone. At 3 percent above baseline happiness, you've achieved basic stability, but

FIGURE 2.4. Happiness Levels by Household Income

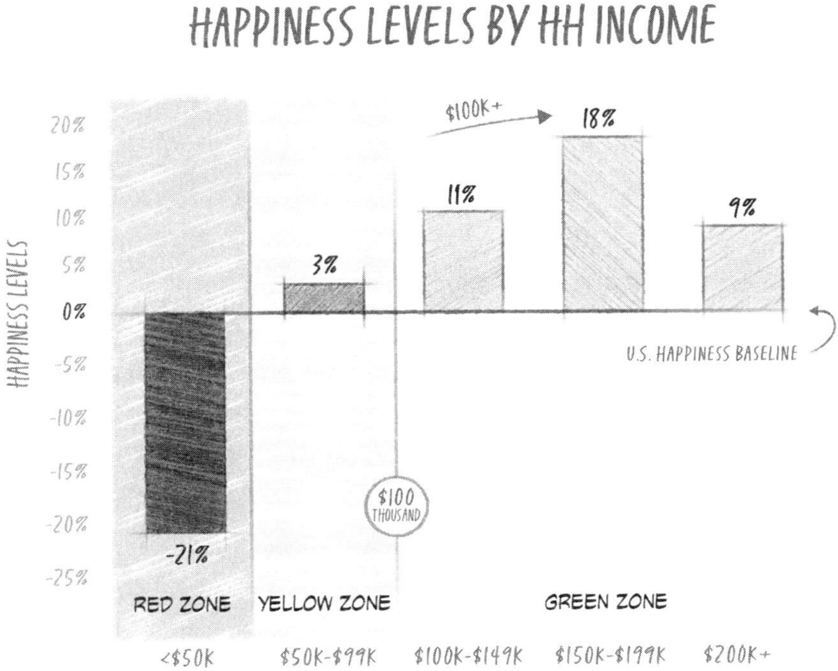

you're not exactly living it up. You can cover your needs and maybe a few wants, but you're still making trade-offs. Do I fix the car or take that weekend trip?

But here's where things get interesting: **Once household income crosses $100,000, happiness levels jump dramatically into the Green Zone. At $100,000–$149,000, we see an 11 percent boost in happiness. Push that income to $150,000–$199,000 and happiness peaks at 18 percent above baseline.**

Notice something curious after that? Just like with assets, there's a plateau effect. Income above $200,000 actually shows a slight dip to 9 percent above baseline. This isn't because money makes you miserable—it's because at some point, you've got enough, and other factors (like time, health, and relationships) matter more than additional dollars.

For retirees, this translates to a practical target zone: Aim for $100,000+ in annual household income during retirement. This isn't some arbitrary number but the empirical sweet spot where financial stress starts to melt away and happiness takes off. Remember, this is total household income from all sources: Social Security, pensions, investment income, rental income, and more—whatever combination works for you.

The beauty of understanding this income threshold is that it makes retirement planning more concrete. If you're not exactly sure how much you will need once you stop working, you could focus on this more concrete level and ask, "How do I generate $100,000 in annual income?" Both questions are leading you down the right path, but finding this Green Zone gives you an actionable income level to target—one that puts you on the path to the financial freedom we're all searching for.

On the subject of adding income, one powerful tool works in reverse: subtracting from your expenses. For most Americans, this means eliminating your mortgage. We'll get to the power of that next.

MORTGAGE PAYOFF: CUTTING YOUR BIGGEST EXPENSE

The third goal is to get within striking distance of paying off your mortgage—or knocking the whole thing out completely.

Our research—look at Figure 2.5 for a handy visual—showed that happy retirees either have their homes completely paid off or are within nine years of making that triumphant final payment. The relationship is clear: As "time to pay off mortgage" goes down, happiness levels tend to rise. Americans with 30+ years remaining to mortgage payoff are 19 percent less happy than the baseline, whereas those with 29 to 10 years left are in a neutral happiness zone. **But once people reach 9**

FIGURE 2.5. Happiness Levels Rise with Mortgage Payoff in Sight

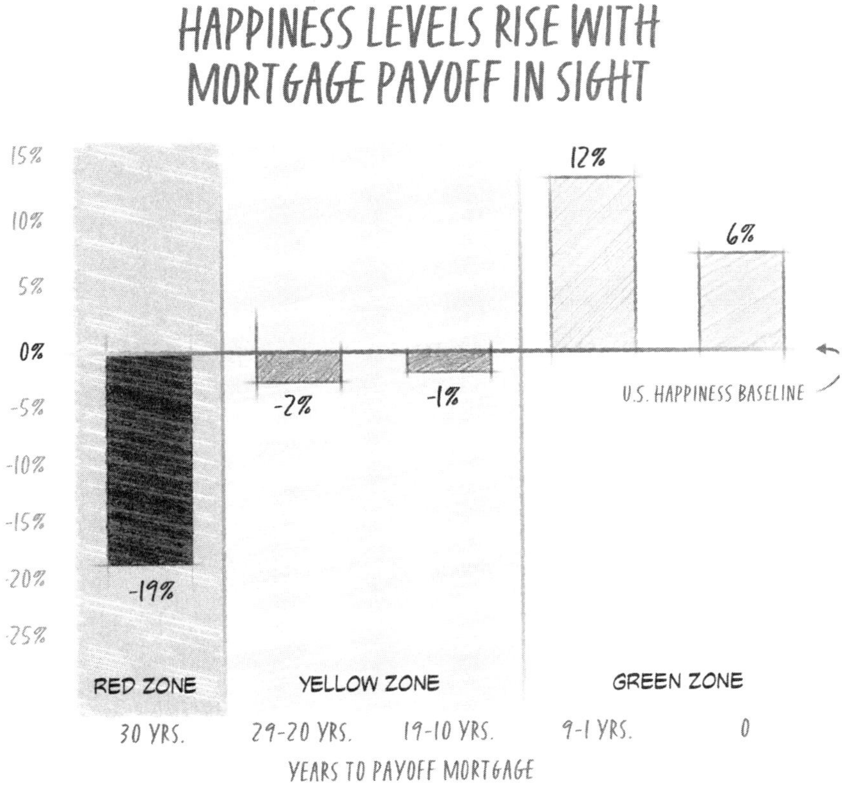

years or less, we enter another financial Green Zone and happiness levels rise dramatically.

Why does this matter so much? Easy: Housing is typically your largest monthly expense, often eating up 20–40 percent of your budget. Eliminate that payment, and suddenly your nondiscretionary spending might drop by $25,000 or more per year. It's like realizing you no longer have to carry the heaviest suitcase through the airport: Everything else instantly feels lighter, easier, and far less stressful.

I'm not necessarily telling you to throw every spare dollar at your mortgage starting tomorrow. The math isn't always that simple, especially in today's mortgage rate environment. If you locked in a 3 percent mortgage rate during the pandemic's golden days of cheap money, congratulations—you basically borrowed money for free after accounting for inflation. In that case, you might be better off investing that extra cash in your nest egg instead of paying down a practically free loan.

However, if you're carrying a mortgage at 6 percent, 7 percent, or higher, that's a different story. Paying off a 7 percent mortgage is essentially giving yourself a guaranteed 7 percent return on your money, tax free. Show me an investment that can promise that kind of certainty, and I'll show you a cat that actually comes when you call it.

The psychological benefits are just as important as the mathematical ones. There's something deeply satisfying about owning your home outright. You sleep better at night knowing that even if everything else goes sideways, you have a roof over your head that nobody can take away. That peace of mind? Priceless.

Ricky and Claudia had completely paid off their $600,000 home the year before we met. When they told me about making that final payment, Claudia literally got teary-eyed. "We had a little celebration," she said. "Ricky wanted to frame the mortgage statement that showed zero balance." That mortgage freedom—and the confidence it gave them—was a big part of the equation when they decided to retire.

If you're currently fifteen or twenty years away from paying off your mortgage, don't panic. You've got options. Consider refinancing to a shorter term if the numbers work. Sometimes moving from a thirty-year to a fifteen-year mortgage doesn't increase your payment as much as you'd think, especially if you can get a lower interest rate in the process. Or simply add extra principal payments when you can—even an extra $200–$500 per month can knock years off your mortgage timeline.

The key is having a plan that gets you mortgage-free—or within nine years of freedom—by the time you want to retire. Your house should be the foundation of your retirement, not the anchor that keeps you working years longer than you want or need.

THE 4+ PERCENT RULE OF THUMB: YOUR NUMBER ONE ANTIDOTE TO RUNNING OUT OF MONEY

Remember how we started this chapter? With the sobering reality that an enormous percentage of Americans are worried about running out of money, no matter what asset level. Well, here's the fourth and final antidote to that fear: the 4+ percent rule of thumb.

If you've been with me a while, you know I'm a big fan of the 4+ percent withdrawal rate. I've yet to find any other approach with the same long-term track record of success that has worked consistently over vastly different decades with vastly different financial realities. It's a surprisingly straightforward formula, and it all started with a guy named Bill.

In 1994, back when a "tweet" was just a bird sound and people thought Blockbuster video stores would be around forever, financial advisor William Bengen revolutionized retirement planning. He published research that answered the question that was keeping pre-retirees (and retirees) up at night: *How much can I safely withdraw from my savings without running out of money?* I think of this as, ***What's the max amount I can take out, without running out?***

Lucky for us, Bengen was an aeronautical engineer-turned-financial planner—a totally lovable nerd. Picture suspenders, pocket protector, giant TI-83 calculator, the whole shebang. After analyzing monthly historical market data going back to the Great Depression, he discovered something remarkable: Retirees who withdrew 4 percent of their initial portfolio in the first year of retirement and then adjusted that amount annually for inflation almost never ran out of money over a thirty-year retirement, as long as they maintained a certain stock–bond asset mix—even during the worst market conditions in modern history.[2]

This became known as the "4% rule," and three decades of additional research and real-world application have only reinforced its validity. It's elegant in its simplicity, yet powerful in its application.

What makes this approach so powerful is its built-in conservatism. Bengen's research showed this strategy would have preserved capital through every major economic calamity of the twentieth century—the Great Depression, World War II, the stagflation of the 1970s, the dot-com bust, and, yes, even the 2008 financial crisis. Even in worst-case scenarios, the money lasted approximately twenty-nine years: almost three full decades of income.

Now, after working with hundreds of retirees over the years, both Bengen and I, independently, adjusted the original withdrawal rate guidelines. While 4 percent works as a baseline, real-world experience shows that retirees can often safely withdraw 4.25 percent or 4.5 percent over time. In fact, Bengen recently upped his safe max withdrawal percentage to 4.7 percent.[3] It may not sound like much, but even moving from 4 to 4.5 percent is a 12.5 percent boost to retirement withdrawals. That's why I call it the 4-*plus* percent rule of thumb. It's a range, a dynamic or even elastic withdrawal target zone rather than an amount that's etched in stone.

Figure 2.6 is designed to give you a visual of the percentage success rates of "money not running out" over a thirty-year period of time, taking inflation into account. The left axis shows the starting withdrawal rate, and across the top you will see various asset mixes (stocks and bonds allocation). **Choosing the 4 percent starting withdrawal range along with a moderately balanced asset allocation of 60 percent stocks and 40 percent bonds gives you a very high level of confidence that money will last for the duration of a long retirement.**

It also shows how an allocation that's very conservative (20 percent stocks and 80 percent bonds) brings down the percentage success rates, while aggressive allocations (80 percent or 100 percent stocks) have led to lower probabilities that money lasts the full thirty-year time span.

When you look at the long arc of retirement—say, thirty or forty years—one thing becomes clear pretty quickly: There's no single "perfect" withdrawal rate or asset mix that works for everyone all the time. If you're too conservative, you may end up spending far less than you need to, making lifestyle sacrifices that simply aren't necessary. On the flip side, leaning too heavily into stocks can reduce your odds of long-term success.

What tends to work best in the real world is balance. A well-diversified portfolio, paired with a flexible withdrawal strategy that can adjust as markets and life change, usually provides the best mix of confidence, sustainability, and the lack of worry about ever running out.

FIGURE 2.6. Effects of Withdrawal Rates and Likelihood of Success After Thirty Years in Retirement Relative to Various Portfolio Allocations

Stock/Bond Allocation

Initial Withdrawal Rate	20/80	30/70	40/60	50/50	60/40	70/30	80/20	100/0	
3%	100%	100%	100%	100%	100%	100%	100%	99%	High Confidence
4%	83%	95%	98%	98%	100%	99%	98%	97%	
5%	41%	62%	71%	78%	83%	84%	84%	83%	Medium Confidence
6%	24%	28%	41%	56%	67%	68%	72%	72%	
7%	15%	18%	25%	35%	45%	51%	56%	61%	Low Confidence
8%	7%	13%	14%	22%	30%	39%	45%	53%	

Source: Capital Investment Advisors, LLC analysis of data from Bloomberg

Let's bring this to life using our $1 million benchmark, the number that gets you out of the Red and Yellow Zones and into the Green. The 4+ percent rule of thumb means you can safely withdraw $40,000 in your first year of retirement (\$1 million × 0.04 = \$40,000). Add that to Social Security, pension income, or other sources, and you can see how you are well on your way to that \$100,000 annual income target. The next year, you adjust your withdrawal amount for inflation, and this pattern continues throughout retirement, ensuring your income keeps pace with rising costs.

Here's how this looks in practice. Several years into retirement, as their Thanksgiving gatherings expanded, Ricky and Claudia began to invite more people from the community—and their home got more crowded. Now that they were entertaining more regularly, they started to dream about renovating to carve out a little more breathing room. Literally! They wanted to expand their blueprint to include a beautiful sunroom in the back of the house. It was something they'd thought about doing for years, but they worried it would take too big a chunk out of their retirement funds.

So we did the math together. For one year, Ricky and Claudia increased their 4 percent withdrawal rate to over 6 percent. This gave them the funds they needed for the extra space. Claudia says the sunroom is now her favorite room in the house. Every morning, she takes her favorite mug of coffee to her favorite chair and looks out on the backyard, where a doe and her fawns nibble grass in the mist.

The year after their modest renovation project, they readjusted the withdrawal rate back down to 4 percent, no sweat. Everyone was happy: Claudia, Ricky, and the deer.

Here's more good news: If your financial needs are less than 4 percent in some years, you can dial it down to 2 percent or 3 percent. Your nest egg gains even more stability and growth potential, and if you have kids and grandkids, you're improving the long-term value of assets that can be passed on to the next generation.

The elegance of the 4+ percent rule of thumb isn't just its mathematical soundness—it's the fact that you can breathe more easily, whether you have a sunroom or not. Once you understand how much sustainable income your nest egg can generate, you can stop obsessing over whether your money will last. You have a clear, research-backed guideline that transforms that number one retirement fear into confidence.

And there you have it. **A $1+ million nest egg, $100,000+ in annual income, mortgage freedom within nine years, and the 4+ percent withdrawal strategy.**

These four strategies work together to help build a solid financial foundation that can get you into the Green Zone—and keep you there. With this base in place, you're ready to focus on what truly matters: living a happy, purpose-filled retirement.

But here's the thing about purpose: It doesn't just magically appear the day you retire. The happiest retirees don't stumble into fulfillment. They actively cultivate it through what I call "core pursuits." These are way more than pastimes—they're the activities that turn empty calendar pages into purposeful adventures. They're how you transform all that financial security into actual joy.

So now that we've got your money working for you, let's explore how to transform your golden years into the adventure of a lifetime.

CHAPTER 3

Secret #2: Super Activities, aka Hobbies on Steroids

280+ Extra Hours of Core Pursuits Each Year

Joe has a confession that would make most working people jealous.[1]

"One thing I do miss about work is using Outlook to manage my calendar," he wrote to me recently. "Now I need to print my calendar off weekly just to track my activities!"

But Joe wasn't just writing to share his scheduling woes; he had more to report. "I wanted to drop you a note and thank you for your books and teachings over the past ten-plus years," his letter began. "I started listening to your weekly radio show at least fifteen years ago, and that led me to your books and podcasts. My wife and I found your insights helpful as we planned our transition into retirement, retiring sooner and happy!"

Joe was thrilled to report that his and Cindy's "core pursuits have exploded" in retirement. But he also revealed something surprising. A few years ago, when he retired at sixty and Cindy at fifty-seven, they weren't entirely sure how they were going to fill their time.

Like many couples, they'd worked hard during their careers. Joe's first post-college job was as a software engineer making $27,000 a year; by the time he was ready to retire, he'd climbed the ranks to become an SVP in Information Technology, leading a team of twelve hundred at a Fortune 15 health-care company. Cindy had worked on the front lines of health care as a critical care nurse. During the pandemic, she'd been a nurse leader in the ICUs an hour north of New York City. When their kids were young, they'd perfected an exhausting tag-team routine: Cindy would head to the hospital for her seven p.m. night shift, getting home at eight a.m. just as Joe was getting their three children ready for school. They'd hand off the kids, and Joe would drive ninety minutes to his own job, then race home that evening before Cindy had to leave at seven p.m. for her next twelve-hour shift. All this to avoid day care expenses!

"I worked around the clock for years," Joe said. "So we were both concerned about what we would fill our day with. But we've replaced work with a ton of the core pursuits you talk about, including many from the Core Pursuit Finder." If you'd like to try your hand at the Core Pursuit Finder, give it a go here:

WWW.YOURWEALTH.COM/CORE-PURSUIT-FINDER

Today, Joe and Cindy are living proof that retirement can be richer and more fulfilling than the working years that preceded it. They've relocated to an active fifty-five-plus desert community in Indio, California, where the weather is always great—"very hot in the summer, but better than a Northeast snow in the winter," as Joe puts it. And if the urge ever hit, they could practically walk to Coachella.

When it comes to core pursuits? These happy retirees are off the charts. Cindy's list reads like a master class in purposeful living: pickleball, hiking, games with friends, volunteering doing street medicine for the unhoused community, biking, exercise classes, book club, puzzles, and travel/camping. Joe's roster is equally impressive: pickleball ("she's a lot better than me," he admits), golfing, hiking, exercise, HOA committees, home improvement projects, biking, travel/camping, and wine club.

Even their vehicles are happy-proofed and primed for excitement: Cindy drives a Lexus 350NX, which Joe calls a "happy car" (he clearly remembered what he read in *You Can Retire Sooner Than You Think*!). Joe has a modified Jeep Rubicon that they tow behind their motor home for their desert off-roading adventures.

Throughout their working years, Joe and Cindy took their three kids to either Disney World or the Caribbean every year, and enjoyed many great camping trips as a family in their RV. Now all three of their adult children are "off the payroll," but they're still a regular part of Joe and Cindy's lives: Two live just 2.5 hours away in North Hollywood and Santa Monica, the third a short flight to San Francisco. "They love to come visit us in the desert on a regular basis," Joe says, "something we didn't expect." Now with their eldest son getting married, Joe and Cindy are already dreaming about the next generation joining their adventures. Lucky grandkids!

Joe and Cindy's transformation from worry to wonder reveals the power of core pursuits: the essential ingredient that can transform a bland or uninspiring retirement into a rich and vibrant one. I've often referred to these as "hobbies on steroids," because they're so much more than playing Solitaire at night and watching that new shark documentary on Netflix. You could also think of them as "super activities," a term coined by my friend—and podcast legend—Joe Saul-Sehy from *Stacking Benjamins*.[2] At their most basic, core pursuits are simply the things you enjoy doing. They're what turn empty calendar pages into meaningful adventures, with or without Microsoft Outlook.

And yet. It can be intimidating to "find your purpose." We'll talk about that phrase later in this chapter—and why it can set people up for failure. Because it doesn't actually have to be hard or complicated. There's no pressure to have a magical awakening. **Purpose is created, not found.**

I am here to tell you that you don't need to save all the lemurs in Madagascar. What are the things you already like to do, love to do, and want to do? Those are how you shape your life purpose. And that's what this chapter is all about.

From our 2025 Money and Happiness in America study, we discovered some crucial insights on the ways happy retirees engage with their core pursuits:

- **There's a magic number of unique/different core pursuits** that separates happy from unhappy retirees.
- **Time spent daily** on these meaningful activities has a great impact on happiness.
- **The right mix of categories** shows certain kinds of core pursuits have a strong lead.
- **Adventure pursuits** are a happiness indicator: activities that keep you exploring and growing.
- **Daily health and fitness** habits don't require an exorbitant amount of time but make a measurable difference in happiness.

- **A strong sense of purpose** is what connects all these activities to deeper meaning.

When you blend these ingredients together, something remarkable happens: Retirement transforms from endless weekends into adventures full of purpose and joy. Though it may sound counterintuitive, retirement is not simply a vacation, and that distinction can be the difference between discontent and fulfillment.

THE MAGIC NUMBER: FIVE-PLUS CORE PURSUITS

FIGURE 3.1. Number of Unique Core Pursuits, Unhappy vs. Happy Retirees

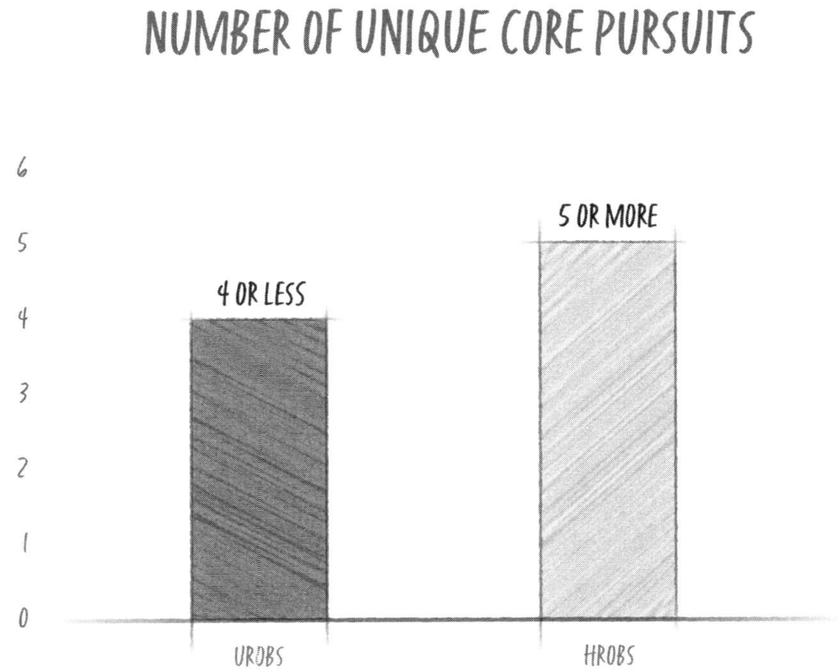

If you're anything like Claudia from Chapter 2—someone who remembers exact figures from my prior books and wants to keep me on my toes—you may remember that fifteen years ago, our research originally found that happy retirees averaged 3.6 core pursuits.

That's out the window. The new research shows a different reality—it's right there in Figure 3.1. **Happy retirees have five or more core pursuits. Unhappy retirees have four or fewer.** Then you've got the show-offs like Joe and Cindy who break the scale.

Why the increase? Did inflation hit the core pursuit market? Actually, I believe it reflects how retirement itself has evolved. Today's retirees are healthier, more active, and living longer than previous generations. They have more time to fill, and healthier life choices have given them more energy to fill it. Along the way, they've discovered that a richer variety of activities creates a more satisfying retirement.

Five isn't just an arbitrary number—it's the inflection point where something magical happens. With fewer than five core pursuits, retirees often feel like something's missing, even if they can't quite put their finger on what. But once you cross that threshold into more than five, you create what I call a "core pursuit cascade." One activity you love leads to another, which makes you hungry for another, which opens the path to still another core pursuit. You always have something to look forward to, something engaging on your calendar that makes you excited to wake up each morning.

Joe and Cindy exemplify this perfectly. Joe counts pickleball, golf, hiking, exercise, HOA committees, home improvement projects, biking, travel/camping, and wine club—that's nine core pursuits. Cindy has pickleball, hiking, games with friends, volunteering, biking, exercise classes, book club, puzzles, and travel/camping—also nine. Some of these they do together; some they do on their own or with friends. No wonder they need to print their calendars to keep track!

But having five-plus core pursuits is only half the recipe. The other half is making sure they get enough time to bake.

SEVEN EXTRA "WORK WEEKS" OF FUN

When we conducted our study, we asked our currently retired participants, "How many hours per week do you spend on each of the core pursuits you're currently involved in?"

The research reveals a striking difference, as you can see in Figure 3.2: Happy retirees spend 18.6 hours per week on their core pursuits versus just 13.2 hours for unhappy retirees. **That's 280+ extra hours per year of purposeful activity—equivalent to 7 work weeks, but instead of work, you're actually choosing the core pursuits you love!**

FIGURE 3.2. Core Pursuits—Time Spent Per Week, Unhappy vs. Happy Retirees

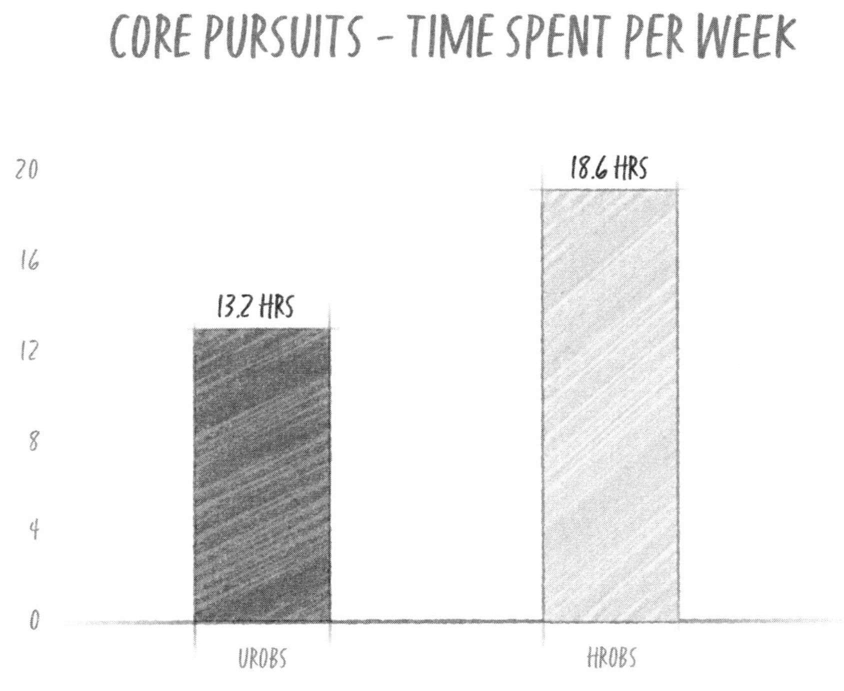

Break this down to daily time and the pattern becomes even clearer. Happy retirees spend an average of two hours and forty minutes per day on their core pursuits, while unhappy retirees average just one hour and fifty minutes. That's nearly three hours per day versus less than two hours. The sweet spot? Aim for at least two and a half hours daily.

This might sound like a lot, but remember: We're talking about activities you genuinely enjoy. This isn't adding 2.5 hours of drudgery to your day—it's intentionally structuring 2.5 hours around what brings you joy and meaning. Think about Joe printing his weekly calendar. Those aren't obligations he's tracking; they're opportunities he's orchestrating.

The beautiful thing about this formula is its flexibility. Some days you might spend four hours hiking and exploring, other days just ninety minutes playing pickleball or working in the garden. The key is that over the course of a week, you're averaging that 2.5+ hours daily. It's like adding the right amount of zest to your retirement recipe—enough to make every day flavorful but distributed in a way that feels natural and sustainable.

Now, if you're thinking, *Okay, Wes, but what should I actually be doing for those 2.5 hours?*—you're asking the right question.

THE RIGHT MIX: CATEGORIES THAT CREATE HAPPINESS

Not all core pursuits are created equal—some pack more happiness punch than others.

In our 2025 study, we asked retirees, "What brings you the most joy and purpose in retirement?" We didn't give them a multiple-choice list to check off. Instead, we let them write in their own answers—and wow, did they deliver! Figure 3.3 shows a beautiful wheel of the passions and core pursuits they shared. This wheel is so beautiful, we wanted Pat Sajak and Vanna White to present it, but we assumed they were too

FIGURE 3.3. Top Categories of Core Pursuits That Bring Americans the Most Joy in Retirement

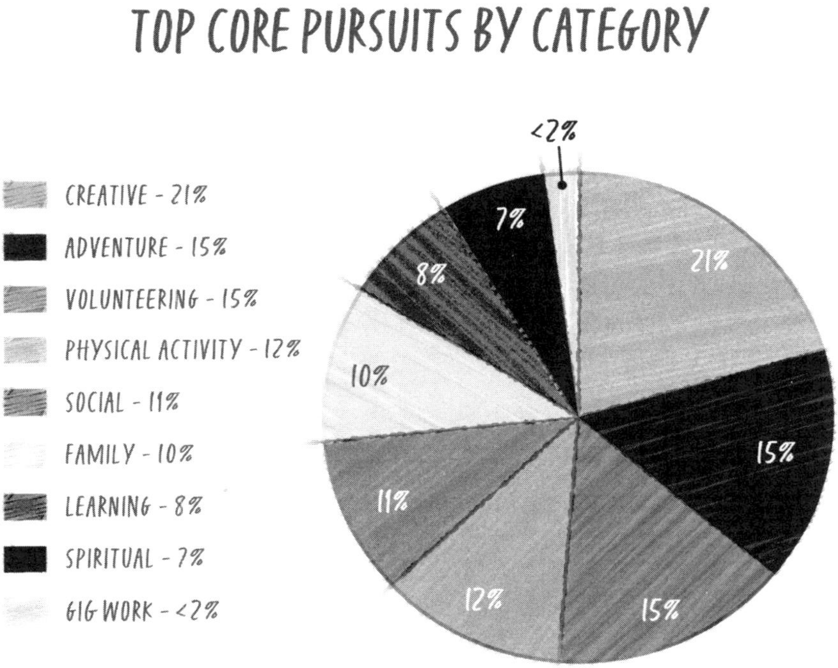

busy enjoying retirement! We collected open-ended responses to the question, and their answers were so creative, so specific, and so inspiring that I knew other aspiring happy retirees needed to see exactly what their peers were up to.

CREATIVITY TAKES CENTER STAGE

Creative pursuits lead the pack at more than 20 percent—and the variety is remarkable. Our participants mentioned everything from painting, woodworking, and photography to blowing glass, restoring old toy trains, and writing a memoir. Gardening appeared repeatedly, which makes perfect sense—you're literally creating life and beauty. Other popular creative pursuits included cooking, sewing, cross-stitch, crocheting, songwriting, and digital video editing. It makes sense when you think about it: After decades of following someone else's agenda, retirees finally have the freedom to express their own creativity.

OTHER CREATIVE CORE PURSUITS OF THE HAPPIEST RETIREES

- Drawing
- Playing music
- Filmmaking
- Spinning (not as in Peloton—this participant said, "I'm in a spinner's guild where we process dyed wool")
- Making healthy meals
- Macramé (I think this has something to do with yarn?)
- Arts and crafts

ADVENTURE MATTERS MORE THAN YOU THINK

Adventure pursuits claim more than 15 percent of the happiness pie—the second biggest category—and reveal something crucial about retirement happiness. In Figure 3.4, you'll see that **happy retirees have an average of 1.9 adventure-related core pursuits compared to just 1.2 for unhappy retirees.** Even more telling: A whopping 57 percent of unhappy retirees have *zero* adventure-related pursuits.

The variety of what counts as "adventure" shows just how personal this category can be. Travel dominated our survey responses—or as one participant put it, "Traveling whenever possible. It brings me joy." RVing makes a frequent appearance, which often coincided with camping and exploring national parks.

FIGURE 3.4. Number of Adventure-Related Core Pursuits

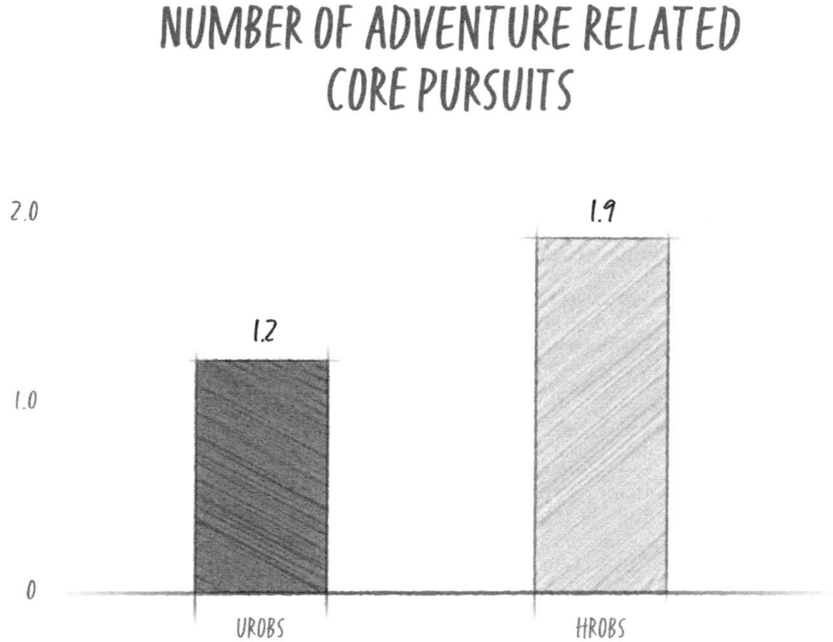

But adventure also includes fishing, boating, motorcycling ("riding my Harley," said one leather-clad grandpa), horseback riding, and kayaking local waterways. One respondent mentioned scuba diving for "five to six weeks a year—I love viewing wonderful coral reefs off the southern Gulf of California."

Why do adventure pursuits matter so much? They create what psychologists call "anticipatory happiness"—the joy you feel looking forward to something exciting. They also provide rich material for storytelling and memory-making. When Joe and Cindy plan their next RV destination or research a new hiking trail, they're not just planning an activity; they're creating anticipation. When they return, they have stories to share and memories to cherish. Towing Joe's modified Jeep Rubicon behind the RV opens up even more adventure possibilities—desert off-roading, exploring remote areas, discovering hidden gems that most tourists never see. They've created a lifestyle where adventure is always within reach.

Many adventure pursuits are naturally social. Whether you're exploring Europe with your spouse, trout fishing in America with your best pal, or meeting other leather-clad Harley riders in your community, these activities create opportunities for connection. We'll talk about the vital importance of socialization and community in Chapter 4.

Adventure is personal. It's a blank page for you to fill however you like. Your adventures might be day trips to explore small towns, photography walks in local parks, antiquing expeditions, or weekend getaways to discover new museums. The common thread is novelty and exploration—activities that take you out of your comfort zone and beyond your routine. So while Indiana Jones might stand an excellent chance of being a happy retiree, you don't have to outrun a giant rolling boulder to have a grand adventure.

OTHER EXCITING ADVENTURES OF THE HAPPIEST RETIREES

- Horseback riding
- Going to the beach
- Bass fishing
- Bird-watching
- Rock hunting ("I tumble rocks and eventually make jewelry")
- Flying planes

WHEN GIVING TIME BECOMES GETTING HAPPINESS

Volunteering was another one of the most popular activities for bringing the most enjoyment in retirement. This category offers something special: the chance to contribute beyond yourself while staying socially connected. Whether you're helping at a food bank, mentoring young professionals, or doing street medicine for the homeless like Cindy, volunteering creates meaning that extends far beyond your own happiness.

The responses our study unearthed reveal the deep satisfaction these retirees find in their service:

- "I volunteer for animal welfare causes. I've always loved all animals, and it makes me feel like I'm doing something important and that I can make a difference."
- "I love spending time with my mom. I didn't get to do that when I was working."
- "I do several volunteer activities, but my very favorite is working with puppies that are going to become guide dogs."
- "Volunteering at my church and belonging to a women's group at church brings me the most joy. First off, my faith is important to me, and I feel I am giving back for all the blessings I have received. I have met some very good friends and a variety of people I never thought I would be friends with."

This connects to something broader we discovered in our research: **Happy retirees are volunteering and working because they want to and they're passionate about it, not because they have to.** We'll talk more about volunteering and other forms of work-related "second acts" in Chapter 5, but for now, the important takeaway is that volunteering is a miracle blend—one driven by passion and purpose rather than financial necessity.

PHYSICAL ACTIVITY: THE FIFTEEN-MINUTE GAME CHANGER

Physical activity was another popular happiness elixir, and the responses reveal how creative people get with staying active. Beyond the expected activities like walking, hiking, and going to the gym, participants mentioned pickleball, tennis, golf (one happy retiree said it best: "I enjoy the thrill of a good shot that goes in the hole"), water aerobics, dancing, yoga, and biking, either the old-fashioned way or with an e-bike (a participant was quick to add, "I try not to use the electric unless I have to!"). Some turned fitness into a social pursuit—one retiree noted being a fitness instructor, while others participate in Zumba or yoga classes.

But here's where it gets really interesting. Happy retirees spend almost an hour a day—approximately fifty-five minutes—on health and fitness activities, while unhappy retirees average just forty minutes. That's only a fifteen-minute difference, but it's statistically significant and shows a measurable divide when it comes to happiness.

Adding just fifteen minutes per day to your health routine might be the simplest happiness tune-up in this entire book. We're not talking about training for a marathon or becoming a yoga instructor (though if that excites you, go for it!). The key insight is that these aren't just workouts—they're enjoyable activities that both groups seem to like to do, but one emphasizes them with more time. Oh, and it just so happens to contribute to your health and vitality.

This finding connects beautifully with the core pursuits framework: Those extra minutes can be "tacked on" to your existing pursuits. If you're already walking with your neighbor for half an hour every morning, extend it by fifteen minutes. If you're playing pickleball twice a week, add a third session. If you're gardening, spend a bit more time digging, planting, and moving around your yard. More is better. Remember, you're looking to spend 2.5+ hours per day on your core pursuits, so that fifteen minutes can be rolled into your overall purpose portfolio.

Joe and Cindy demonstrate this perfectly. Their health activities aren't separate from their core pursuits—they're integrated into them. Hiking, biking, pickleball, and even their RV adventures that involve walking and exploring all contribute to their physical activity. They're getting their health boost while doing things they genuinely enjoy.

The beauty of this approach is that it doesn't feel like "exercise"—it feels like living. When your health activities are also your core pursuits, you're not forcing yourself to do something you don't enjoy; you're simply extending activities you already love.

OTHER PHYSICAL ACTIVITIES OF THE HAPPIEST RETIREES

- Yardwork
- Weight lifting
- Stretching
- Running and fitness
- Water aerobics
- Swimming
- Scuba diving

THE FULL SPECTRUM OF JOY

You may have noticed that many of these activities overlap across categories. We love to hear that! When you tap into these core pursuits, your happiness quickly gets exponential. Take scuba diving, for example. It's simultaneously an adventure pursuit (exploring coral reefs) and physical activity (swimming). Rock hunting combines adventure (discovering treasure in the great outdoors) with creativity (making jewelry), while group fitness classes blend physical activity with social connection. Once

FIGURE 3.5. Top Core Pursuits By Activity That Bring Americans the Most Joy in Retirement

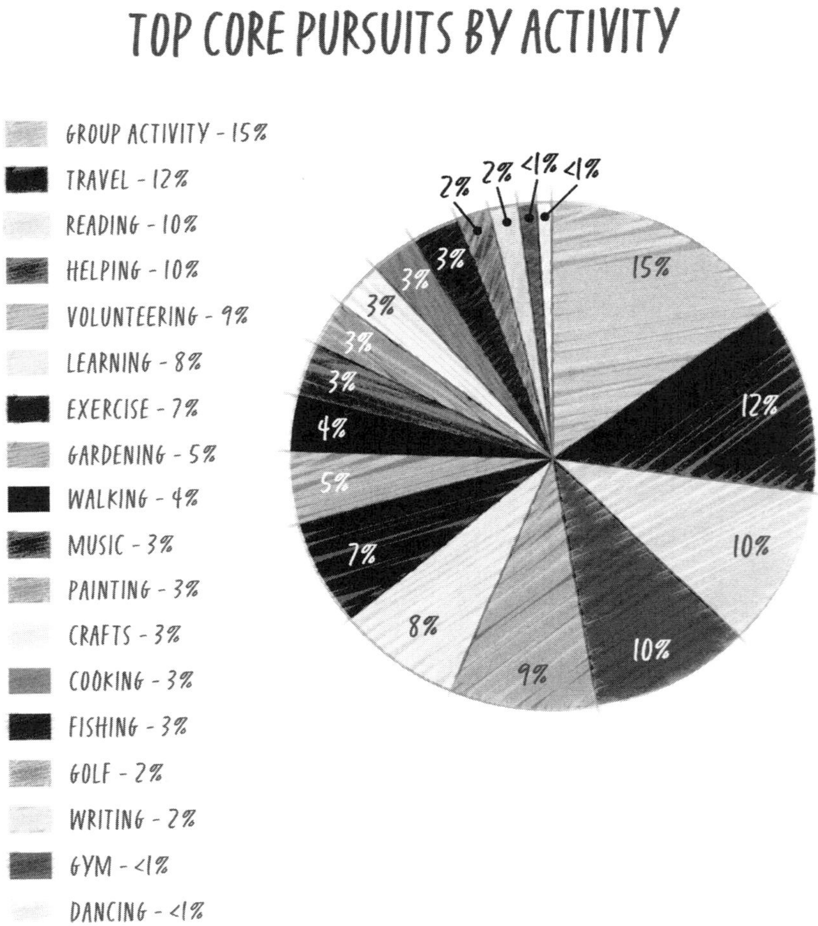

again, RV trips really do it all: There's built-in adventure (exploring new places and cultures), social connection (meeting fellow adventurers), and physical activity (hiking new trails). Throw in plein air painting of those gorgeous gorges—which I think means painting outside landscapes while you're outside—and you've got creativity covered, too.

If you're thinking, *But I'm not an RV person*, don't sweat it. I harken back to RVing simply because it pops up a lot in the research. But there are limitless ways to engage with the world around you. As our team drilled down even further into the specific activities that bring happy retirees the most joy, we discovered just how wonderfully diverse core pursuits can be. Group activities lead the pack at 15.4 percent, followed by travel at 11.5 percent and reading (yes, reading!) at 10.3 percent. The complete roster includes traveling, reading, helping, volunteering, exercising, gardening, walking, playing music, painting, crafting, cooking, fishing, golfing, writing, and going to the gym. And for all you aspiring acolytes of Fred Astaire and Ginger Rogers who are putting on your tap shoes: Yes, dancing made the list!

Think of core pursuits as your building blocks for constructing purpose. As we're about to see, building a powerful purpose portfolio is easier than you think.

FIGURE 3.6. Percentage of Americans Who Report Having a Strong Sense of Purpose

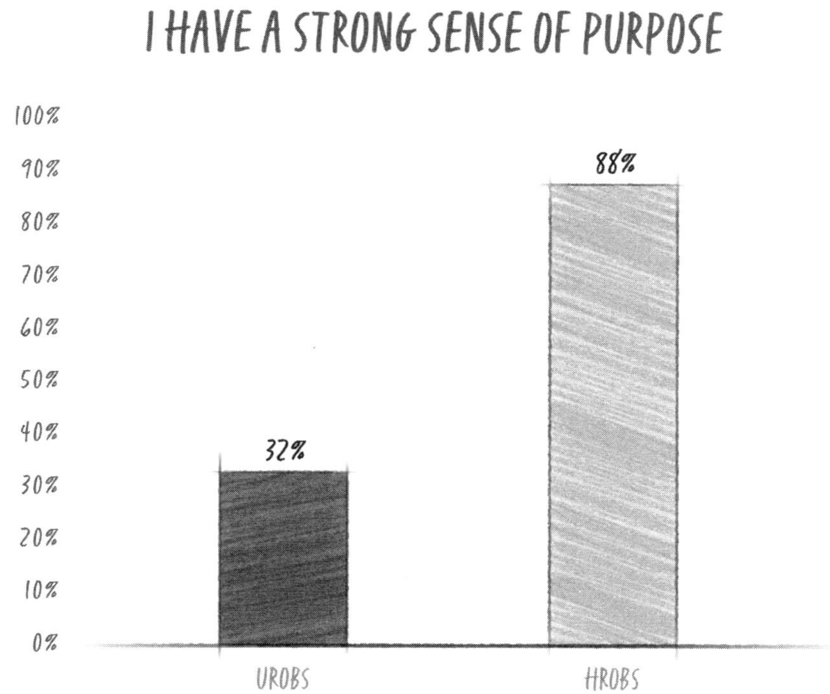

THE PURPOSE CONNECTION

By now, you can see the pattern emerging. It's laid out in Figure 3.6. Five core pursuits 2.5+ hours daily. Adventure elements. Health habits. Each of these things matters individually, but here's what ties them all together: **Our research shows that happy retirees are nearly three times more likely to have a strong sense of purpose.**

Want to know the most eye-opening truth of all?

Purpose isn't something they found; it's something they created. Purpose is built one core pursuit at a time.

This flies in the face of our cultural mythology around purpose. People are always talking about "finding your purpose"—and by people, I mean bumper stickers and inspirational posters with forests and waterfalls. Is it any wonder that many retirees believe their big *raison d'être* is hiding somewhere in the far-off distance and they have to spare no expense to hunt it down? (I don't speak French, but my editor tells me those words mean "reason for being.")

We've been conditioned to believe that if we book that trip to save those lemurs, we'll uncover our epic Mother Theresa–level life purpose that was waiting for us in Madagascar all along. It's a seductive idea, albeit a misconception. This is where the pressure comes in. *Find your purpose! Discover your purpose!* This sounds terrifying, doesn't it? It doesn't need to be. **We can simply *create* our purpose from the core pursuits we're already doing and already love.** Low pressure. It doesn't have to be an Indiana Jones treasure hunt or an Ayahuasca retreat in Peru.

But you, and only you, get to fashion your purpose in whatever way suits you. And it's available to you *right now*, not floating around the universe playing hard to get. Purpose is something you get to create.

Because here's what I've observed in thousands of happy retirees: They didn't stumble upon some cosmic destiny. They built purpose deliberately, often from ordinary elements of their lives—relationships they value, skills and interests they already have, and communities they care about. The happiest retirees understand that purpose isn't discovered like a diamond in the rough; it's crafted like a fine piece of Amish furniture: with intention, effort, and personal touches that reflect who you are.

You don't have to wait passively for meaning to find you. You actively construct it, piece by piece, choice by choice, day by day. And the most empowering thing is that because you're the creator, you have the freedom to reshape and expand your purpose as you evolve.

THE TWO FACES OF PURPOSE: DAILY AND YEARLY

After more than a decade of research, I've discovered that purpose operates on two essential levels: daily purpose and yearly purpose. Both are critical to retirement happiness, but the way they work in tandem is special. It takes the pressure off the ubiquitous cultural idea that to live a purposeful life, we must solve world hunger before breakfast.

Daily purpose consists of your core pursuits—the regular, intentional activities that give meaning to your everyday life. They're doable, manageable, and rooted in what brings you joy. This could be tending your garden three mornings a week, coaching your granddaughter's soccer team every Saturday, practicing guitar for thirty minutes after breakfast, or volunteering at the local animal shelter every week.

Yearly purpose is where your core pursuits build toward something more substantial in retirement. Your daily gardening rolls up into a yearly purpose of planting a substantial new vegetable garden and making fantastic salads all summer (your spouse better get used to eating healthy greens). Those Saturday coaching sessions provide a way for you to strengthen family bonds and help develop your granddaughter's confidence. Your daily guitar practice inspires you to play in the local senior band's holiday concert series. And those weekly shelter hours grow into a larger vision: Help one thousand dogs find forever homes, thereby becoming a valued part of your community's animal welfare network.

See how easy it is to roll your daily purpose into yearly? It's taking what you already love to do—and expanding it. This approach naturally widens your circle of social connections, adds richness to your schedule, and extends your regular routines into rewarding journeys. Your 5K becomes a 10K, then a half-marathon. Maybe even a marathon! 26.2 miles. Wow. I bet it's the last 0.2 that really kills. Just watch out for those knees—they're expensive to replace.

Both types of purposes pull their weight in the happiness equation. Daily purpose keeps you engaged and energized throughout your week, while yearly purpose transforms those individual activities into something long-lasting. It's like the difference between placing a single brick (daily purpose) and seeing the beautiful home you've built brick by brick over time (yearly purpose)—something you can step back and admire.

It really is that simple: five-plus core pursuits, 2.5+ daily hours, adventure elements, 15 extra minutes of physical activity, and purposeful intention—a satisfying and transformative recipe. Joe and Cindy's story shows us what's possible when you follow this regimen. They've gone from worrying about filling their days to needing printed calendars to track all their activities. They've replaced the structure of work with the joy of purpose-driven living.

Start where you are. If you currently have three core pursuits, work toward five. If you're spending ninety minutes daily on meaningful activities, gradually expand toward 2.5 hours. Plot out an adventure, even if it's close to home. No one says a trip to the local plant nursery can't be an adventure. Incorporate fifteen extra minutes of health activity. Most importantly, begin thinking about how your daily activities can roll up into your yearly triumphs. Step by step, you'll build a purpose portfolio you can be proud of.

STOP GIVING YOUR CORE PURSUITS SHORT SHRIFT

Now I want you to do a writing exercise.

Before getting married, the bride and groom dedicate time to writing their "I Do's." And rightfully so. But I think the "to-dos" deserve just as much attention. (Don't tell my wife.)

Set aside thirty minutes and then follow these steps to reframe your favorite to-dos:

1. Start by making a comprehensive list of all possible core pursuits you could see yourself doing over the next five years.
2. Next, take your top five or ten and reframe them to focus on their deeper meaning to you and your life. Here are some examples of how to make what you might think of as just an activity into something with a deeper purpose:
    a. "I like golf" becomes "I like golf because I'm building camaraderie with friends while challenging myself to improve."
    b. "I love to garden" becomes "I love nurturing life and enjoying the satisfaction of creating something tangible."
    c. "I enjoy playing an instrument" becomes "I enjoy expressing creativity and connecting with others through music."
    d. "I'm cool with babysitting" becomes "It's meaningful to build lasting relationships and pass on family values."

The happiest retirees have learned how to align their daily activities with what brings them long-lasting, self-replenishing joy. As your daily purpose evolves into yearly purpose—expanding what already exists and taking unexpected turns to find new treasure—simply lean into what you love.

But here's something I've learned: Even the most electrifying core pursuits can feel hollow when experienced in isolation. The woodworker who builds beautiful furniture but has no one to share his craft with. The avid reader who devours fascinating books but lacks a community in which to discuss them. The master gardener whose stunning roses bloom for an audience of one. Core pursuits provide the foundation for happiness, but they reach their full potential when paired with genuine human connection.

That's the not-so-secret formula that happy retirees use to build lives of authentic fulfillment. Now you're ready for the secret sauce that transforms a good retirement into a great one: other people.

CHAPTER 4

Secret #3: Get a Life! (i.e., a Community)

Four or More Close Connections, aka Friends

When Jerry and Elise moved to their fifty-five-plus community outside Sacramento ten years ago, they didn't know a soul.

They'd chosen the development for all the usual reasons retirees gravitate toward active adult communities: mild California climate, lush golf course, the promise of an active lifestyle among peers their own age. The development was also brand new, which was a nice perk. When Elise and Jerry moved into their home, the walls still held that crisp, newly constructed smell—a blend of fresh paint and possibility.

What they didn't expect was that the timing would be absolutely perfect for something far more valuable than any perk or amenity.

"We were one of the first families to move onto our street," Jerry said. "The whole phase had just been completed, so within the first six months, we had a dozen new neighbors who were all in the exact same boat—didn't know anybody, looking to make friends, and wanting to get involved in the community."

What happened next was pure social magic. Because everyone was new, everyone was eager to connect. Evening cocktails on the cul-de-sac became a weekly tradition. Dinner parties rotated from house to house. Nature walks turned into monthly hikes. Jerry's "exact same boat" metaphor went literal as he took their neighbors out on the lake every Sunday. Within a year, Jerry and Elise had transformed from strangers in a new town to the heart of a tight-knit community.

"It was like a restart button on our social lives," Elise said. "We went from knowing nobody to having more close friends than we'd had in decades. And that's really why we love it here so much. It's not the golf course or the weather. It's the community."

I've heard this story countless times from happy retirees. They move somewhere for the scenery—the mountains, the beach, the desert—but they stay for the people. I don't know about you, but when I sit in an Adirondack chair watching a gorgeous sunset, it's even better with my gorgeous wife in an Adirondack chair beside me. And you can tell her I said that.

Jerry and Elise's story and thousands of similar tales from happy retirees all point to the same fundamental truth: Socialization isn't just a nice thing to aim for in retirement; it's nonnegotiable. Yet the odds are stacked against us culturally—and as we'll see, genetically, too.

In this chapter, we'll talk about how to beat those odds.

FACEBOOK IS LYING TO YOU: THE SAD STATE OF MODERN FRIENDSHIP

We all know the social media spin: Every day we sign in to our accounts and see our thousands of "friends" all around the country and the world.

But the research says otherwise. Look at Figure 4.1, which shows an overall decline in close friendships among Americans from 1990 to 2024. The percentage of people who have two or fewer friends has risen from 16 percent to 37 percent—more than twofold. Having more than three to four close friends has stayed essentially flat, while having five or more close friends has declined substantially.

If that's not depressing enough for you, here's a sobering statistic: 17 percent of Americans report having *zero* close friends outside of family members. This is a dramatic shift from just a generation ago. **In 1990, only 3 percent of Americans reported having no close friends. We've gone from 1 in 33 people being socially isolated to nearly 1 in 5.**[1]

FIGURE 4.1. Close Friendships Among Americans

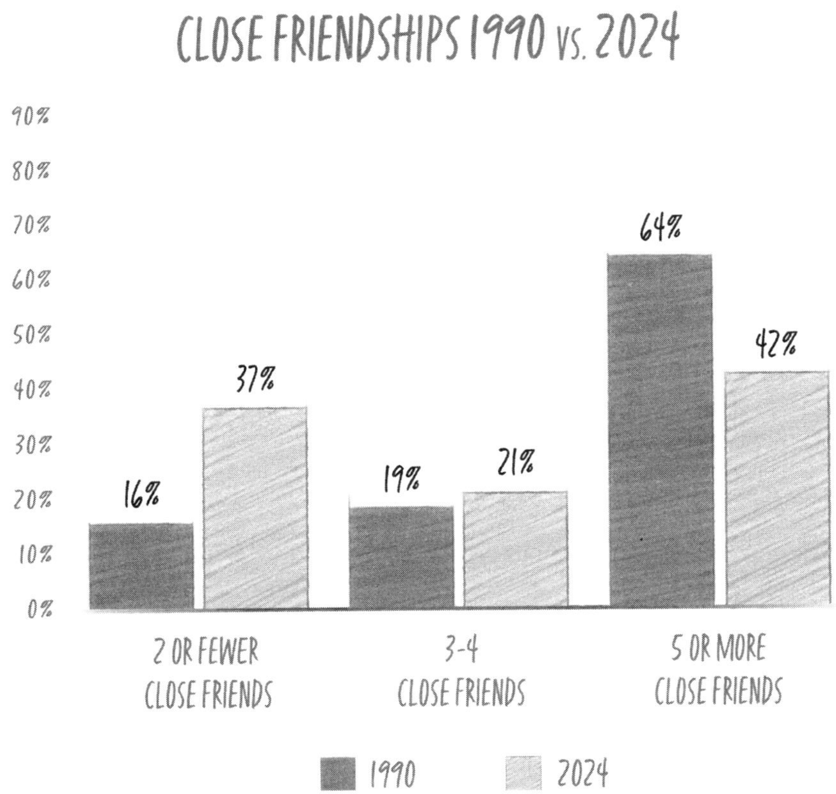

Source: Daniel A. Cox and Sam Pressler, "Disconnected: The Growing Class Divide in American Civic Life," Survey Center on American Life, August 22, 2024, https://www.americansurveycenter.org/research/disconnected-places-and-spaces.

Americans are significantly less likely to have large social networks and more likely to experience social isolation compared to previous generations. This isn't just a sad statistic—it's a retirement crisis in the making. As we're about to see, making and maintaining meaningful social connections is standard practice for the happiest retirees. But these connections are becoming increasingly rare, which makes our focus on them more crucial than ever before.

COMMUNITY: THE ONE WORD TO RULE THEM ALL

By now you know I spend a lot of time studying the habits of happy (and unhappy) retirees—more time than I sit around in Adirondack chairs, that's for sure. This latest study generated 54,000 data points covering everything from financial levels to core pursuits, from education levels to personality traits.

But if I were forced to boil all of that research down into a single word, the lynchpin of retirement happiness, it would be this: *community*.

This struck me most powerfully when I analyzed the open-ended responses to our survey question, "What brings you the most joy and purpose in retirement?" We didn't provide multiple-choice options—we let people write in their own answers. The responses were wonderful and wide ranging, covering everything from creative pursuits to adventure activities to volunteer work.

Take a look at the pie chart in Figure 4.2. If it seems familiar, that's because you saw the same one in Chapter 3. But this time, I want you to look at how many of these activities have a social component.

As we crunched the data from our study, here's what really caught my attention: Whether respondents mentioned creative activities like music or woodworking, adventure pursuits like RVing or hiking, volunteer

FIGURE 4.2. Top Core Pursuits By Activity That Bring Americans the Most Joy in Retirement

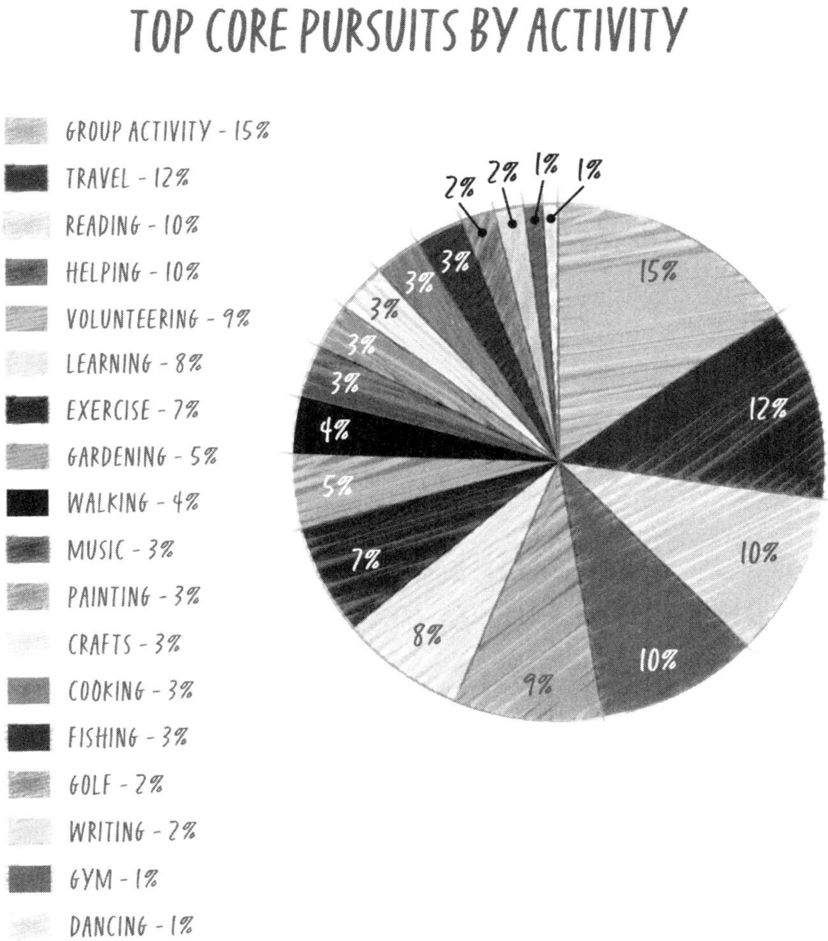

work at food banks or churches, or physical activities like biking or pickleball, the vast majority described doing these activities *with other people*—family, friends, neighbors, fellow volunteers.

Adventure activities were described as trips *with spouses or friends*. Volunteer work emphasized serving *with others* and meeting like-minded people. Physical activities were about walking *with groups*, playing tennis *with partners*, and hiking *with clubs*.

The pattern was unmistakable. It's not just the activity itself that brings joy—it's doing it with others.

You might say that the other secrets behind the Retire Sooner Method ultimately serve this deeper purpose. Having enough money gives you freedom to build community. Your core pursuits provide structure for socializing. Good sleep keeps you awake and energized to maintain and nurture strong relationships. Even having a written plan reduces stress so you can focus on what truly matters: your family and your social network.

But don't take my word for it. There's hard science behind why friendship and socialization matter so much to our well-being. I learned all about it from a man named Michael.

THE NEUROSCIENCE OF CONNECTION: WE'RE WIRED FOR THIS

One of the best things about hosting the *Retire Sooner* podcast is that I get to meet fascinating people and have enlightening conversations. One of my all-time favorite interviews was with Dr. Michael L. Platt, a neuroscientist at the Wharton School who studies social connection in both humans and primates.[2] What he revealed about our brains blew mine wide open.

Michael explained that we are biologically wired for connection from birth. "When a newborn emerges from the womb," he said, "they have a preference for looking at faces." The human brain is hardwired to seek out faces and make eye contact and read emotional cues, because our survival has always depended on other people.

It makes sense, if you think about it. Throughout human history, being part of a group or tribe meant safety, productivity, food, and reproduction. Being alone meant danger. Even if today you're not likely to get attacked by a lion on your way to the office, that same wiring persists and shapes how we feel, think, and behave. It's no surprise the social brain network—a dedicated system for managing relationships, reading emotions, and responding to others' behavior—lights up when we communicate, laugh, and share with people. At a biological level, it's core to our survival to bond with others and feel understood.

It doesn't stop there. Regular social connections release oxytocin, the bonding hormone that reduces stress, boosts trust, and helps regulate cortisol levels, heart rate, blood pressure, and even inflammation. Michael's research shows that connection can literally reduce inflammation in our bodies, while loneliness activates the opposite response—a threat response that increases stress hormones and slowly damages the body over time.

One of the most compelling concepts Michael shared was "synchrony," the measurable alignment of brain activity, physiology, and behavior between two or more people during meaningful interactions. When we're in deep conversation with someone we connect with, our brain waves can literally become synchronized. "What's really cool with regard to synchrony," Michael added, "is that every culture on the planet has rituals in which we do rhythmic activities together. We sing, we dance, we march. What we now know is that those activities turn up physiological synchrony. When we move together, we get in sync."

This isn't telepathy. It's real-time brain alignment. And you don't have to get out your marching baton to experience it. "The process of having a conversation begins to bring your brains into closer alignment," Michael said. Through perceptual cues—eyes, voice, gestures—combined with brain chemistry, we unconsciously sync up with people we click with, even when all we do is talk.

The science is clear: We're not just social creatures by choice—we're social creatures by design. Fighting against this biological imperative makes retirement harder and less fulfilling. Embracing it unlocks extraordinary happiness potential.

"I spend half my time studying monkeys," Michael confessed. "Their brains are wired in exactly the same way ours are. They depend on each other. The more friends a monkey has, the longer and healthier life they lead."

Now let's take a look at Figure 4.3. This chart measures the impact of the number of close connections, aka friendships, and their impact on happiness. There's a clear correlation between happiness and connection—a substantial one. Americans who report one to two friends fall

FIGURE 4.3. Happiness Relative to Number of Close Connections/Friendships

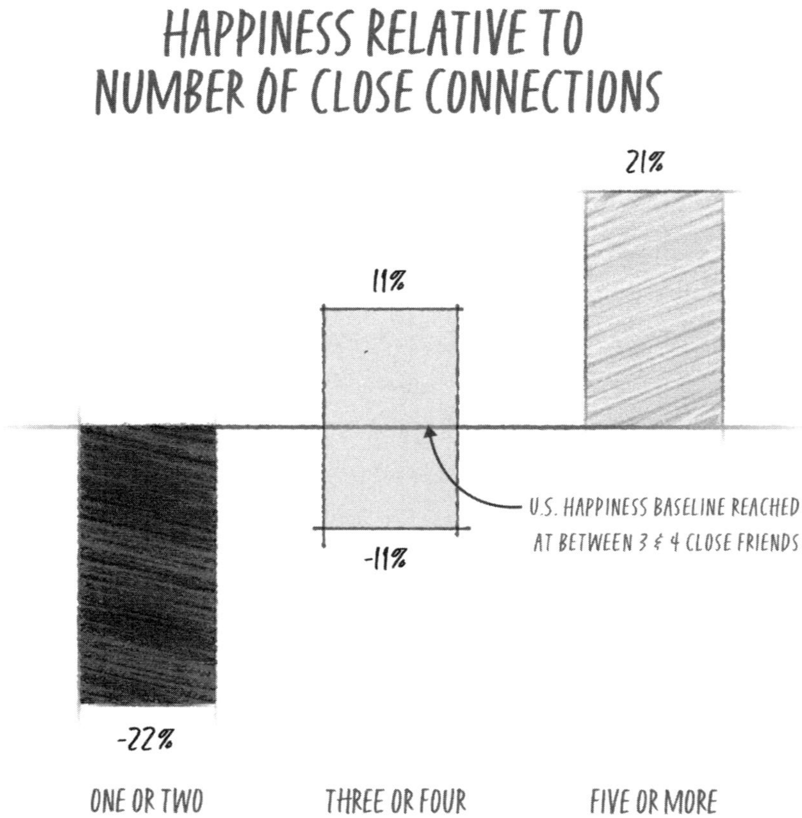

Source: Capital Investment Advisors, LLC analysis of data from *What the Happiest Retirees Know*. Wes Moss, *What the Happiest Retirees Know: 10 Habits for a Healthy, Secure, and Joyful Life* (McGraw Hill, 2021)

FIGURE 4.4. I Have Enough Close Friends, UROBs vs. HROBs

significantly below the US happiness baseline. Conversely, Americans with five or more friends are significantly above the baseline.

Looking at the middle of the chart, our research shows that having three to four friends lands us close to the US happiness baseline. Statistically, 3.6 close friends is the tipping point. If you zoom out of the statistics, what that means for you is that it's great to have three to four friends—it puts you solidly in the neutral zone. But clearly, when it comes to friendships, connections, and socialization, more is better. If you want to get you into that other fabled Green Zone, shoot for the five-plus camp.

Once again, there's more research that bears this out. As you can see from Figure 4.4, **happy retirees (HROBs) are twice as likely as unhappy retirees (UROBs) to say they have "enough" close friends.** When we asked retirees whether they felt they had sufficient close personal connections, aka friends, 81 percent of happy retirees answered yes, compared to just 38 percent of unhappy retirees. Essentially, happy retirees are two times more likely to say they have enough close friends. This isn't about having dozens of acquaintances—or dare I say, Facebook "friends." It's about having enough meaningful relationships to feel socially supported and connected.

What the data suggests is that crossing a threshold of "enough" creates a dramatic happiness inflection point. When you feel like you have sufficient close connections, everything else in retirement becomes more enjoyable, and happiness levels soar.

THE CHALLENGE: MAKING FRIENDS GETS HARDER WITH AGE

Here's both the bad news and the good news about friendship in later life.

The bad news: Our research confirms what many people intuitively know—making close friends gets significantly more difficult as we age. Figure 4.5 is sobering. Americans find it relatively easy to make friends in their twenties and thirties, but starting in their forties and continuing through each subsequent decade, forming new close connections becomes increasingly challenging. "We see the exact same thing in monkeys," Michael said. "The most intense interest in socializing is during adolescence . . . then it begins to fall off as we get older."

According to Michael, who studies this kind of thing, it's harder for men to make and sustain friendships later in life than it is for women. Men die at younger ages than women do, too. Coincidence? I—and, more importantly, Michael—think not. There's a proven relationship between social support and your health and vitality in old age.

Even happy people acknowledge that making friends gets harder over time. However—and here's where it gets interesting—older Americans who are happy in their current life stage are significantly more likely than neutral or unhappy older Americans to say making

FIGURE 4.5. How Easy or Difficult Do You Think It Is to Make Close Personal Friends or Connections in Your 20s, 30s, 40s, etc.

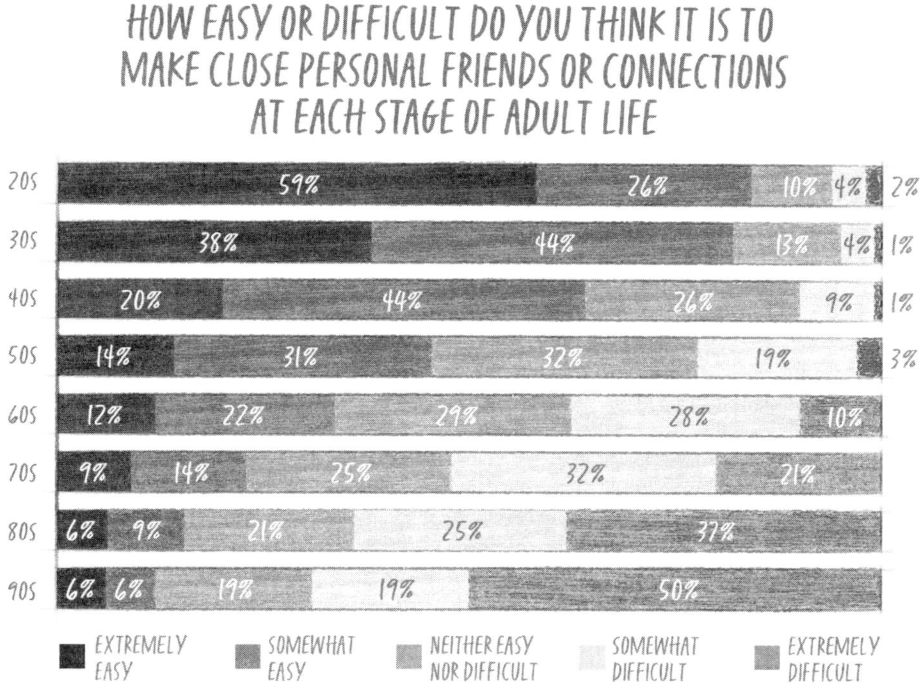

friends is "extremely" or "somewhat" easy in their forties, fifties, sixties, seventies, eighties, and even nineties.

My personal theory on this is that when you're content with your life, you're more approachable, more optimistic, more likely to participate in anything—all of which makes forming new friendships more natural. It's a symbiotic cycle. Be happy, make more friends, have more friends, get happier. You can't make old friends, but you can lose them, and the only way to fight against this is to make new ones.

I promised you some good news, so here it is: Recognizing that friendship becomes more challenging with age means we can be intentional about addressing this challenge. Just like financial planning requires more effort and strategy as we approach retirement, social planning requires deliberate action to maintain and build the relationships that will sustain us.

"It's really a question of just making it happen," said Michael. "Put the devices down, put the paper down, and put yourself out there. I liken it to a gym. If you haven't worked out in a while and you go to the gym, what's it like? Painful. You get out of breath, but you have to keep at it to get in shape. The same is true for making friends."

When I asked Michael if he had any tips, he said every conversation matters. "Your social brain network is like a muscle," he explained. "The more you use it, the more it grows. Every little interaction—even talking to the barista at Starbucks—is like getting on the treadmill for your brain. You have to keep working at it to keep your brain healthy, vital, and alive."

MAKIN' MONEY, MAKIN' FRIENDS

While chatting up your barista is one way to flex that social muscle, here's another game changer: solid financial planning. Because guess what? More money makes pretty much everything easier—including making friends.

People with higher levels of wealth report that making friends is easier across all life stages. **Americans with $3 million or more in assets are 38 percent more likely to say making friends is easy compared to those with lower asset levels.**

Why is this the case? I don't know, but I have a few guesses. Maybe it's because wealth provides more opportunities for social activities—joining clubs, traveling, dining out, entertaining at home. Maybe it's because financial confidence can translate into personal confidence. Again, I'm not sure. But this does give us one more reason to hit the financial Green Zone.

FIGURE 4.6. Share of Retirement-Age Individuals Who Report Being Married

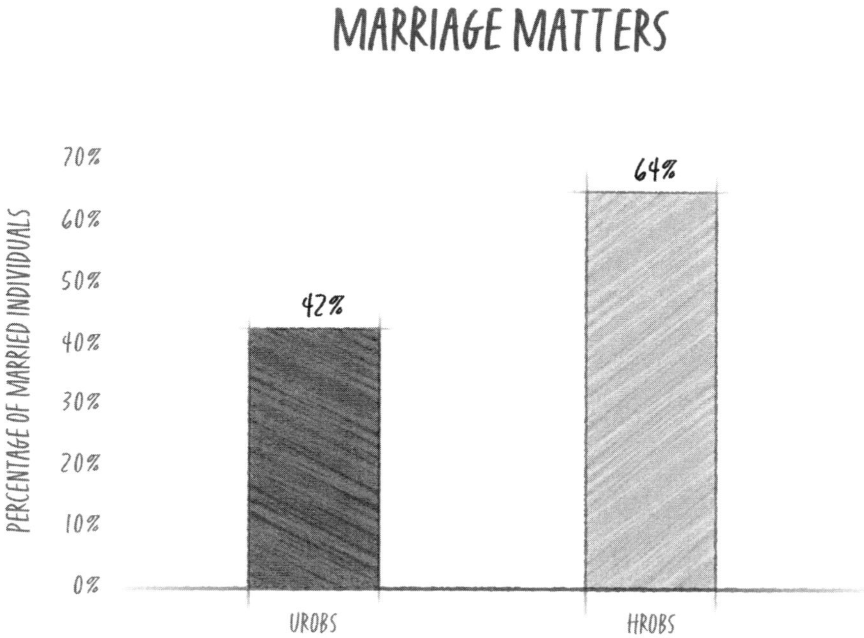

MARRIAGE MATTERS

Our research made it abundantly clear: **Happy retirees are 50 percent more likely to have a spouse or partner.** You may not think sharing morning coffee and arguing over the thermostat is the secret to happiness, but one glance at Figure 4.6 and you'll see why that daily dose of human connection matters more.

And if you're not married, you're not doomed. In our Money and Happiness in America study, we asked participants, "What is your current living situation?" Then we gave them several options: Did they live alone, with their spouse or significant other, with a roommate, with their parents, in a senior living community, or with a relative? Figure 4.7 sums up our research: **Unhappy retirees are 60 percent more likely to report living alone compared to happy retirees.** Sure, living with a spouse or

FIGURE 4.7. Share of Retirement-Age Population Who Live Alone

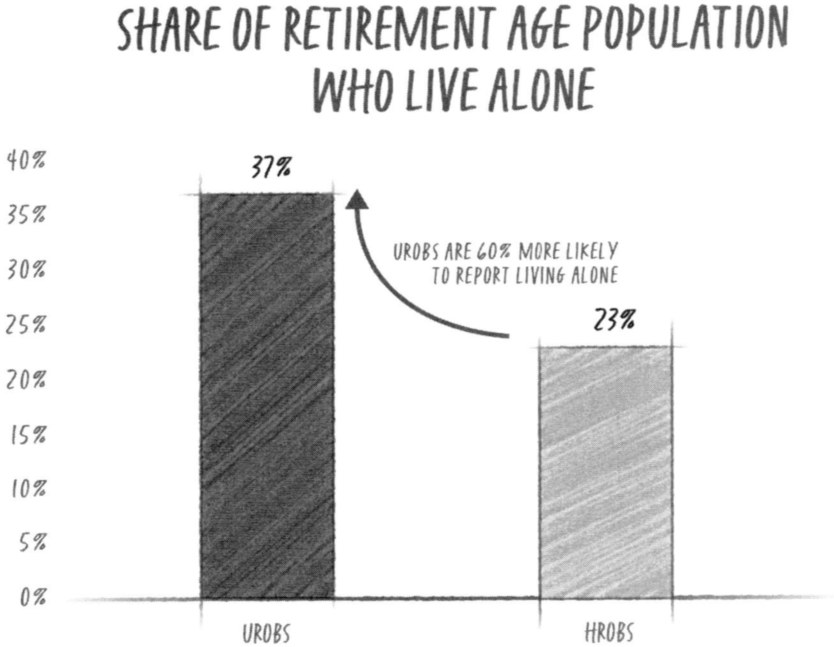

partner saw the highest levels of happiness, but retirees living with anyone—siblings, other relatives, friends, etc.—were consistently happier than those living alone.

For retirees who do live alone, whether by choice or circumstance, this data underscores the importance of building robust social networks outside the home. Regular commitments to social activities, volunteer work, clubs, or community organizations become essential for maintaining the daily social interaction that coupled retirees get naturally.

THE KIDS ARE ALL RIGHT (BUT YOU SHOULD PROBABLY LIVE CLOSE ENOUGH TO CHECK)

Family relationships play a significant role in retirement happiness, particularly when it comes to involvement with adult children and grandchildren. **Among happy older Americans, 36 percent say involvement with adult children and grandchildren is extremely important to their happiness, compared to only 26 percent of neutral or unhappy older Americans.**

This doesn't necessarily mean happy retirees live in the same house as their adult children—in fact, multigenerational living can create its own stresses. But proximity matters. Many happy retirees have made deliberate choices to live near their adult children, whether that means staying put in a longtime family neighborhood or relocating to be closer to where their children have settled.

Remember Jerry and Elise? When they moved to California, one factor in their location choice was being within driving distance of their adult children: one a casting producer in Los Angeles, the other a doctor in San Francisco. Now their kids and grandkids regularly visit their Sacramento community, enjoying that lush golf course and Jerry's boat out on the lake—and meeting their parents' new friends.

This creates a beautiful compound effect: The retirees get regular family time, the adult children get a vacation destination, and the grandchildren get to see their grandparents embedded in a thriving community rather than isolated and dependent.

THE COMPOUND EFFECT OF SOCIAL CONNECTION: WHAT *HAPPY GILMORE* TAUGHT ME ABOUT BEING HAPPY

What makes social connections so powerful in retirement is their compounding effect. Unlike investments that grow through mathematical formulas, social connections grow through what economists call "network effects": Each relationship you build makes it easier to build additional relationships.

I recently experienced this firsthand. For years, my family has spent time in Michigan every summer—visiting, enjoying the lake, chatting with other visitors. But by and large, we've been vacationers, socializing with our fellow vacationers in pleasant short-term relationships rather than building long-term friendships with residents of the town.

As I worked on this book—and after my eye-opening conversation with neuroscientist Michael Platt on the podcast—I began to think more about the importance of socialization. I realized I didn't want to be "just a vacationer" anymore. I wanted to connect with the community.

So I joined the local golf club, even though I only knew a handful of people in town. Within weeks, I wasn't just playing golf—I was meeting families, getting invited to community events, and building a real network.

Midsummer, one of my new golf buddies, a class act who relocated to Michigan with his family five years ago—we'll call him Kevin—mentioned it would be fun to have a screening party for the upcoming *Happy Gilmore 2* movie. "I wish we could go all out and do it at the Lyric Theater," Kev said. "But I don't think we can since it's on Netflix, not in theaters."

"Actually," I said, "I know the guy who runs the Lyric."

I was able to connect with the local theater director, whom I'd met at a fundraiser, and a quick text later, we had permission for a private community screening.

After that, everything fell into place. Kevin and I organized a hundred-person event with an open bar and costume contest where people dressed up like *Happy Gilmore* characters. It became the capstone event of the summer—everyone had a blast. And all because I'd decided to stop being a tourist and start being a neighbor.

It was a wake-up call. It had been a long time since I'd had to do that kind of social building from the ground up. I've lived in Atlanta for twenty years, so I don't have to work at building a community there; we already have one. But when you don't know anybody and nobody knows—or frankly cares—who you are, it doesn't matter how many books you've written or how many balanced portfolios you've helped create. You're starting from scratch.

So how do you actually meet people? It takes serious effort. Real effort. You've got to choose to participate . . . in anything. Re-enliven your social brain network and flex that muscle before it's atrophied. When my boys asked why it was so important to me to join the golf club, I told them, "Guys, trust me—you want people to play golf and grab drinks with—people who are actual friends. That's what really matters in any town."

And there you have it: the compound effect in action. Getting into that golf club, making an effort, initiating conversations—it was all a reminder that you have to build community intentionally. It doesn't just happen the moment you roll in for the summer and kick back by the lake. Once you start putting in the effort, one connection leads to another, which opens the door to another. Before you know it, you're not just a visitor anymore—you're in a thriving community of people in costumes, watching as Happy Gilmore (spoiler alert!) accidentally kills his wife with a golf ball on the big screen.

The happiest retirees are a little more careful with their swing. They also understand that social networks, like any network, become more valuable as they grow. Close friendships provide emotional support and deep connection. Casual friendships spark variety and fun. Activity-based relationships create a strong bond over shared interests. Community involvement lays a path for purpose and belonging.

Sometimes a golf buddy becomes the catalyst for the event of the summer. You never know where connections will lead—that's what makes building them so worthwhile.

PRACTICAL STRATEGIES FOR SOCIALIZATION

The research is clear: Social connections are nonnegotiable for retirement happiness. But how do you actually build and maintain these relationships, especially if you're starting from scratch or facing the biological reality that making friends gets harder with age?

Fortunately, Michael shared some actionable strategies for strengthening social connections. Combined with insights from our research, here are some tips and tricks for how to socialize during retirement:

- **Be intentional about location.** Jerry and Elise's story illustrates a crucial point: Where you choose to live in retirement matters enormously for social connection. If you're considering relocating, don't just think about climate, cost of living, or amenities; think about community. Are there built-in opportunities for social interaction? Is it a walkable neighborhood where you'll encounter people naturally? Are there active clubs, organizations, or social groups? If not, what would it take to start your own?

  Active adult communities, while not for everyone, do solve many social challenges by concentrating like-minded people in similar life stages with shared interests and plenty of time for socializing. And don't forget: Living near your kids and grandkids is a potent happiness factor too.

- **Put yourself out there early and often.** Michael's research suggests that every social interaction, no matter how small, exercises your social brain network. Don't wait for perfect opportunities or until you feel completely ready. Start with small, low-pressure interactions and build from there. Perfect opportunities don't exist, and knowing that can release you from the expectation or pressure to find them.

  Join groups based on interests you already have. If you love reading, find a book club. If you enjoy walking, join a walking group. If you're interested in volunteering, contact local non-profits. The activity itself matters less than the commitment to regular social interaction.

- **Find ways to accelerate connection.** Michael talked about "Fast Friend" exercises—structured conversations that help people move beyond small talk to deeper connection relatively quickly. While you don't need formal exercises, the same principle applies: Meaningful relationships develop when people share more about themselves and learn about others.

  Don't be afraid to invite people to coffee, suggest continuing conversations outside of group settings, or propose new activities. The people who seem most socially connected are usually the ones willing to take the initiative in deepening relationships.

- **Embrace the investment mentality.** Michael's monkey research reveals friendship requires investment—time, energy, and attention. Monkeys invest in relationships through grooming. Personally, I don't suggest you try combing other people's hair. Humans invest through shared activities, quality time, and meaningful conversations.

  Think of social connection as requiring the same intentional investment as financial planning. You wouldn't expect your retirement accounts to grow without regular contributions and attention. Similarly, relationships require ongoing investment to flourish.

BE SOCIAL, BE HAPPY

Community isn't an isolated component of a happy retirement but rather a powerful underpinning. Without strong social connections, even the most financially secure retirement feels hollow, as you sit alone in your castle on the hill.

Here's the beautiful thing: Social connections can begin improving your life immediately. Every conversation you have, every person you meet, every group you join adds up to something greater than the sum of its parts.

The goal isn't to become a social butterfly or to build a network of hundreds of acquaintances. The goal is to reach that threshold where you feel you have "enough" close connections—people who know you, care about you, and enhance your daily experience of being alive.

As our monkey friends can attest, we're literally wired for this. Our brains are designed to find joy, meaning, health, and longevity through connection with others. Why fight biology?

Jerry and Elise could have chosen to live anywhere for their retirement. They could have prioritized the biggest house, the best view, or the lowest cost of living. Instead, they stumbled into something far more valuable: a community of people who became true friends.

That's the power of socialization. It transforms a house into a home, a location into a community, and a retirement into an adventure shared with people who matter.

Now it's time for the secret that provides structure and confidence for all the rest: a plan to get you where you want to go.

CHAPTER 5

Secret #4: Mapping Out Your Future

A Written Financial Plan and/or Happy Retiree Life Map

Winston Churchill said it best: "Failing to plan is planning to fail."

Some people attribute that enduring gem of wisdom to Benjamin Franklin, but either way, for a couple of dead guys, their thesis is alive and well. We saw it in our research for this book. Look at the bottom portion of Figure 5.1. **Happy retirees are 2.25 times more likely to have a written financial plan than unhappy retirees.**

That's right: more than twice as likely. As you can see in the upper part of Figure 5.1, **they're also about half as likely to be anxious about their financial future.** If you're wearing nerdy glasses and have a pocket protector, you might say, "Wes, correlation does not imply causation." Okay, nerd. But it's pretty clear to me there's a connection.

FIGURE 5.1. Confidence Around Financial Future

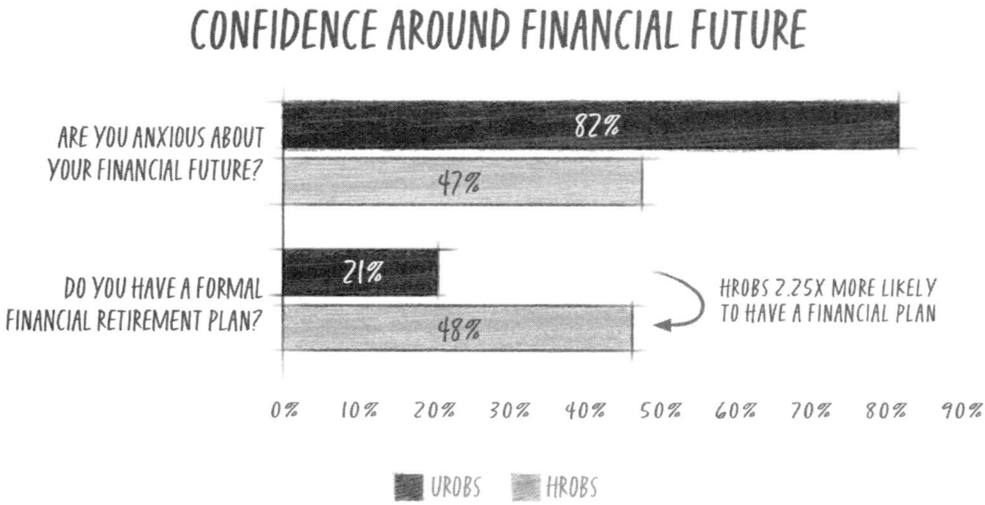

Planning isn't just about the money. A written plan serves as a blueprint to navigate both your financial and lifestyle goals. By reducing the decision fatigue that plagues so many retirees—Should we downsize now or later? Can we afford that trip to Europe? Is it safe to help the grandkids with college?—a plan provides a solid framework for your financial choices *and* your purpose portfolio.

Think of retirement planning as having two complementary sides of the same coin. The *financial side* deals with the numbers: income streams, rates of return, inflation assumptions, withdrawal rates, tax rates, and more. It answers the question, "Can we afford the kind of retirement we want?" But the *life side* is equally crucial—it maps out your daily and yearly sense of purpose, your core pursuits, your relationships, and how you want to spend the freedom that financial security provides. To know whether you can afford it, you first have to determine what life you actually want.

Without the financial side, even the most inspiring life plans remain fantasies. Without the lifestyle side, even the most sophisticated financial projections feel hollow and meaningless. But when you've got a plan where both sides work in harmony, something powerful happens: You stop merely hoping your retirement will work out and start actively designing it instead.

Here's the cool thing about having a plan: Making one doesn't have to be boring. Gone are the days when financial planning meant drowning in spreadsheets and mind-numbing projections that put you to sleep faster than counting sheep. The "fun" in this chapter title isn't a typo. I'm going to show you how fun mapping out your future can actually be. We'll talk about creating a financial plan—both a software and pen-and-paper timeline version—and a hand-drawn happy retiree life map.

But before we roll up our sleeves and reach for the colored pencils, I want to introduce you to two people who took completely different approaches to retirement planning. Both were financially secure and both had successful careers. Yet ten years into retirement, one was flourishing while the other was anything but.

A TALE OF TWO RETIREES

In 2014, back when Germany clapped Argentina to win the World Cup and people all over the world were dumping ice water over their heads as part of the Ice Bucket Challenge, five researchers from Harvard Business School were doing something quite different. The same year *You Can Retire Sooner Than You Think* came out, these researchers launched a groundbreaking ten-year study on retirement that spanned the next decade.[1]

The study focused on two groups. The first group was 106 participants, a mix of people pre-retirement and post-retirement, drawn from different industries and regions across the US. That larger sample gave them a broad view of the patterns, challenges, and differences in how people experience retirement. The second group was a much smaller set of fourteen participants, but this group was studied more intensively. The researchers followed them longitudinally—meaning they tracked their transition into retirement over time, capturing the nitty-gritty of what actually shifted as work receded and retirement life took shape.

Participants shared insights into how they navigated the challenges of retirement and were asked to explore their current and ideal future life structures, detailing daily routines, relationships, activities, and self-identity. By tracking these two groups, the researchers aimed to figure out what makes the difference between a retirement people love and one they end up wishing they'd done differently.

The study led to a book, of course—kind of like the book you're reading right now. The book led to an article called "Retire Without Regrets" in *Harvard Business Review* that featured two unrelated retirees—Irene and Lawrence—whose retirement experiences couldn't have been more different.[2] Irene absolutely nails her post-work life. There's no doubt she would fall into our happy retiree camp. Lawrence, on the other hand . . . Lawrence is a cautionary tale. He literally ends up in rehab, alone and at the end of his rope.

Irene approached retirement like a project worth planning. She didn't just leave a job; she built a new life. She figured out early that what she'd miss most wasn't the paycheck but the structure—the reason to get up in the morning, the conversations with colleagues, the small daily rituals that gave her days shape.

So she created new ones. Irene signed up for art classes, started taking long morning walks, joined a community group that met every Thursday. She gave herself a new rhythm and new people to see. None of it was accidental. She designed it. And it worked: Irene woke up feeling like her life was still full of purpose, only now with more daylight hours and less email.

For the *HBR* article, the researchers had both Irene and Lawrence sketch out a vision of their retirement. I call this a "happy retiree life map" (more on that shortly). The results of the sketches are telling. Irene's life map features many friends and family to the north, south, east, and west. She drew a wide variety of activities, including watching birds in nature, travel, cooking, ocean conservation, art, writing, and reconnecting. She even drew a picture of herself on her paddleboard.

Irene not only took the time to plan for her retirement but also incorporated how her husband's might factor in. Lawrence, by contrast, made no mention of friendships or socialization. He did say he intended to spend more time with his local grandson, but his only nod to core pursuits was "games and fun" and "watch movies." He denoted that he was "*thinking* about volunteering," not actually volunteering. He had an entire circle devoted to "chores, pay bills, and manage money." And he made no mention of physical activity whatsoever.

Lawrence assumed retirement would simply "happen." He figured his family would fill the space, his hobbies would magically blossom, and the rest would fall neatly into place.

Unfortunately, it didn't. Without the scaffolding of work, his days sagged. The social interaction he thought would come naturally never quite materialized. Instead of walking into a full calendar, he walked into long, unstructured mornings and afternoons. At first it felt like a vacation. Eventually it felt like drift. And with drift came frustration, loneliness, and the creeping sense that something had gone wrong, though he couldn't quite put his finger on it.

The implication was clear: It isn't just financial planning that lays the foundation for retirement success; it's the lifestyle choices. Without addressing and preparing for the financial reality of retirement, you won't have the resources to support the lifestyle you envision. And without thoughtfully designing that lifestyle, even substantial savings can leave you feeling adrift and unfulfilled in what should be your most rewarding years.

It's hard to disagree with the findings of this longitudinal study—maybe because I've seen it in practice and have been writing about this for over a decade. Irene's success stemmed from her willingness to create purpose rather than wait for it to find her. She went into retirement with a clear vision of what she wanted her days to look like. She deliberately built both daily and yearly purpose through multiple avenues—spending time with family, taking art classes, staying physically healthy, and getting involved in coastal conservation. A wide range of hobbies, social connections, and meaningful core pursuits made her feel engaged and satisfied. Even better, she planned for her husband's eventual retirement, knowing their dynamic would shift and that she'd need to adapt. This approach is precisely what I've observed in the happiest retirees.

Lawrence, by contrast, didn't put nearly as much intentionality into his plan. It's not as if he didn't have any ideas for retirement—he had vague notions of (thinking about) volunteering and visiting family. But he didn't take action on any of them. Without intentionally creating daily or yearly purpose, Lawrence fell into what I call the "purpose vacuum," that dangerous empty space full of time and regrets. And as one might expect, a vacuum sucks. His hope to spend more time with his toddler grandson went up in flames when family circumstances changed, which eventually led to a period of isolation and struggle. Before long, his casual drinking spiraled into addiction, ultimately leading him to a residential rehab program. Lawrence's story underscores why waiting until retirement to get specific about your purpose—and never taking the time and thought to build out a diverse and multifaceted purpose portfolio—is like waiting until you're thirsty to dig a well. By then, it may be too late.

The Harvard researchers identified "adaptability" as a key factor in successful transitions, but I'd take it a step further. **The happiest retirees I've studied don't just adapt—they proactively design their purpose portfolio well before the retirement party. They start building those daily purposes while still working, gradually cultivating activities**

that will seamlessly roll up into yearly purposes. This doesn't require dramatic reinvention; it's more like adding new rooms to a house you already love, creating space for parts of yourself that were always there but may not have had time to flourish.

Irene had savings, plans, location flexibility, etc. But she didn't stop there. She used her financial security as a launchpad, a foundation for exploring new identities and activities: art classes, beach walks, paddle-boarding, moving full-time to Cape Cod, reconnecting with family. That financial foundation meant she didn't have to keep working to pay bills, but more importantly, it meant she could choose what her retirement looked like.

Retirees who thrive match their "life structure" to who they are. They know what gave their old life meaning, and they figure out how to carry those elements forward—or reinvent them in new ways. They're willing to act, not just wait for something to happen. And they're flexible enough to adapt when things change, as they inevitably will.

Retirement isn't a finish line; it's the sequel to the book of your working years. And like any good sequel, it needs a plot. Irene wrote hers. Lawrence forgot to pick up the pen.

So how do you write that sequel?

You plan it out.

HOW TO MAKE YOUR WRITTEN FINANCIAL PLAN

There are many different kinds of financial planning software available. Our team loves eMoney, which is one of a handful of amazing financial planning tools that can essentially solve for any potential scenario you could ever think of. Platforms like eMoney allow you to input a nearly endless list of variables, including different income streams, part-time wage income, rate-of-return assumptions, spending assumptions, cash flow, withdrawal rates, inflation, tax consequences, RMDs, charitable gifts, qualified versus unqualified accounts, etc. You can fill it all in and figure out what you would like to spend, and eMoney will help you figure out the rest. It'll even give you what's called a Monte Carlo analysis, which includes a percentage of likelihood of you meeting your financial goals.

But planning doesn't require complex platforms or expensive tools. It can be as simple as putting pen to paper, forcing yourself to think concretely about your future. In my work with families, I often begin with something deceptively simple: **Draw a line from where you are today to a date you want to plan toward in the future.**

I used to do this exercise with colored pencils and highlighters spread across my desk. These days I use my trusty reMarkable tablet. The very act of sketching out your timeline with someone—your financial advisor, your spouse, your adult children—creates something magical in your brain. You're not just thinking about retirement anymore; you're visualizing it, making it tangible and real.

Here's what fascinates me: Though these hand-drawn timelines will never be perfectly accurate, when people revisit them one, five, or even ten years later, the numbers can end up remarkably close to reality. Why? Because the act of creating the timeline forces you to think seriously about your assumptions and goals. It transforms vague hopes into concrete targets. When you see a desirable object in the distance, you tend to head in that general direction.

Your timeline is your map. Like any good map, it will need updates as conditions change—market fluctuations, health considerations, family circumstances, the fall of the Ottoman Empire. You just never know. You may need to make course corrections along the way. But now you know where you're going and what your goals are, giving you the clarity and forward momentum to hit your marks.

CREATING YOUR RETIREMENT TIMELINE

Now it's time to draw your timeline. If you are in your twenties, thirties, or forties, the timeline will be longer, with the intention of focusing on the potential (and most critical) time zone, which is your target retirement zone when you would like to stop working full-time.

If you are thirty-five, the "target retirement zone" might be fifteen, twenty, or twenty-five-plus years from now. If you are fifty or sixty, maybe your zone is right now, next year, or a few years out.

(Please note that in the upcoming examples, I've rounded some numbers for the sake of simplicity.)

Step 1: Draw Your Basic Retirement Timeline—Number of Years You're Planning For, Your Target Retirement Zone, and Assets Today

Start with something simple. Draw a horizontal line across a large piece of paper or your tablet screen, like the one you see in Figure 5.2. Then add dates, your age(s), liquid assets today, and your "target retirement zone."

FIGURE 5.2. Retirement Timeline: Step 1

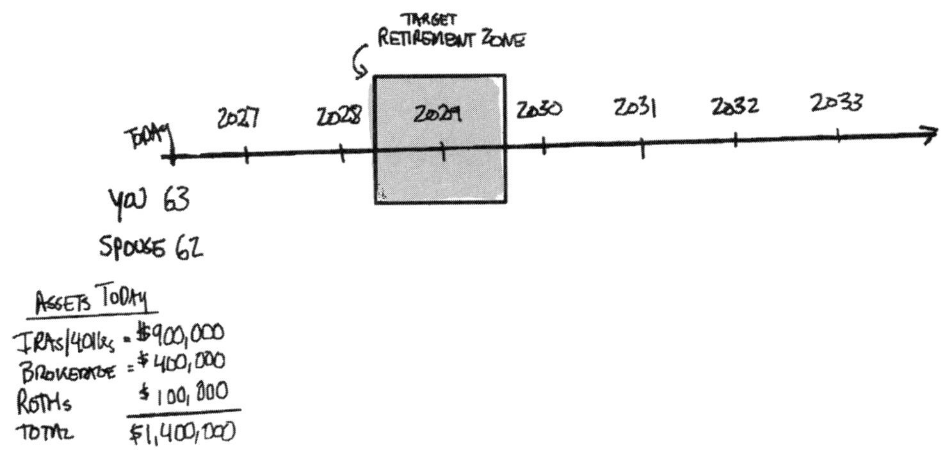

Step 2: Add Key Financial Years/Ages and Assets Tomorrow

Next, add in some of the key years when important financial milestones kick in, like sixty-five for Medicare. For Social Security, pick an age when you might want to start receiving benefits: age sixty-two (earliest possible start, but with permanent reductions), age sixty-seven (full retirement age for most people), or age seventy (maximum benefits). The optimal age you choose to start Social Security can be debated infinitely; don't get stuck on the exact year or age right now, but do pencil in when you think you might want to turn on this income stream. If you're fortunate enough to have a traditional pension—a dying unicorn—mark when you'll become eligible to receive the monthly income. (Don't forget to research whether your pension includes cost-of-living adjustments.)

Finally, estimate what your assets today might be worth in the year of your target retirement zone. Start with your assets today, then project how these balances will grow using conservative assumptions: 5-6 percent annual returns depending on your risk tolerance and asset allocation. While stocks have historically had higher returns in the long-term, conservative projections help you avoid unpleasant surprises.

Don't forget ongoing contributions. If you're still working and maxing out your 401(k), include those annual additions. The combination of investment growth plus continued contributions creates powerful compounding. For example: $500,000 today + $30,000 annual contributions + 6 percent returns = over $1.3 million in ten years. These projections give you solid "future balance" milestones to track against as the years unfold.

In Figure 5.3, you can see that today's $1.4 million with $40k per year in savings and a 5 percent rate of return (ROR) in three years would be approximately $1.75 million. Your own "assets tomorrow" target might be lower or much higher—for some households it may be $1 million, while for others it could be $5 million, $10 million, or more. The timeline simply helps you see what's possible and map a path forward.

FIGURE 5.3. Retirement Timeline: Step 2

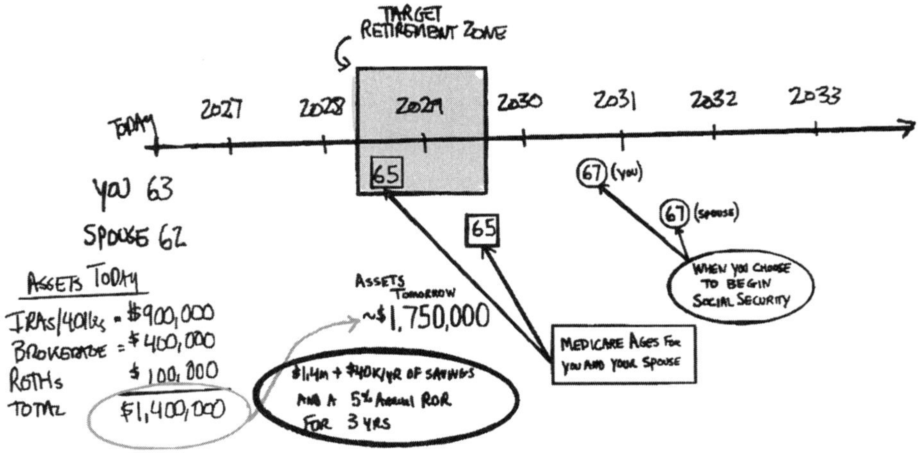

Step 3: Add Up Your Income Streams

Here's where you will add in what your income streams will total up to. For assets tomorrow, apply the 4+ percent rule of thumb, plus estimate your annual Social Security payments. Add these—plus any other income streams like rental income, pensions, annuity payments, deferred compensation, etc.—to arrive at a total annual income amount once all or multiple income sources have kicked in.

Here are a few guidelines for how to get realistic estimates:

- **Investment income:** This will come from your 401(k), IRAs, and other investment accounts using withdrawal strategies we'll calculate in the next step.
- **Social Security benefits:** Use the Social Security Administration's online calculator to get realistic estimates based on your earnings history and planned retirement age.
- **Rental income:** If you own rental properties, project the net income after expenses, accounting for potential rent increases and maintenance costs.

- **Pension payments:** If applicable, contact your HR department for projection statements showing monthly benefits at various retirement ages.
- **Part-time work:** Many retirees continue earning some income through consulting, seasonal work, or passion projects. Be realistic about how long you'll want to maintain this income. Again, this can and probably will change, so approximate numbers are fine.

Put it all together, and you'll have something akin to Figure 5.4.

FIGURE 5.4. Retirement Timeline: Step 3

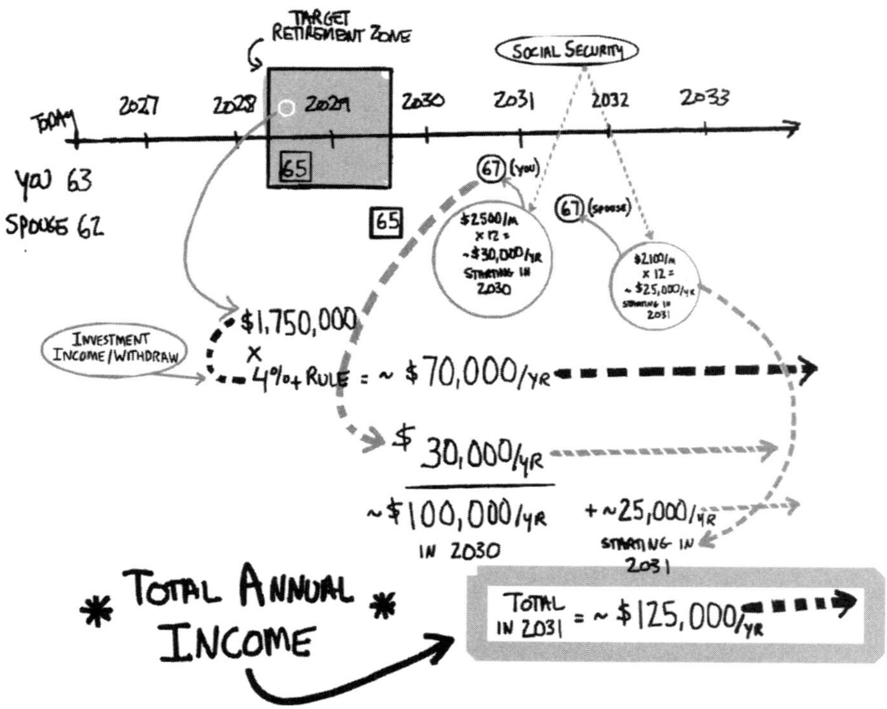

As you can see from step 3, you now have a very good idea of what your main income sources will add up to once you reach your target retirement zone year. In the aforementioned example, this hypothetical couple is eyeing retirement starting in 2029. Their first income source to kick in is their investment income based off the 4+ percent rule of thumb. This is approximately $70k/year based on $1.75 million x 4 percent starting in 2029.

In 2030, the first Social Security income stream kicks in for a total of $30,000/year ($2,500 x 12 = $30,000). Now this couple has about $100,000/year in income. Next, in 2031, the next Social Security income stream kicks in of a total of $25,000/yr ($2,100 x 12 = $25,000), for a total of $125,000 a year. This three-income combo—and keep in mind, you may have more than this—sets an income baseline that, if managed properly, should both last a lifetime and increase over time to protect you from inflation.

Step 4 (If Needed): Add in Other Important Financial Goals

If you have more moving parts than in step 3, you can continue to add to your timeline and customize as needed. The following timeline in Figure 5.5 does the same work in figuring out your projected income (in this case in 2032) when multiple income streams have kicked in.

In this example, you will see a married couple, both fifty years old, eyeing a target retirement zone six years from today when their investment income will be approximately $60,000/year, with one pension for $36,000/year and the addition of part-time work. The decision to work part-time here could last three years or more, but it supplements their overall income and helps this couple reach $126,000/year. Note that, for this Retire Sooner couple, seven years after their "target retirement zone" another significant annual amount could start if they choose

FIGURE 5.5. Retirement Timeline: Step 4

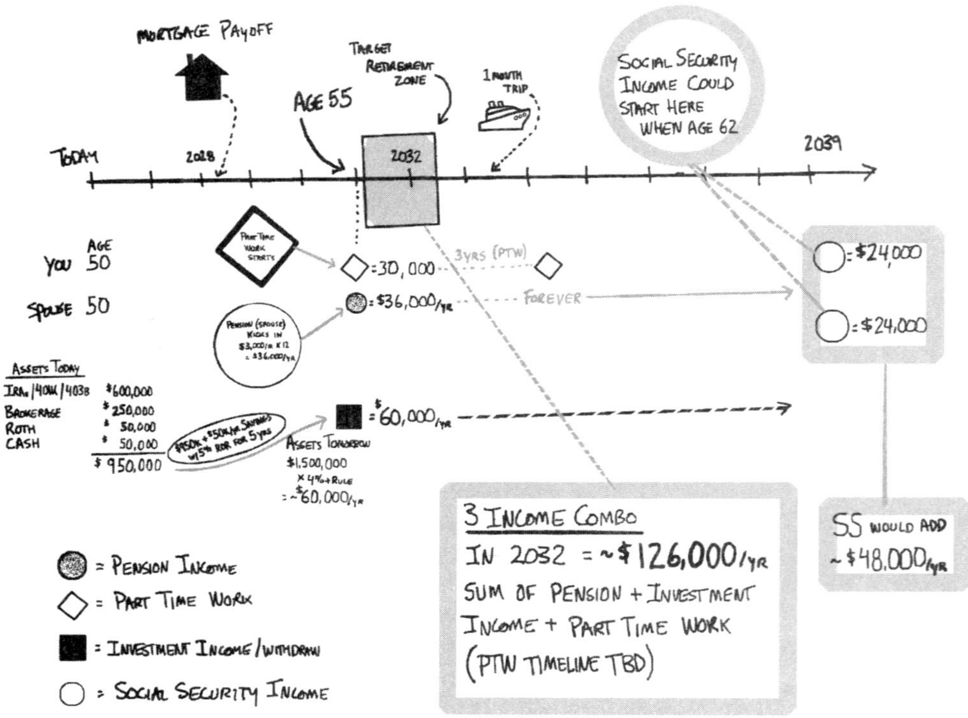

to take Social Security in 2039. At this point, there are multiple full-fledged income streams in play.

Note that, like this example, you can pencil in your mortgage payoff year target, plan for a significant trip, add an income source legend, or include any other significant financial milestone that you wish.

The beauty of this timeline exercise is that it works with whatever tools you prefer. There's the old-school approach we just outlined: large sheets of paper, colored pencils, highlighters, a calculator, and the tactile experience of drawing by hand. There are digital options, like eMoney or MoneyGuidePro, that provide sophisticated modeling if you're working with a financial advisor. There's even good ol' Excel spreadsheets that offer calculation power and easy updates. Modern

AI tools can help model complex cash flow scenarios given your inputs, running multiple what-if analyses to stress-test your assumptions. And you're always welcome to join me on a Microsoft Surface or reMarkable drawing tablet as we map out the future, one hand-drawn timeline at a time.

The tool matters less than the thinking process. You're training your brain to think systematically about your financial future rather than squeezing your eyes shut and hoping it will all work out.

When you complete this exercise, you'll have something most people never create: a visual representation of your financial journey through retirement. Your personal version of Figure 5.5 will show you exactly when different income streams activate, how your nest egg evolves, and whether your projected income supports your desired lifestyle.

More importantly, you'll have transformed abstract anxiety about "running out" into substantial knowledge about your financial trajectory. Instead of losing sleep over vague money worries, you'll know specifically what adjustments might be needed and when to make them.

This financial roadmap becomes the foundation for everything else—from deciding when to retire to determining if you can afford a second home to calculating whether you can help with your grandkids' education. **It's the difference between financial hoping and financial planning.**

IT'S NEVER TOO EARLY TO PLAN

By the way, I encourage planning no matter what age you are: thirtysomethings who are finishing off student loan payments and building good credit; fortysomethings who are juggling their careers and raising families; fiftysomethings who are

continued →

actively saving for retirement and paying for their kids' overpriced colleges; and, of course, sixtysomethings who are often on retirement's front stoop—anyone and everyone can tap the power of a plan. In the years before retirement, your focus should be on accumulation, long-term growth, and consistent savings; you've got the benefit of time to recover if unexpected challenges arise.

YOUR HAPPY RETIREE LIFE MAP

If you're dying to create a colorful life map like Irene, your time has come. Gather your satellite imagery, aerial photographs, and land surveys, because we're about to draw one together. While the financial timeline gives you the means to retire, the life side of mapping ensures you'll have compelling reasons to wake up each morning. This time, you're mapping meaning rather than money.

One of the best perks of having a podcast and radio show is when people reach out to me to share stories from their own retirement journey. Wendy was one of those. After I talked about retirement life maps on the *Retire Sooner* podcast, she sent me hers. I've recreated this absolute gem in black and white for Figure 5.6. Please draw yours in color!

Wendy's map is as heartwarming as a flock of puppies. I couldn't love it more. For me, seeing her take this idea and run with it makes the work I do worthwhile. As an extra special bonus, from her detailed rendering of southeastern Pennsylvania, it looks like she might know exactly where my dad lives. Maybe she'll drive past and find my dad, John Moss, writing cowboy poetry or riding his horse Hammy (two of his core pursuits) while my stepmom, Anne, wheels pottery and tends to her garden (two of hers).

FIGURE 5.6. Retirement Life Map

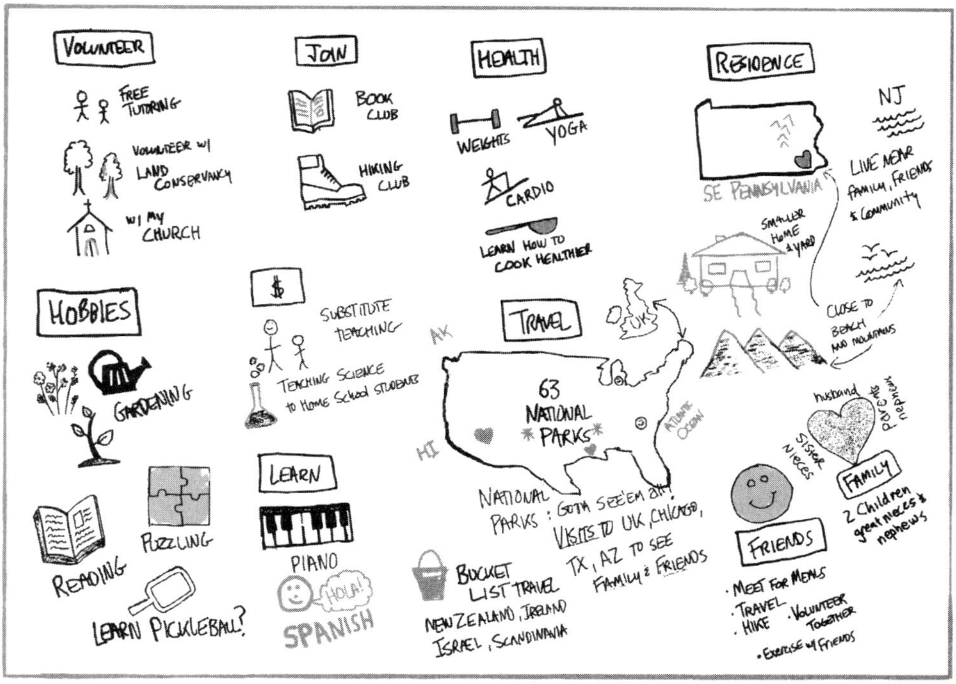

Wendy has woven together continued professional engagement through teaching science with intellectual stimulation via her book club. Her spiritual life remains anchored through church, while her creative side flourishes with piano lessons. Physical vitality is clearly a priority with her comprehensive fitness regimen—weight training, yoga, and cardio—complemented by outdoor activities like hiking. Under hobbies, she even asks, "Learn pickleball?" I'm guessing she already has by now.

What's particularly striking about Wendy's map is her balance between mastering new skills (Spanish, piano, pickleball) and deeper engagement with established passions (teaching, gardening, land conservancy work). Her ambitious goal to visit all sixty-three national parks demonstrates how daily purpose can beautifully scaffold toward meaningful annual milestones.

Wendy's map teaches us something profound: The most fulfilling retirement plans often blend continuing expertise from our working years with long-deferred curiosities we finally have time to explore. Her map doesn't just list activities—it reveals a thoughtful integration of physical health, intellectual growth, social connection, and environmental stewardship. This isn't a random collection of hobbies; it's a holistic vision for a life where daily activities build toward purpose and joy.

For more ideas, flip back to Chapters 3 and 4 where we talk about core pursuits, daily and yearly purpose, and the power of socialization. In the meantime, here's a quick recap of some ideas that bring the happiest retirees the most joy:

- **Physical pursuits:** Activities that keep your body engaged and healthy—hiking groups, tennis leagues, yoga classes, gardening clubs, or volunteer work that involves physical activity. When in doubt, think of the "ings." And don't forget the easiest happiness hack in this book: Add just fifteen minutes a day to your exercise routine.
- **Intellectual challenges:** Learning opportunities that stretch your mind—audit university courses, join book clubs, learn new languages, master technology skills, or teach others in areas of your expertise.
- **Social connections:** Regular interactions that combat isolation—volunteer organizations, religious communities, hobby groups, neighborhood associations, or mentoring relationships.
- **Creative expression:** Outlets for imagination and self-expression—writing, painting, music, crafts, cooking, or any artistic pursuit you've always wanted to explore.
- **Service to others:** Ways to contribute to your community and feel needed—tutoring, environmental work, animal rescue, political engagement, or helping other retirees navigate their transitions.

My advice? Start building and growing these purposes, practices, and core pursuits as early as possible, making sure they're aligned with your core values. You can't manufacture meaning overnight, but you can cultivate it gradually while you still have the energy and structure that work provides.

WHEN IN DOUBT, MAP IT OUT

Remember when your kids were younger and had those connect-the-dots coloring books? There's something surprisingly satisfying about watching a picture emerge from what initially looks like random points on a page. Creating purpose in retirement works in much the same way—except you get to decide where the dots go.

I'm a big believer in making your retirement life map with actual colored pencils. Yes, the same pencils your grandkids use for their dinosaur pictures can be your secret weapon for retirement happiness. (And no, you don't need artistic talent—stick figures work perfectly fine.)

When I did this with my family a few years ago, I was amazed at how illuminating it was—even for someone who thinks about retirement planning every day. It made me all the more convinced that retirees should take time to visually map out their days and years. The life map exercise gives you a way to home in on your daily and yearly purpose by drawing, without withdrawing from your retirement accounts!

HOW TO CREATE YOUR HAPPY RETIREE LIFE MAP

Let's walk through the systematic process for creating your own retirement life map. This isn't about artistic perfection—it's about visual clarity that transforms abstract hopes into concrete plans.

Step 1: Warm-Up Lists

First, set aside a good chunk of time. If you're making your life map with your spouse or kids, make sure they can also set aside time so that they're not rushing off to a prior commitment. Eliminate as many distractions as you can, which probably means turning the alerts off on your phone and computer or—better yet—hiding all your devices in another room. If you feel inspired by nature, you might go outside, though if you're doing this exercise by hand, I recommend finding a table or bringing something hard to write on so that you don't end up with a topographical map informed by the grass and sticks you wrote it on.

Now take a piece of paper—or open a fresh screen on your tablet—and start with some warm-up brainstorming.

1. **Start by identifying your core values**—what matters most deeply to you? Family relationships? Intellectual growth? Physical health? Community service? Creative expression? Environmental stewardship? Write six to ten values across the top of your page, then circle your top three or four. These become the nonnegotiables that should appear prominently in your retirement map.
2. **Underneath each value, begin brainstorming specific core pursuits or commitments** that would honor that value in retirement. Don't edit yourself initially—let your imagination run wild. The goal is to generate possibilities, not perfect plans.
3. **Next, organize these possibilities into daily purposes** (activities that could provide regular structure and meaning) and **yearly purposes** (bigger projects or goals that give shape to longer time periods). Daily purposes might include morning walks, volunteer shifts, or creative practices. Yearly purposes might include travel goals, major learning projects, or significant volunteer commitments. If some of these are current routines and

activities that bring you joy, all the better. This baseline helps you see what's already working in your life.

Step 2: Spot the Alignment Gaps

This is where honest self-assessment pays dividends. Compare your current weekly activities against your core values. Are you spending time on what matters most to you? Many people discover significant gaps—perhaps they value creativity but have no creative outlets, or they prioritize family relationships but spend more time on solo activities than connecting with loved ones.

Identify these underrepresented areas now, while you still have time to address them gradually rather than scrambling to fill purpose vacuums after retirement.

Step 3: Draw Your Map

Now that you've brainstormed the things you love and the gaps you'd like to fill, it's time to make the actual map. This time, grab a large sheet of paper and your colored pencils or fire up your digital whiteboard anew.

Now write out the most important things that come to mind. I find it helpful to use different colors for different categories. These may include family, church, your social network, and your favorite core pursuits. There's no particular structure, except to start scribing the most important variables you see in your future. Once you start drawing these out, more specifics will come to mind. If they're important to you, write them down and/or create a visual for the activity, just like Wendy drew a yoga pose, a US map, hiking boots, and a bucket to symbolize her bucket list of travel. Hand-drawn icons and emoji are welcome here.

Again, it doesn't have to be pretty, just meaningful to you. The goal is to create a visual representation where you can quickly see whether you're balanced across all your values. Include both continuing pursuits (activities that build on your existing expertise and passions) and new adventures (those curiosities you've been putting off for decades). Draw arrows or timeline elements showing when you'll start different activities—which can begin while you're still working versus what requires full retirement.

The key is making it visual and specific enough that anyone looking at your map would have a good idea of what your ideal retirement looks like.

Pro tip: Make your map actionable. This is where many retirement life maps fail—they remain too vague to be useful. Instead of writing "travel more," specify "two international trips annually plus four weekend getaways." Rather than "stay healthy," detail your actual fitness regimen. Don't fall into the trap Lawrence did with "games and fun" and "watch movies." Include specific learning goals, volunteer and part-time work commitments, and relationship priorities. The more concrete your vision, the more likely you are to achieve it.

When your map is complete, place it somewhere you can see it—on your office wall, next to the microwave, or on the fridge. The point isn't to outshine your three-year-old grandson's crayon drawing of Jesus; it's to give you a daily reminder of the happy retirement you've mapped out.

You're not trying to eliminate all uncertainty. Life will surprise you regardless of how well you plan. The goal is to enter retirement with both the financial security and the sense of direction that allow you to adapt confidently to whatever comes next. When you've mapped both sides of the retirement coin, you're not just calling heads or tails; you're making change.

WHY THIS ACTUALLY WORKS

The power of visual life mapping extends far beyond the feel-good exercise of playing with colored pencils. Research consistently shows that people who create specific, written goals are significantly more likely to achieve them than those who keep plans in their heads.

Clarifying priorities ensures your daily activities actually match your stated values rather than defaulting to whatever seems urgent or convenient. Highlighting gaps lets you see what's missing before it becomes a problem—much easier to add Spanish lessons to your routine now than to realize five years into retirement that you're intellectually understimulated, putting you at a real disadvantage during that trip to Marbella on the Costa del Sol.

Your map provides a flexible blueprint that can adapt as circumstances change, health evolves, or interests shift. Most importantly, it helps you make intentional choices rather than drifting into someone else's retirement agenda or filling time with activities that don't truly fulfill you.

When you combine this visual life map with the financial timeline we explored earlier, you create something powerful: a comprehensive vision for retirement that addresses both the means and the meaning of your post-career years. You're not just hoping your golden years will be golden—you've actively designed them to shine.

See? Planning doesn't have to be hard or boring. It doesn't even have to be black and white. Maybe you're the by-the-book spreadsheet type, or maybe you prefer colored pencils and bright yellow poster board; all approaches are welcome. But regardless of your method or materials, having a written financial plan and life map helps ensure you retire like Irene, not like Lawrence.

Ironically, once you have that plan in place, the fifth and final secret is going to send you straight to bed—literally.

CHAPTER 6

Secret #5: The Happy Retiree Superpower

A Generous Portion of Quality Sleep

I've got four growing boys who play every sport imaginable—football, basketball, golf, and lacrosse. The carpooling situation alone is a crisis. Their mom—my wife, Lynne—is a nurse, which means she believes in two core tenets of life: sleep and hydration.

According to Lynne, eight hours isn't enough. She'll tell you flat out: Teen boys need at least ten to twelve hours of sleep. And water? Don't get her started. Hydration is basically a religion in our house.

Picture this: I'm on a lacrosse trip, hustling kids between back-to-back games somewhere in Delaware. I like to think I'm a fairly responsible dad, who keeps the boys safe and healthy. But inevitably, my phone rings. It's Lynne. Her first question isn't "How's the game going?" or "How was the flight?" It's always, "Did you get a case of water at CVS after you landed? Do you have the liquid IV packets? What time is Jake going to bed?"

If the answer isn't "nine p.m. sharp," she's not happy. Because in her world, Jake has a ten a.m. game, which means warm-up starts hours earlier, and with three games in one day, he needs every minute of sleep he can get.

Lynne's fixation on sleep and hydration has become a running joke in our house. The boys roll their eyes, but deep down, they know Mom is right. According to the American Academy of Sleep Medicine, children ages six to twelve should get nine to twelve hours of sleep a night, and teenagers ages thirteen to eighteen should get eight to ten.[1] Even if Lynne the RN insists on the upper end of those recommendations, she's not far off the mark.

Of course, this creates an impossible math problem. If you have to be at school by seven thirty a.m. and need to wake up at six thirty, that means bedtime should be at eight thirty p.m. What teenager is going to bed at eight thirty?

The truth is, whether they're fifteen or sixty-five, kids and retirees face the same fundamental challenge: How do you get enough sleep? Teenagers need to balance impossible schedules with growing bodies that demand rest. Retirees need to navigate changing sleep patterns while maintaining the energy for an active, happy retirement.

When we started analyzing the results from our 2025 study, there were plenty of "tipping points" I expected would make an appearance. After all, I've been studying happy retirees for years. I suspected purpose would likely play a role, as would socialization, planning, and income levels that lead to a feeling of financial security.

But sleep was the one finding that surprised me. It's just not something I'd thought a lot about before.

It seems deceptively simple. Everyone knows they need sleep, right?

But our research revealed something striking: Happy retirees are nearly *twice as likely* as unhappy retirees to say they get enough sleep. To

FIGURE 6.1. I Get Enough Sleep

put numbers on it, head over to Figure 6.1: **69 percent of happy retirees on balance report getting enough rest compared to only 38 percent of unhappy retirees.**

That one word—*enough*—is the whole ball game. Not "as much as possible." Not "as little as you can grind by on." Simply enough.

Enough sleep doesn't just mean you feel rested; it supports and enables the other four secrets. Sleep clears your mind to make smart financial decisions and map out your future, fuels your energy for your core pursuits, and helps you fortify your social circles by supporting your health and lowering your anxiety. Without enough sleep, your ability to implement the Retire Sooner Method is compromised.

So what is "enough"?

WHAT "ENOUGH" SLEEP REALLY MEANS

Most adults—yes, even in their fifties, sixties, and seventies—still need seven to eight hours of sleep per night. Contrary to popular myth, sleep needs don't shrink dramatically with age. What changes is our ability to sleep deeply and consistently.

As we age, our internal sleep systems naturally shift. Our circadian rhythms become less reliable, melatonin production decreases, and we spend significantly less time in the deep, restorative sleep stages that help us feel refreshed. The result is lighter sleep, more frequent night-time awakenings, and earlier wake times that can leave retirees feeling less rested despite spending more time in bed.

The American Academy of Sleep Medicine and the Sleep Research Society both recommend a minimum of seven hours per night for adults.[2] The research confirms that regularly falling short of this target increases risks for cardiovascular disease, obesity, diabetes, depression, and cognitive decline.

One Harvard study following nurses over decades found that chronic short sleep—less than six hours—was associated with higher rates of heart disease and stroke.[3] Another study from the NIH showed that people who consistently sleep poorly are more likely to develop dementia.[4] Those who reported steady, restorative sleep had better memory, mood, and longevity.

And you can't just pick up sleep at CVS; you have to do it on your own.

The point isn't to obsess over hitting exactly seven to eight hours every night. The point is to aim for *enough*—and to protect the consistency of your sleep patterns.

THE CULTURAL CONFUSION AROUND SLEEP

In America, we've developed a strange relationship with sleep.

For much of the twentieth century, eight hours was simply assumed.

Parents told their kids, "Get your eight hours." (My kids still hang on to that number and use it to argue with their mom.) Farmers and factory workers alike built their days around sunrise wake-ups and sunset bedtimes. If you go back a hundred years, before electricity was commonplace, there wasn't much to do after the sun went down except light your candle and march off to bed. Why stay up late when there's no Netflix and chill?

But somewhere along the way—particularly in recent years—skimping on sleep became a badge of honor. Executives boasted about running on four hours a night. Entrepreneurs claimed they were too tough to need rest. The hustle culture glorified exhaustion fueled by an all-or-nothing work ethic.

Look no further than this *Wall Street Journal* front-page article from 2025: "AI Startup Founders Tout a Winning Formula—No Booze, No Sleep, No Fun."[5] The article starts by detailing a twenty-eight-year-old founder who's recently posted on LinkedIn that he put in three ninety-two-hour weeks in a row. He confesses to taking one single vacation—as in, one vacation total since founding the company—but "flew home early because he was too stressed about work." His goal is to build a $10 billion company in ten years. That's the winning formula he's settled on.

I'm not sure what he's winning exactly, but he better hope he never comes face-to-face with my wife.

What I find tragic is that "No Booze, No Sleep, No Fun" basically requires these guys to give up everything but their laptops. That means they have to eliminate stuff we take for granted. No pets. No relationships. No kids. No life. All in the pursuit of getting rich.

Happy retirees are not like that. They don't need $10 billion to live an amazing life.

Make no mistake: I'm not completely dismissing what these guys believe. In full transparency, I've certainly worked seventy-hour weeks in my life, and probably a few ninety-twos during crunch time. Does Lynne approve? Absolutely not. (I probably wasn't hydrating enough, either. Sorry, honey.) But I grew up watching my dad work seven days a week as a large-animal veterinarian. Animals don't abide by a schedule. Milk fevers and calving would happen at the worst possible times—Saturday night at eleven p.m., Sunday morning at four a.m.—and Dr. John Moss would pack up his red pickup truck and go to these farms without complaint.

Many retirees showed just as much zeal and dedication during their working years. Sometimes they feel guilty for hitting the snooze button. I get it. Once there's no job waiting and your morning's not dictated by the screeching siren of the alarm, it's easy to feel sheepish or embarrassed about sleeping in or taking naps. When you've worked hard your whole life, often getting by on less sleep than you really needed, it can be hard to feel like it's okay to get a full eight hours. I've had many retirees tell me, "Whenever I sleep past seven a.m., I feel lazy."

Both extremes miss the point. The happy retirees in our research don't brag about needing less, nor do they apologize for needing more. They simply prioritize *enough*.

In what researcher Dan Buettner famously termed the "Blue Zones"—including Okinawa, Japan; Sardinia, Italy; and Ikaria, Greece—rest and stress-reduction practices like afternoon naps and midday breaks are woven into the fabric of everyday life.[6] While it's difficult to prove direct causation, these communities where people routinely live to one hundred and beyond share several common practices, and prioritizing rest is one of them (others include strong social bonds, nutrient-dense diets, and staying physically active well into old age). Rest appears to be not just a luxury in these longevity hot spots but an essential component of a life well lived.

For me personally, when I stick to a regular sleep schedule, I have a lot more mental clarity, which makes me want to exercise and socialize more because I have more energy to engage in my core pursuits. The more core pursuits I do, the more I enjoy better, deeper sleep. And when I sleep more deeply, I feel better and have higher levels of emotional regulation and less anxiety—which can help with anxiety around your finances.

Guess what? With lower anxiety, it's easier to sleep. And the cycle continues.

This is the flywheel of sleep, health, and happiness. It's one of the most efficient compounding systems in life. When you sleep enough, everything else improves. And when everything else improves, you sleep enough.

There is no substitute for hard work. But when you shift into retirement, you're playing with a different playbook. As the happiest retirees know, sleep should be a priority. If you've ever felt guilty about "too much" or "too little" sleep, let this be your permission slip to drop that guilt. There's no shame in eight hours, no medals for five. You worked enough during your working years. Now it's time to sleep enough, too.

As long as there's a case of water involved, my wife will be thrilled.

THE FINANCIAL SIDE OF SLEEP—AND HOW TO SWAN

So what's really keeping Americans up at night? A recent Allianz study found that **64 percent of Americans worry more about running out of money than death itself.**[7] That worry has real consequences on sleep quality. In another watershed study from the American Academy of Sleep Medicine (AASM), **two-thirds (66 percent) of respondents reported that they sometimes, often, or always have lost sleep at night due to worries about their finances.**[8]

If our friends at the AASM need more anecdotal evidence, I've got plenty. Over the years, I've noticed that, as people get older, they tend to worry more. The irony is that we can't live in a world where we don't have financial resources, and yet financial resources inevitably cause stress. Either you don't have enough and you're worried about it, you have some and you're worried about losing it, or you have a lot and you're worried about how to manage it, who to leave it to, and where it should go.

Before I started hosting *Money Matters* on WSB radio, the show was hosted by the late Mike Kavanagh, a beloved financial advisor here in Atlanta. Mike had this wonderfully deep radio voice, and when he answered a caller's financial question, he would often end his response with the same reassuring phrase: "So you can SWAN"—in other words, Sleep Well at Night. Mike loved this acronym.

No matter how much money you've saved, retirement brings inherent anxieties. Will it be enough? What if the market crashes? What if health-care costs spiral out of control? That's precisely why the secrets we've shared so far focus on getting you to a point where you truly do have enough—and where you *know* you have enough. It's also why we dedicated Chapter 5 to planning and mapping out your financial future. Because when you have a clear, written plan that accounts for the realities of retirement, you can finally do what Mike Kavanagh always hoped his listeners would.

What I've noticed over the years is that families achieve peak SWAN status right after they've reviewed their overall roadmap. People don't necessarily sleep well because their portfolio performed well or because they got a bonus—they sleep well when they have a clear vision of what they need to do. Whether that clarity comes from a retirement timeline, a comprehensive financial plan, a happy retiree life map, or all of the above, the goal is the same: to eliminate the persistent worry that keeps them up at night.

But here's the catch: Clarity doesn't last forever. Life happens, things change, and our vision of the future invariably gets fuzzy over time. We start thinking, *Wait, what was the plan again? Does this market volatility throw me off course? Has something fundamentally changed? Maybe I'm not protected after all.*

This is why financial peace of mind operates in cycles. We achieve clarity, it gradually fades to fuzziness, then we need to get clear again. The retirees who sleep best at night are the ones who stay current on their plans and regularly revisit their roadmaps. They understand that maintaining financial clarity is an ongoing practice, not a one-time event.

THE RICH RATIO: BETTER THAN MELATONIN

One key metric that provides clarity and security is knowing your Rich Ratio, the simple formula we use with the families we work with. To calculate it, take all the steady income you expect each month in retirement (Social Security, pensions, rental income, investment withdrawals, etc.) and divide it by the monthly expenses needed to enjoy the retirement you want.

That's it: *have* divided by *need*. If your Rich Ratio is over 1, you're rich—not because you have a certain dollar amount but because you have more than you need.

Let me show you with two examples. Biff loves to travel and figures he needs $10,000 a month in retirement. His income streams add up to $7,000: $1,000 pension, $2,000 Social Security, and $4,000 from 401(k) withdrawals using the 4 percent rule (all after taxes).

Biff's Rich Ratio is 0.7. He's not rich.

McFly, on the other hand, lives more simply in his paid-off home and only needs $5,000 monthly. His income streams consist of a $1,500 pension, $2,000 Social Security, and $2,500 investment withdrawals for a total of $6,000. His Rich Ratio is 1.2.

McFly is rich.

The beauty of this metric is its simplicity and personalization. It's not about keeping up with the Joneses and the yacht they bought the day after they retired; it's about understanding whether your specific lifestyle—the way you want to live—is financially sustainable.

Money worries are like a persistent mosquito buzzing in your ear at two a.m. You can't ignore it, you can't reason with it, and you can't stop worrying about financial West Nile. That mosquito is not going away until you deal with it. A clear financial plan is like bug spray for your brain.

Which brings us to Charlotte and Ray, a couple who discovered first-hand how the right plan can turn financial anxiety into peaceful sleep.

FROM SLEEPLESS TO SWAN: THE RICH RATIO IN ACTION

Charlotte and Ray seemed pretty frazzled when I first met them in my office. Both in their early sixties and still too young to turn on the Social Security spigot, they had saved diligently throughout their careers and were among the most active people I'd ever encountered. Ray rode his fat-tire mountain bike through the streets of Atlanta and the crowded Beltline four days a week, navigating potholes and pedestrians with equal enthusiasm. Every weekend, he and Charlotte would drive somewhere within a few hours of the city to tackle a new hiking trail—they had a whole spreadsheet of Georgia state parks they wanted to conquer. They'd been passionate tennis players while their kids were in high school but had dropped the sport due to time constraints and busy schedules. Recently, they'd discovered pickleball at their local recreation center. As Ray put it, with a grin, "I'm not sure pickleball's a real sport, but I sure do love it."

With their kids fully through school and starting families of their own, Charlotte and Ray's financial situation put them in position for early retirement—something they'd dreamed about for years. So, they took the leap. Charlotte left her comfortable job at one of Atlanta's big banks after nearly three decades, Ray wrapped up his successful home renovation business and sold off his equipment, and they embarked on their starry-eyed early retirement adventure with visions of endless hiking trips and pickleball tournaments where they would rule the court.

But despite being well into the financial Green Zone with their investment assets, they couldn't shake a growing sense of dread that seemed to intensify with each passing week. No longer having the security blanket of steady wage income meant relying entirely on their investments, and eventually Social Security payments—but those were still years away.

Since they'd stopped working, every news headline threw them off course. Stories about economic uncertainty, rising inflation, geopolitical tensions, wars halfway around the world, artificial intelligence threatening to reshape the job market—suddenly, everything felt personally threatening. They found themselves obsessing over questions they'd never considered while working: Would AI create mass unemployment and trigger economic collapse? What if another financial crisis wiped out their savings? Were they witnessing the beginning of societal breakdown?

The irony wasn't lost on them. Charlotte and Ray weren't anxious people by nature—in fact, they were both quite grounded. During their working years, they'd been rarely flustered by world events. But now that they had all the time in the world, the constant barrage of troubling news was driving them to distraction. Despite maintaining their active lifestyle—still hiking every weekend, still playing pickleball twice a week—they literally had trouble sleeping at night, lying awake worrying about their uncertain future. In short, they were not gettin' their SWAN on!

"We wake up at two or three sometimes," Charlotte told me, her voice tinged with exhaustion, "wondering what tomorrow's news will bring. What crisis will hit next? Did we retire too young? Was this whole thing premature? Should we go back to work while we still can?"

When they first came to see me, Ray and Charlotte had been early retired for six months. They should have been on top of the world, but instead, they were an emotional mess. They had all the traditional markers of happy retirees—substantial savings, active core pursuits, good health, and a strong marriage. But without a clear understanding of their financial plan beyond "we have plenty of money to do this," their anxiety wouldn't go away. That buzzing mosquito of financial worry was keeping them up at night, turning their dream retirement into a waking nightmare.

Charlotte and Ray were tired. They were restless. They didn't look so good.

But once we sat down and mapped out the complete picture—how their income streams and investment portfolio stacked up against their actual spending needs—the transformation was immediate. Their Rich Ratio was a solid 1.4. We ran their financial scenario through thousands of different market conditions and economic environments. The result? A 99 percent probability of success over the next thirty-plus years, even accounting for market volatility, inflation, and unexpected expenses.

Together, we laid out their entire financial timeline: when Social Security would kick in at full retirement age, how their investment withdrawals would be structured to minimize taxes, which accounts they'd tap first and when, and, most importantly, how much "dry powder" they would maintain—three years' worth of spending and safety assets to allow time for a stock market recovery and any risky assets, which we'll talk more about in Chapter 8, to weather any economic storms without having to sell stocks during market downturns.

"I don't know why we didn't do this sooner," Ray said, visibly exhaling for what seemed like the first time in months. "We thought we were in pretty good shape based on our account balances, but now we actually have mathematical confidence that we're good. All this time we were flying blind when we could have had a flight plan."

Charlotte nodded emphatically. "We kept telling ourselves we had 'enough,' but we made our plan so long ago that we'd forgotten what 'enough' looked like in practice. Now we can see exactly how our money will flow for decades to come."

A month later, I received a call from Charlotte that made my day. "Wes," she said, and I could hear the fresh energy in her voice, "we haven't slept this well in years."

Now, I'm not a sleep doctor; I'm just a financial advisor and podcaster. I can only tell you what Charlotte and Ray told me: Despite being highly active and physically exhausted from their daily workouts, they still weren't getting quality rest, because their minds were racing with financial worries—and getting clarity literally transformed their ability to sleep at night.

This pattern shows up constantly in my practice. Retirees with vague or uncertain financial plans frequently find themselves tossing and turning at night, waking up in cold sweats as they replay worst-case scenarios in their heads.

But retirees who have done the math—who know their Rich Ratio shows they have more income than they need, who've diversified into multiple income streams that kick in at different times, and who've eliminated major debts like their mortgage—tend to sleep more soundly. They've replaced uncertainty with clarity, anxiety with confidence.

Think of financial anxiety as excess caffeine for your brain. No matter how tired your body feels, worry keeps your mind wired and alert, replaying problems long past the point when you want to rest. Financial security, on the other hand, acts like a natural sleep aid—it signals to your nervous system that it's safe to unclench and truly relax.

This is why comprehensive financial planning goes far beyond spreadsheets and investment returns. It's about creating the peace of mind that lets you rest easy at two a.m., knowing that whatever crazy news tomorrow's headlines hold, it can't and won't derail your carefully constructed plan. When you have financial clarity, you can finally give yourself permission to sleep those seven to eight hours—and wake up refreshed, rejuvenated, and reassured.

THE RHYTHM OF REST: STRUCTURE AS SLEEP MEDICINE

I want to share an insight that's been hugely important to me on the path to better sleep: the power of daily structure and consistency.

Research backs this up in compelling ways. A comprehensive review by the National Sleep Foundation analyzed sixty-three published studies covering over forty thousand people and found that irregular sleep timing is consistently linked to negative outcomes—impaired mood, disrupted metabolism, and poor overall sleep quality.[9] The message is clear: Your body craves predictability.

Of all the factors that contribute to quality sleep in retirement—and believe me, I've seen them all in my years of working with retirees—physical activity matters, eating well certainly helps, and having engaging core pursuits is essential. But above everything else, I've become convinced that structure is the secret ingredient most people overlook. I'm talking about having a consistent schedule for when you'll pursue your core pursuits, when you'll exercise, when you'll socialize—and yes, when you'll sleep. When you wake up knowing you have tennis at nine, volunteer work at two, and dinner with neighbors at six—early enough that you can still be in bed by eleven—your body learns to anticipate these patterns. That kind of structure naturally leads to more consistent bedtimes and wake times.

The most successful retirees I work with don't treat their weeks as blank canvases to fill however they please. Instead, they build purposeful frameworks around their core pursuits, volunteer commitments, exercise routines, and social activities. This isn't about rigid scheduling—it's about creating gentle rhythms that signal to your body when it's time to be active and when it's time to rest. You're dropping anchor points that help regulate your internal clock. Your body learns to anticipate these patterns, making it easier to wind down naturally when evening arrives.

While you should certainly build big-picture retirement dreams—the yearly cruise, the major renovation project, the cross-country RV trip—the research suggests focusing on the day-to-day might be the ticket to overall sleep quality. I like to think of it as "consistency over heroics." Having something meaningful to wake up for tomorrow in addition to next week, next month, and next year creates the kind of forward momentum that naturally leads to better rest. As James Clear says in his mega-hit book, *Atomic Habits*, "You do not rise to the level of your goals. You fall to the level of your systems."[10]

And here's a bonus tip I've found particularly effective: What you do in the hour before bed can make or break your night's rest. Research consistently shows that the blue light emitted by phones, tablets, and televisions suppresses melatonin production—the hormone that signals your body it's time to sleep. A study published in the *Proceedings of the National Academy of Sciences* found that people who read on light-emitting devices before bed took longer to fall asleep, had reduced REM sleep, and felt groggier the next morning compared to those who read printed books.[11] Additional research out of Harvard Medical School indicates that exposure to blue light in the evening can shift your circadian rhythm by as much as three hours.[12]

You may not need to go this far, but some retirees I know have developed intentional wind-down rituals that don't involve screens: reading physical books, journaling about their day, spending time in prayer or meditation, or listening to calming music. You can also get glasses that change the blue light to orange/yellow light. These activities signal to your brain that it's time to transition from the stimulation of day to the restoration of night.

Of all the factors that contribute to happy retirement—financial security, physical activity, close relationships—maintaining a structured approach to your days might be the most underrated. Deep, restorative sleep keeps you energized for whatever adventures lie ahead.

Sleep might seem surprisingly passive to have snuck its way into the five secrets. After all, you're not even conscious while doing it. But as Charlotte and Ray discovered—and as my wife intuitively understands—quality rest is the foundation that makes everything else possible.

The path forward isn't complicated, but it does require the same intentionality you've brought to saving for retirement. Prioritize getting those seven to eight hours. Build structure into your days. Create wind-down rituals that don't involve screens. Most importantly, give yourself permission to rest without guilt. You've earned it.

Mike Kavanagh's simple sign-off wasn't just about financial security; it was about creating a life where peace of mind comes naturally, where you can SWAN, truly resting in the knowledge that you've built something sustainable and meaningful to buoy you through the coming years.

THE ENOUGH PHILOSOPHY

Here's what makes sleep such a perfect fit for the Retire Sooner Method: It embodies the philosophy of "enough." This common thread runs through all the secrets we've discussed.

- **Enough money** doesn't mean the most—it means enough to live with freedom.
- **Enough core pursuits** doesn't mean filling every hour—it means enough to feed your purpose.
- **Enough social connection** doesn't mean a hundred friends—it means enough close ones to confide in.
- **Enough planning** doesn't mean spending ten hours a week tweaking your financial plan—it means enough of a roadmap to quiet that buzzing mosquito of worry.
- **Enough sleep** doesn't mean marathon slumbers or proud deprivation—it means the right amount to stay healthy and fuel joy.

This philosophy—*enough*, and in this case, enough sleep—is a nice reminder that retirement isn't a money or sleep competition. It's a balance. The plateau effect we saw with wealth in Chapter 2 applies here too. Just as there are diminishing returns to happiness beyond a certain asset level, there are diminishing returns to sleep beyond seven to eight hours for most people. The difference between five hours and seven hours of sleep is life-changing. The difference between eight hours and ten hours? Much smaller.

This is the wisdom of "enough"—not settling for less than you need but also not obsessing over exceeding what serves you. Whether it's money or sleep, the happiest retirees have mastered the art of enough.

Congrats! You've collected all five secrets. You're done, right?

Not so fast.

You may have noticed there are still quite a few more pages in this book. The next two chapters dive into the financial mechanics that make it possible to say yes to retirement.

Chapter 7 is all about inflation—how to protect your dollars from slowly wilting away. Because trust me: $1 million today won't be worth $1 million forever.

Chapter 8 introduces the five pillars of income investing. Yes, another five—but these are different. The secrets tell you *what* happy retirees do. The pillars show you *how* to invest your money so you can afford to do those things for the next twenty, thirty, even forty years.

PART TWO

MONEY MATTERS

CHAPTER 7

Wilting Dollars and Withered Dreams: The Truth About Inflation

Since the dawn of the American economy, inflation has been as reliable as people insisting there's a "The" before Ohio State University. No matter how much you hate it, it's not going anywhere.

The data from our 2025 Money and Happiness in America study showed retirees are far more anxious about inflation than they are about rowdy Buckeye football fans. Take a peek at Figure 7.1. **Uncontrollable economic conditions—market volatility, inflation (the rising cost of living), etc.—nabbed the #1 spot, ranking as the most prevalent overall concern for retirees.** This was even higher than declining health (#2) and an overall worry about running out of money (#3).

FIGURE 7.1. Americans' Reported Biggest Challenges When Contemplating Retirement

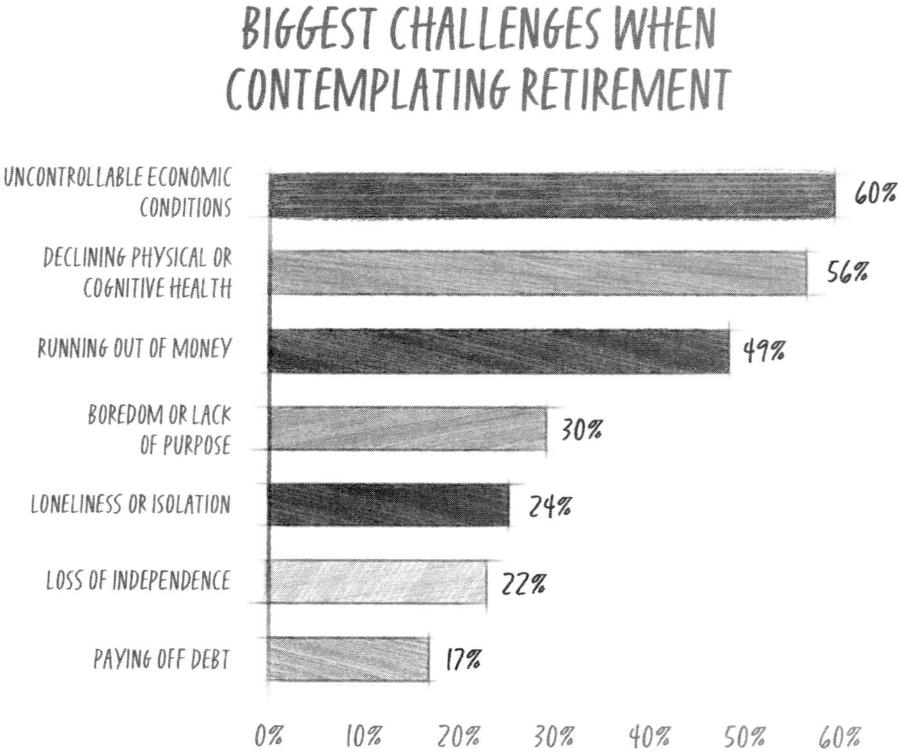

Here's something that might surprise you: Inflation isn't always the villain it's made out to be. In fact, a dash of inflation over time is actually an important part of the recipe for a functioning US economy, like a pinch of salt in your grandmother's biscuits. Just enough enhances the flavor; too much ruins the meal.

Mild inflation puts healthy upward pressure on the value of goods and services. Meanwhile, static investments—like those crisp twenty-dollar bills sitting in your wallet—slowly lose purchasing power. This natural erosion motivates people to spend on goods today rather than waiting until they become more expensive tomorrow. It also encourages investing in assets that appreciate over time instead of keeping cash under the mattress or in a checking account earning an amount of interest that wouldn't even interest a squirrel saving for winter.

Just for clarity: **inflation up = the purchasing power (or value of the dollars sitting in your wallet) down.** For a visual representation, feast your eyes on the slow descent of Figure 7.2. You can clearly see that the purchasing power of the US consumer dollar, aka the dollars sitting in your wallet, is a one-directional chart that bleeds lower and lower over time. From January of 2000 through 2025: minus 48 percent. Relentless.

But the relentlessness is not all bad. Think of stable inflation as a gentle nudge, prompting us to put our money to work before it weakens. It's the economic equivalent of those sweet summer peaches ripening on your counter: Use them today and whip up an award-winning peach cobbler; let them sit around and in a week, you'll be feeding your garbage can congealed, moldy pulp.

In the US, we've experienced brief periods of *deflation*, where prices actually decline over time. While paying less for things might sound

FIGURE 7.2. US Consumer Price Index Decline in Purchasing Power Since 2000

Source: Capital Investment Advisors investment research using Bloomberg data

appealing, deflation is actually a more pernicious problem than mild inflation. If prices are steadily dropping, consumers have no incentive to purchase anything today, since waiting would give them better deals tomorrow. If we lived in a world of persistent deflation, nobody would want to spend unless absolutely necessary, grinding economic activity to a halt.

That's why the Federal Reserve—essentially the governing body of our economy—has two explicit priorities (fancy term: "dual mandate"). One is for maximum employment, which makes intuitive sense. Of course we want Americans working. But the second is price stability, which in the Fed's view means maintaining a mild dose of inflation around 2 percent per year—not negative 2 percent, not positive 20 percent, but a steady inflation rate that keeps the economic engine purring without overheating.

The Fed doesn't want inflation bouncing up and down like a kid in a bouncy house at a birthday party. That creates confusion and uncertainty, which leads people to hold off on spending and investing. If the Fed had its way, we'd experience a consistent 2 percent inflation rate, something you could always count on, like sweet tea at a Southern summer picnic. Even if the price of your glass of tea is increasing by 2 percent every year.

Here's where retirement planning gets interesting. Since inflation is literally woven into our economic fabric, the physical dollars in our wallets are slowly wilting by let's say 2 percent each year, even if from the outside your wallet looks just as full. And that's if the Fed hits their dream target. From 2009 through 2020, inflation was actually a touch lower than the Fed's ideal, averaging around 1.5 percent a year. But once the pandemic hit, inflation spiked to levels not seen in decades, with rates hitting 9 percent in 2022. Suddenly, that slow wilting turned into rapid withering.

While 9 percent may seem staggering, it's child's play compared to economic crises we've seen elsewhere in the world. In the late 1980s,

Argentina experienced inflation rates exceeding 1,000 percent, turning grocery shopping into a daily race against rapidly increasing prices and causing widespread social unrest.[1] In 1923 Germany, inflation in the Weimar Republic ran so rampant that workers were paid twice daily because money lost value so quickly. People famously burned stacks of currency for heat because it was cheaper than buying firewood.[2]

Thankfully, we're not likely to find ourselves burning bundles of cash in our fireplaces anytime soon. The Fed has powerful tools to keep inflation from reaching such catastrophic levels. But even a steady 2 percent target rate is quietly siphoning off your retirement savings year after year. A dollar in 2000 would only be worth fifty-two cents today: 48 percent less.

So what can you do to protect the purchasing power of your hard-earned nest egg?

That's exactly what we'll explore in this chapter: how to think about inflation and recalibrate your mindset. Inflation isn't going anywhere, but that's okay. We just have to face that reality and be prepared for it. Retirement isn't only about having enough dollars—it's about ensuring those dollars maintain their strength to fund your purpose for decades to come.

FROM THE DRIVEWAY TO THE DINNER TABLE

When we talk about inflation, it's easy to get lost in the macro level of abstract percentages and economic jargon. I find it much more revealing to look at how inflation affects specific goods we all purchase. This paints a detailed portrait of exactly where and how quickly our dollars are wilting.

Let's hit the road with a concrete example most Americans can relate to: buying a car.

Imagine you set aside specific "car dollars" in 2020: $30,000 earmarked specifically for purchasing a nice, reliable used car. In honor of my first book, we'll say you were eyeing up a Lexus—a staple of happy retirees—and *not* a BMW. You had your eye on a particular model, the ES 350, but decided to wait a bit before you took the plunge. What a judicious and fiscally responsible decision, right?

Maybe not. Fast-forward to 2025 and—according to the Consumer Price Index (CPI) for Used Cars and Trucks—equivalent used vehicles in the US cost over $40,000.[3]

Wait a second. You haven't lost any actual dollars! You've still got $30,000 in your special "car dollars" account. And yet, through no fault of your own, your car dollars have wilted. You can't explain to the salesman that the car is supposed to cost $30,000. Those dollars are weaker than they were five years ago, simply because they don't have the same buying power they once did. Check out Figure 7.3. **Your original $30,000 has shrunk by about 25 percent. Put another way: One car dollar from 2020 was worth only about $.75 of car-buying power by 2025.** To maintain the same purchasing ability, you'd need an extra 34 percent on every dollar you had saved—or an additional $10,000 on your original $30,000.

It's not just your car dollars that wilted. By 2022, when used vehicle prices had surged by over 56 percent (Figure 7.3), you were also feeling the effects of inflation on the groceries in your back seat. Remember the panicked run on grocery stores in early 2020? A few years later, people weren't exactly lining up for great deals on cereal. From January 2020 to December 2025, food prices in the US saw a significant increase, with the all-food CPI rising by 31.6 percent.[4] Eggs got more expensive. Milk got more expensive. Bread got more expensive. Let me tell you: As my wife and I fed four growing boys, every trip to the grocery store started to feel more and more like paying college tuition. They never stop eating!

FIGURE 7.3. Consumer Price Index for All Urban Consumers: Used Cars and Trucks

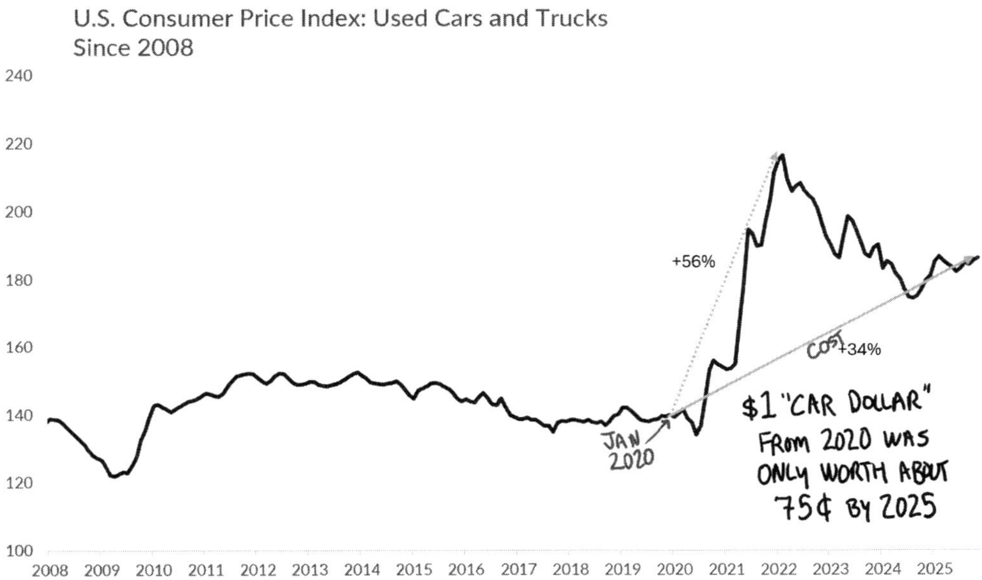

Source: Capital Investment Advisors research based on "Consumer Price Index for All Urban Consumers"

And what about the house you're lugging those groceries to? You guessed it—real estate prices went up too. The numbers of Americans who moved during the pandemic increased, in part incentivized by the Fed slashing interest rates.

The inflation dragon had been awakened. And we all felt the fire.

TAMING THE DRAGON

As much as people may wring their hands and wail at the moon about the cost of living, inflation is nothing new.

In the 1970s and early '80s, Americans were living in an inflation nightmare. Prices doubled in under a decade. The dollars in your wallet weren't just wilting; they were being shredded and engulfed in flames—something KISS might have done onstage at a concert.

In the late '80s and '90s, the inferno dwindled to a glow. The value of US dollars became less flammable—though inflation's simmer still charred the edges of purchasing power.

Then we entered what many perceived as a golden age. In truth, we were being lulled into a false sense of security. For a solid decade, inflation rose and fell gently, like a softly rolling wave. We started in a period of deflation in 2009, -0.4 percent, then watched as the rate went up and down in small increments, reaching a modest apex of 3.2 percent in 2011, then down to 1.8 percent in 2019.[5] By and large, Americans enjoyed this period. The great inflation dragon was hushed into an icy hibernation, frozen beneath reasonably priced grocery items. (Who doesn't love a good deal on eggs?) Many younger Americans had never experienced meaningful inflation, and even us older folks had largely forgotten its fiery breath.

That all changed abruptly with the flood of economic stimulus the pandemic unleashed. This unprecedented financial injection acted like a flamethrower, melting the ice and freeing the inflation dragon from its frozen slumber.

As prices increased, our dollars wilted once again, leaving our wallets and bank accounts far lighter than before. It wasn't just the price of cars, food, and houses that skyrocketed. *Everything* suddenly cost more, which meant our saved dollars bought less and less.

Here's the hard truth: The inflation dragon is not going into hibernation. That's just not how our economy works. The Federal Reserve will do everything in its power to keep inflation alive; they don't want 10 percent inflation per year, but they do want to maintain that 2 percent rate. The dragon may have been subdued from its wild, *Game of Thrones*–level bloodlust, but it is still flying overhead, quietly breathing smoke on your retirement dollars. **That means for the rest of your life, you need to have a plan to combat inflation.** And that plan should be proactive, not just reactive: You must have a shield *and* a sword.

Fortunately, there are many elixirs for this problem, strategies to tame the dragon to keep your retirement funds from losing their power. As you might expect, they all hinge on investing, which we'll get into more in Chapter 8. The key is to invest your dollars in a way that either keeps up with inflation or outpaces the rate of inflation over time.

PRACTICAL INFLATION-FIGHTING TACTICS

Very simply, if we want to maintain our purchasing power, we have to invest in assets that inflate along with inflation.

This is why investing in companies that are tasked with this same inflation-fighting job is one of the primary ways to protect your purchasing power. Imagine a potato chip company. The price of potatoes has gone up 10 percent, which means the cost of making potato chips has gone up a commensurate 10 percent. Does the potato chip company eat the difference? Nope. They raise the price of a bag of potato chips by—you guessed it—10 percent. As long as consumers keep buying, the company has figured out an effective way to combat inflation.

As much as we hate paying 10 percent more for that bright and shiny yellow bag of salt, we're now on the other side. We own shares in the company that makes potato chips, and that company continues to grow its revenue and its earnings, propelling its dividend-paying power and overall value higher. Isn't it better if I invest my dollars in the potato chip company than sit around complaining about overpriced Super Bowl snacks?

This same phenomenon happens in other sectors, too. That's why I believe any balanced portfolio should include equities—broad stock indexes using ETFs, growth stocks, dividend stocks, international stocks, small- and mid-cap stocks, many of which have a long track record of success.

Here are some examples of how certain sectors of the economy pass on increased cost with relative ease to us as consumers:

- **Utilities:** Everyone needs electricity and water regardless of economic conditions—even during a recession, people still flip on the lights. Utility companies typically operate as regulated monopolies with the ability to request rate increases to offset rising costs. While they're about as exciting as watching paint dry at your in-laws' house, utilities often combine inflation-resistant revenues with above-average dividend yields—a particularly attractive combination for retirees.
- **Energy:** Oil, gas, and energy infrastructure investments have traditionally served as excellent inflation hedges. When inflation heats up, energy prices frequently lead the way. Companies in this sector often see their hard assets (oil reserves, pipelines, refineries) increase in value during inflationary periods, while their product prices rise in tandem with broader inflation. It's like owning the only gas station at a busy interstate exit. People may buy fewer Big Gulps when prices go up, but they still need to fill their tanks.
- **Health care and pharmaceuticals:** Medicine is one of the last things people cut from their budgets, regardless of price increases. Have you seen anyone comparison shopping from an ambulance gurney? Pharmaceutical companies maintain strong pricing power and can generally pass along inflationary pressures to consumers and insurance companies.
- **Consumer staples:** Companies producing essentials like food, beverages, and household products tend to maintain their pricing power even when consumers are feeling the pinch. Should I be eating all those chips? In light of my recent cholesterol levels, my doctor would say no. But dammit, I can still invest!

These are examples of how companies are able to combat price increases by charging more. We are fortunate enough to be able to invest in companies whose earnings also inflate along with inflation, acting as a protector of our purchasing power. **Our job is to invest in assets that inflate along with inflation.**

While stocks might get most of the attention in investment discussions, real estate deserves its own spot in our inflation-fighting arsenal. There's something deeply satisfying about owning a tangible asset you can actually see, touch, or even live in—especially when that asset has a rich history of keeping pace with or exceeding inflation.

REAL ESTATE

For many Americans, your house isn't just where you live—it's likely your largest single investment, and it can be one of your most effective inflation fighters. Unlike the dollars sitting in your wallet or checking account, which quietly lose purchasing power over time, your home's value tends to rise alongside inflation, and often faster. During the inflation surge from 2020 to 2023, when cumulative inflation reached roughly 20 percent, home values in many markets increased by 30 percent or more.[6]

This is a very different kind of asset than cash. When inflation drives up the cost of building materials, labor, and land, it typically pushes the value of existing homes higher as well. Even if you never plan to sell your home, this appreciation provides a significant buffer against inflation's corrosive effects on your overall net worth.

Better yet, if you've paid off your mortgage (like we talked about in Chapter 2), you've locked in your housing costs at a relatively fixed level (annual property taxes, insurance, etc.). It's like having price protection on one of your biggest monthly expenses—an invaluable advantage during inflationary periods. They say "home is where the heart is," to which I'd add: home is where the hedge is. The inflation hedge, not the one in the front yard that your spouse is always asking you to trim.

For those who own rental properties, the inflation-fighting benefits are even more pronounced. Not only does the property itself tend to appreciate with inflation; the income it generates can be adjusted upward as well. When your costs increase, you raise rents accordingly.

Let's say you own a rental property generating $20,000 in annual income. If inflation runs at 5 percent, you may be able to increase rents to $21,000 the following year. Meanwhile, many of your expenses—particularly the mortgage, if you have one—remain fixed. This creates a powerful combination of appreciating asset value and growing income stream that few other investments can match.

Even during the rental market disruptions of the pandemic, real estate proved remarkably resilient. After a brief period of uncertainty, rental rates in most markets not only stabilized but surged to new highs, demonstrating once again real estate's ability to adjust to inflationary pressures. Being a landlord has its perks—and lords are good at defeating dragons.

Of course, not everyone wants to be a landlord, dealing with midnight calls about clogged toilets and broken water heaters. Fortunately, publicly traded real estate investment trusts (REITs) offer many of the inflation-fighting benefits of direct property ownership without the management headaches. REITs are companies that own, operate, or finance income-producing real estate across a range of property sectors. By law, they must distribute at least 90 percent of their taxable income to shareholders annually in the form of cash distributions. This makes them particularly attractive for income-focused retirees.

BONDS AND MORE CONSERVATIVE WAYS TO OUTPACE INFLATION

While stocks and real estate are powerful ways to outpace inflation, sometimes we're simply looking for investments that won't lose ground. This is where bonds, fixed-income securities, and money market accounts come into play. These investments typically pay interest rates similar to or slightly ahead of the rate of inflation. The way I look at it is that, even though historically, bonds don't dramatically outrun inflation the way stocks can over time, they at least help you keep pace with rising prices, preventing your dollars from shrinking—while also typically providing more stability than the stock market (more on this in Chapter 8). Think of stocks as your inflation offense and bonds as your inflation defense: Both play crucial roles in protecting your purchasing power throughout retirement.

A 5 percent yield on a two-year treasury note (which will certainly change depending on the interest rate environment) might not sound thrilling at your neighborhood cocktail party (unless you're at a really boring party), but when inflation is around 3 percent, you're actually maintaining or slightly increasing your purchasing power.

Remember, a solid inflation defense strategy doesn't mean avoiding *all* risk—it means taking calculated risks appropriate for your stage in life. Your bonds might not be the star players that hit financial home runs, but they can be reliable fielders that prevent runs from scoring against your retirement.

PRIVATE BUSINESSES AND INVESTMENTS

Investing in private equity or private companies—or your own company—offers yet another powerful way to combat inflation, with some unique advantages. Unlike publicly traded companies where you're one of thousands of shareholders, owning a private business gives you more direct control over pricing. When inflation pushes up costs, private ones can adjust prices accordingly—often more nimbly than large corporations. Whether it's a small manufacturing company, a professional services firm, or a local retail establishment, private business ownership can provide inflation-fighting power while often avoiding much of the bureaucracy.

Even if you're not running the business day-to-day, private equity investments and stakes in privately held companies can offer similar benefits for qualified and accredited investors. These businesses face the same inflationary pressures as public companies, but without the quarter-to-quarter scrutiny of Wall Street, they can often make more strategic long-term decisions about pricing and operations. While these investments typically require more capital and come with less liquidity than stocks or bonds, they can serve as powerful inflation antidotes in a well-diversified portfolio.

Take Barbara, who owns a large landscaping business serving Atlanta suburbs. When equipment costs spiked during the pandemic, she didn't need board approval or shareholder meetings—she adjusted her service rates and route efficiency within days. Her business not only weathered the inflation storm but actually expanded its client base by staying nimble while larger competitors struggled with cumbersome pricing processes.

This control extends beyond just pricing. Private business owners can quickly adjust inventory levels, switch suppliers, modify product offerings, or change marketing strategies in response to inflationary pressures. It's like having your hand directly on the inflation thermostat rather than hoping someone else notices the temperature change. This agility is particularly valuable during periods of unexpected or rapidly accelerating inflation, when slower-moving entities often find themselves playing an expensive game of catch-up.

For those who aren't entrepreneurs themselves, investing in private businesses can still provide significant inflation protection. Whether through direct investments in local businesses, private equity funds, or family business interests, these alternative investments often follow different cycles than public markets. Instead of being at the mercy of inflation, you can position yourself to benefit from it.

That's the big secret, inscribed in some ancient rune in an old fortress . . . the fortress being your financial plan. Rather than running from the inflation dragon, you can learn to ride it—or at least keep it from burning through your savings. This multilayered approach doesn't just protect your purchasing power; it can actually help your wealth grow despite inflation's constant presence. By strategically investing in companies that pass along price increases, owning real estate that appreciates with inflation, and maintaining defensive fixed-income positions, you can build a comprehensive shield against inflation's fiery breath.

The bottom line? **Your retirement portfolio needs to include enough growth-oriented investments to combat inflation, or your supposedly "safe" withdrawal rate won't be safe at all.** We don't want you reaching into your wallet twenty years into your retirement just to discover that those wilted dollars buy only half of what you need.

So how do you build a portfolio that can both generate the income you need today and grow enough to protect your purchasing power tomorrow? How do you balance the safety you crave with the growth you require? How do you create an investment strategy that lets you sleep well at night while still keeping pace with rising costs?

That's exactly what we'll tackle in the next chapter. It's time to seize the reins and dive into the nuts and bolts of income investing—a systematic approach designed to give you the best of both worlds. Fair warning: We're about to get into the weeds with enough numbers, percentages, and equations to give you an honorary degree in math. But stick with me, because by the end of Chapter 8, you'll have a roadmap for building a portfolio designed to weather any economic season while keeping your retirement dreams fully funded.

CHAPTER 8

The Five Pillars of Income Investing: An Antidote to Wilting Dollars

There are infinite ways to invest. If you spend a few minutes online, you'll get thousands of different "best" strategies. You'll see advertisements for stock-picking newsletters, day-trading options, crypto tokens, commodities, venture capital, angel investing. The list is endless.

The challenge isn't finding something to invest in; the challenge is cutting through all that noise—which is constant and loud—and finding a framework that makes sense to you that is simple, durable, and easy to understand. An approach you can stick with through thick and thin.

Unless you've been living under a rock, you've heard of the Magnificent 7: Apple, Microsoft, Alphabet, Amazon, Meta, Nvidia, and

Tesla. These seven tech titans have grown so enormous—each sporting trillion-dollar-plus market caps—that together they account for nearly 35 percent of the entire S&P 500's market cap, aka total weight. Think about that for a second. Seven companies out of 500 make up about a third of the entire index. Make no mistake: These companies we all know by name have enjoyed exceptional success. But investing is not about yesterday. It's about tomorrow.

Pure growth investing can work beautifully—but it gets trickier when you reach retirement and actually need the money. Sure, you can always sell stocks that have gone up in price. But when your paycheck stops and you're relying on your portfolio to fund your monthly expenses, core pursuits, and a family trip to Turks and Caicos, it can present you with a timing problem. You're relying on appreciation which, as we all know, can come in dramatic fits and starts. When eyeing retirement, it's not crazy to want to add a little more predictability into your investment portfolio approach.

Would it be great to find the next small-cap company that turns into a trillion-dollar behemoth? Maybe the magical Mag #8? Of course it would. But with thousands of companies to choose from, betting on finding the next diamond in the rough runs counter to adding that predictability.

So how do we do this? What does the Retire Sooner Method, from an investment standpoint, tell us to do?

Let's start with the simple philosophy hanging on the wall of our office that guides everything our investment team does: **Make It Simple**. Not *keep* it simple, not *be* simple, but do the work to *make* it simple. And when it comes to investing for retirement, the master formula couldn't be more straightforward: Total Return = Growth + Income (TR = G + I).

That's investing. That's all it is.

Growth gives you the potential for appreciation and a decrease or rise in price. Income gives you cash flow. Growth can be wildly unpredictable—just ask anyone who lived through 2008 or early 2020. But income? Income shows up like clockwork, providing steady cash flow that becomes essential once your wage income has ceased to exist.

When we work with families, we expect appreciation from growth over time—but we also like to have some measure of control over the formula. That's where income comes in. I wrote about this philosophy more than a decade ago for the original *You Can Retire Sooner Than You Think*, and I believe in it today more than ever. The world may have changed, presidents may have come and gone and come back again, and ChatGPT has made us question whether humans are still necessary (jury's still out), but the fundamental math of retirement income hasn't budged—and the five pillars of income investing have carried the banner through good times and bad.

Before we start constructing those pillars from the ground up, I need to level with you. As I said way back in Chapter 1, the majority of this book has been about data—understanding the research we've collected on happy retirees and explaining how you can apply the same habits and behaviors. In other words, it's been less about my opinion and more about what the research tells us.

But this chapter is different. When we get into the specifics of how I believe investing works for happy retirees, this becomes very much my opinion based on how I've helped families invest for decades. I'm a firm believer in the investment principles I'm about to share, but there are certainly other paths people could take and be very successful. All of this could be prefaced by "In my opinion . . ." or, as the kids say, IMHO. (Btw, the *H* is for humble.)

THE FIVE PILLARS OF INCOME INVESTING

1. Multi-asset-class income investing
2. Dividend growth
3. Dry powder principle
4. The 4+ percent rule of thumb
   (you'll remember this one from Chapter 2)
5. Tax efficiency

Let's go.

PILLAR #1: MULTI-ASSET-CLASS INCOME INVESTING

This one's the big kahuna, the pillar on the hill I'd die on. If I were to give it an official name on Wall Street—a wonky one no one would like—it would be multi-asset-class income investing (MACII). But that's a mouthful, so let's call it what it really is: **a balanced, simplified approach harnessing both G (Growth) and I (Income) that can work for you in the accumulation phase if you're reinvesting dividends, and particularly well during retirement when you need cash flow.**

Keep in mind our make-it-simple equation: TR = G + I. Growth is when the value of your assets goes up, also known as appreciation. Buy a stock for $10 and it grows to $20? That's growth. Buy a house that appreciates by $100,000 over ten years? That's growth.

Growth is exciting. But it's unpredictable. It comes in peaks, retracements, deep valleys, and bursts of glory.

Income, on the other hand, should be steadier, more predictable, and generally more within our control. Dividends from stocks, interest we expect to receive from bonds, distributions from energy pipeline companies or real estate investment trusts (REITs), rent from a property you own—income tends to show up on a schedule. That makes it much easier to measure and plan around.

Companies that pay dividends typically pay them every single quarter, on or around the same date. Bond interest is typically paid semiannually, while dividends come monthly or quarterly, usually around the same day each period. Rent is due the first of the month, every month. In all of these examples, the income tends to be highly repeatable.

We know that once companies start paying dividends, they're loath to ever cut them or stop paying them. In fact, most companies like to raise their dividends each year. As a landlord, you don't expect to get rent for just a year; you expect to get rent for the life of the property until you sell it. When investing in bonds, you don't expect to get interest income once in a while. You expect to get it on a regular schedule—whether monthly, quarterly, or semiannually—until the bond matures and gives you back your cash.

Of course, none of this is guaranteed. Companies can cut their dividends and renters can stiff their landlord. But by and large, these income streams are ongoing, barring extreme events.

One of the beauties of income investing is that, despite the name, it doesn't force you to pick between growth or income. As you can see from Figure 8.1, both can yield great returns. Income investing allows you to harness G *and* I by spreading your investments across multiple asset classes, each with its own way of generating cash and appreciation and compounding over time.

Everything you're about to read in this chapter hinges on different categories of assets—which ones to use, what they're used for, and how big a part of your portfolio they should be. So before we dig into the intricacies of MACII, the stock ticker nickname no one asked for, let me break down the asset classes.

TURNING $10 INTO $20

A hypothetical example of "pure growth" vs. "pure income" investing

FIGURE 8.1. Turning $10 into $20 Using Two Very Different Approaches

All Growth Example	Beginning	Year 1	Year 2	Year 3	Year 4	Year 5	Year 6	Year 7	Year 8	Year 9	Year 10	Total
Stock ABC												
Stock Price	$10	$11	$12	$13	$14	$15	$16	$17	$18	$19	$20	$20
Dividends	$0	$0	$0	$0	$0	$0	$0	$0	$0	$0	$0	
												$20
All Income Example	**Beginning**	**Year 1**	**Year 2**	**Year 3**	**Year 4**	**Year 5**	**Year 6**	**Year 7**	**Year 8**	**Year 9**	**Year 10**	**Total**
Stock XYZ												
Stock Price	$10	$10	$10	$10	$10	$10	$10	$10	$10	$10	$10	$10
Dividends		$1	$1	$1	$1	$1	$1	$1	$1	$1	$1	$10
												$20

Stocks: The Volatile Star Quarterback

Stocks are the well-known first-round draft pick when it comes to beating inflation. This is your star QB, running back, and offensive attack who can be maddeningly unpredictable. He takes risks, running on fourth down rather than setting up a field goal. His talent often shines through, but sometimes those risky plays lead to losses or injuries. During periods where he spends extensive time on the sidelines, you sometimes question if this is the right team to begin with. They're over there sulking on the bench while you're sitting in the coach's box, alone with your dark thoughts. *Should we trade them?* You wonder. Or even, *Should we fire the whole team?*

The stats here are very clear. Over time, the S&P 500 has enjoyed extraordinary inflation-fighting power. Take a look at Figure 8.2. Due to the US Consumer Price Index rising over time (aka inflation), the purchasing power of the US consumer dollar has fallen over 40 percent just since 2005 (the descending line at the bottom).[1] Meanwhile, the

FIGURE 8.2. Impact of Inflation: US Consumer Dollar (Cash) Purchasing Power vs. Stocks

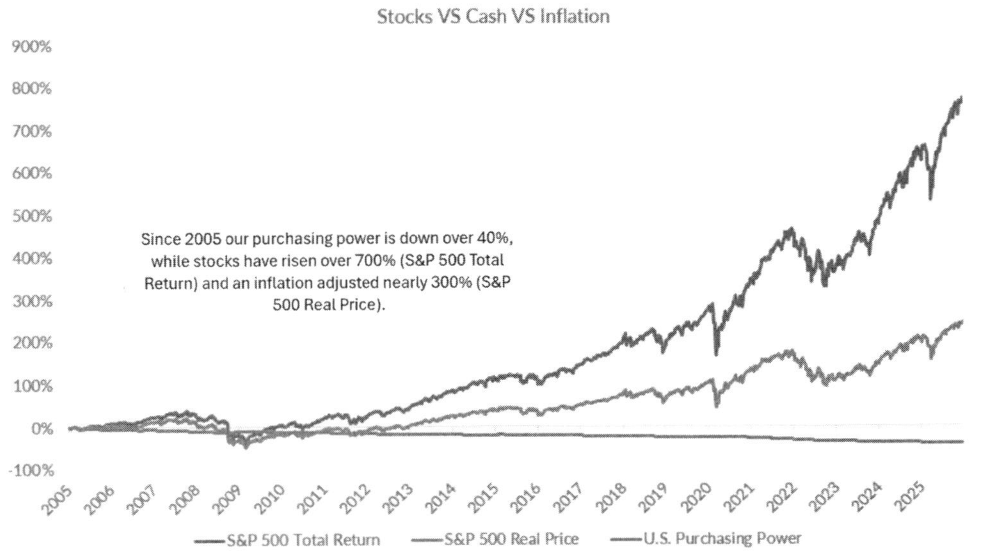

Source: Capital Investment Advisors investment research

S&P 500 total return (including dividends) during that same period is up over 700 percent (the ascending line at the top). That means *even adjusting for inflation*, the S&P 500 is up nearly 300 percent during this same period of just over twenty years.

Now, these gigantic returns for the market come with a heavy emotional price. As you can see from Figure 8.3, even though the S&P 500 has achieved an average annual return of about 12 percent since 1928, the average intra-year drawdown has been 16.3 percent, meaning that getting that nice average 12 percent has come with staying invested during a very regular barrage of pullbacks—each one with its own scary reason, prompting investors to worry, *Wait, maybe this time is different, and we won't recover?*[2]

Here's where behavioral finance gets brutal. The psychological research on "loss aversion" has shown that losses feel 2.5 times more painful than equivalent gains feel good.[3] That's why investors are tempted to

FIGURE 8.3. S&P 500: Maximum Intra-Year Drawdown vs. End of Year Total Returns

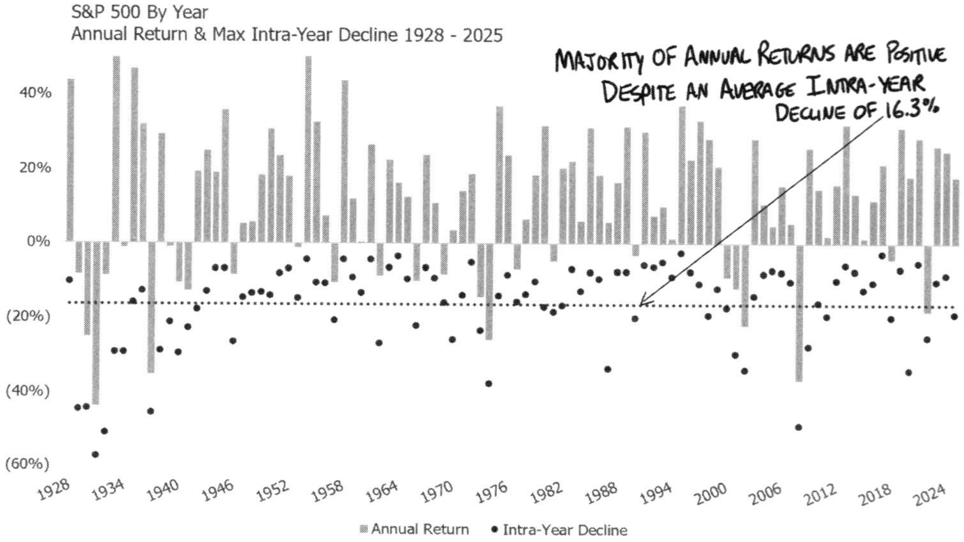

Source: Capital Investment Advisors investment research using S&P data

consistently sell at the worst possible times. The DALBAR Quantitative Analysis of Investor Behavior report measures how investor actions—buying, selling, and switching investments—impact long-term portfolio performance. Figure 8.4 reveals a shocking reality: The average investor earns far less than the very markets they're investing in, mostly due to poor timing decisions. This chart shows twenty years of performance from 1995 to 2024. While stocks averaged 10.4 percent and a balanced 60/40 stock–bond portfolio returned 7.8 percent, the average asset-allocation investor earned only about 3.8 percent—less than half the return of a balanced portfolio—largely due to poor market-timing decisions.

Consider this sobering statistic: If you'd stayed fully invested in the S&P 500 from 1995 to today, you'd have earned roughly 8.8 percent compound annual growth. But for a truly blood-curdling horror story, look at Figure 8.5. Miss *only* the best ten days during that period—yes,

FIGURE 8.4. The Average Investor Underperforms Due to Market Timing

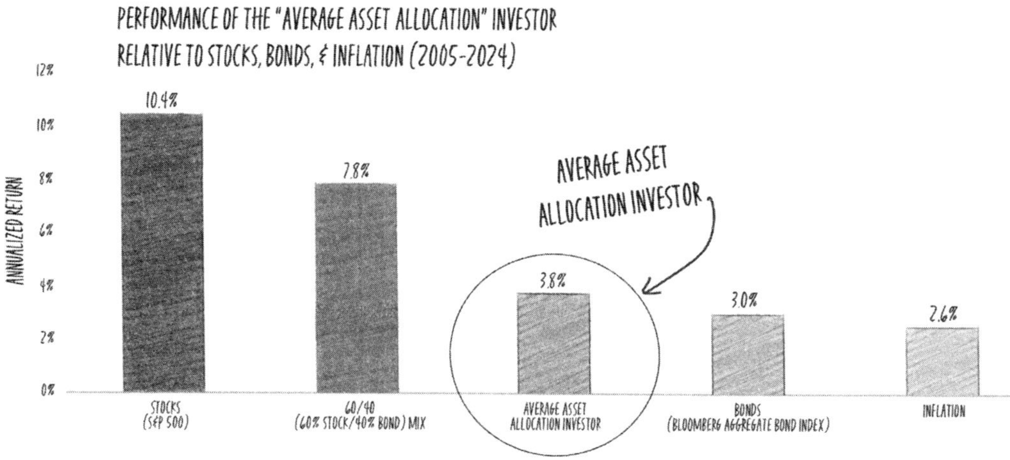

Source: Capital Investment Advisors investment research utilizing Bloomberg and DALBAR data

FIGURE 8.5. Missing the Best Days in the Market

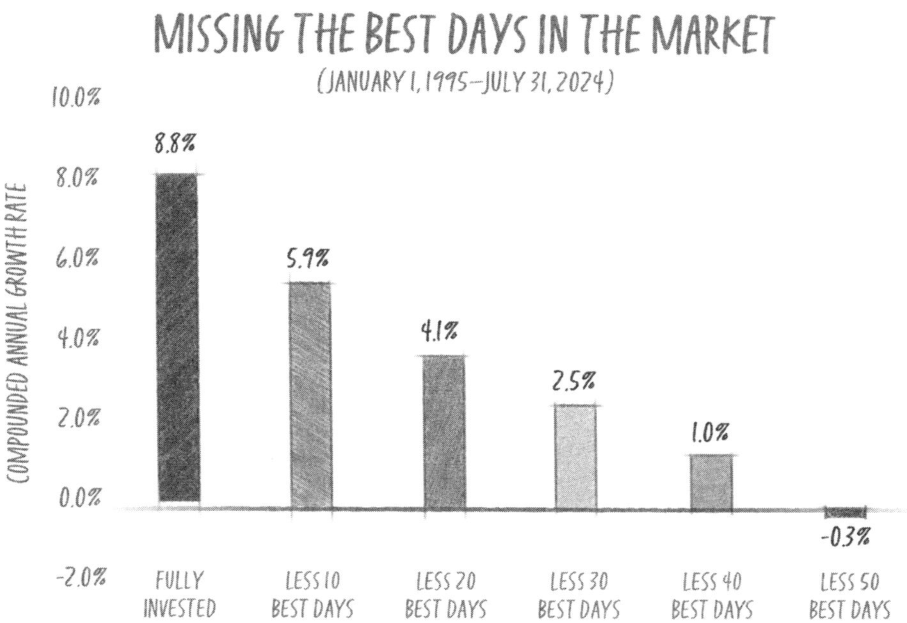

Source: Capital Investment Advisors investment research

FIGURE 8.6. S&P 500 Bull and Bear Markets

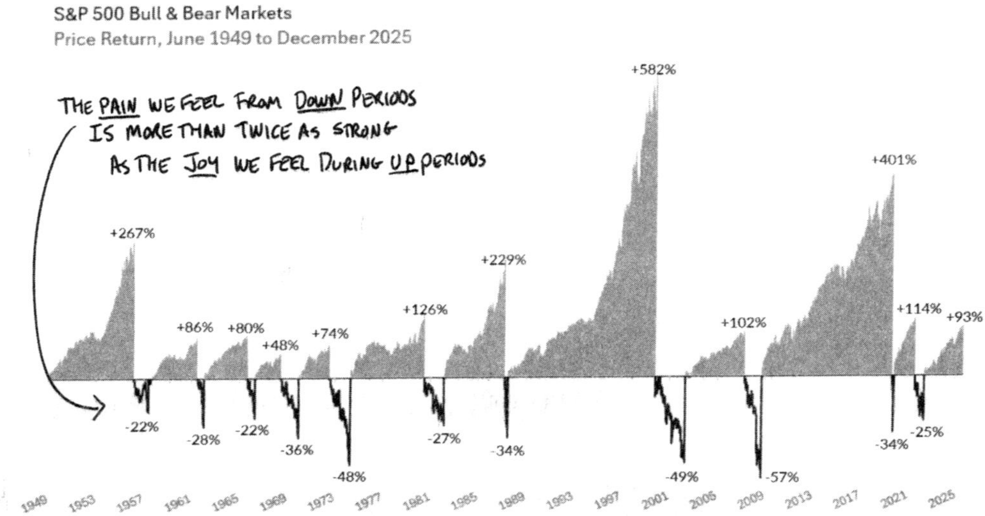

Source: "S&P 500 Index Historical Trends," Guggenheim Investments, https://www.guggenheiminvestments.com/advisor-resources/interactive-tools/sp-500-historical-trends.

ten days out of twenty years—and your returns drop to around 6 percent (a full third less). Miss the best twenty days, and your return has been cut in half. The cruel irony? The best days often cluster right near the worst days, making market timing nearly impossible.

Figure 8.6 perfectly illustrates the emotional roller coaster that comes with stock ownership. The upper solid gray sections represent bull markets—those glorious stretches when everything feels brilliant and you're convinced you're an investing genius. Bull markets have averaged 5.3 years and delivered an average return of +254 percent.[4] But notice the bottom of the chart, where periods of decline are shown. The pain of these stretches feels 2 to 2.5 times more powerful than the joy we get from the positive ones.

While bear markets are shorter and less frequent, they pack an emotional punch that drives many investors to make terrible decisions.

There's a few of them: selling at the bottom right before the next positive stretch begins, or not investing in stocks at all. As you might imagine, investors who stay the course through both the pain and the pleasure are handsomely rewarded, but it requires the mental fortitude to endure those inevitable negative periods without panicking.

The takeaway is simple: **Stay invested.**

Bonds: The Unsexy, Unsung Hero

If stocks are the growth engine, bonds are the ballast. At their simplest, bonds are IOUs—promises to repay borrowed money with interest. While they typically won't make you Bollywood rich like stocks can, they serve a crucial role as your portfolio's seat belt.

The long-run record speaks for itself: Bonds (measured by the Bloomberg US Aggregate Bond Index—Total Return) have returned over 1,750 percent over the past forty-five years versus 320 percent inflation—meaning bonds have indeed beaten inflation over the long haul, just not as dramatically as stocks.[5]

Why own bonds? Three key reasons: stability during stock market downturns, predictable cash flow through regular interest payments, and the "seat belt effect"—which allows you to invest more on the stock side of the ledger than you maybe otherwise would. Put simply, **owning the right percentage of bonds allows you to be a better stock investor**.

The bond universe offers multiple flavors: Treasuries and TIPS (Treasury Inflation-Protected Securities), both with government backing; corporate bonds for higher yields; municipal bonds for tax advantages; high-yield bonds for income seekers willing to take more risk; and floating-rate bonds that adjust with interest rates. Each serves different purposes in a well-constructed portfolio.

Alternative Income: The Quirky but Lovable Uncle

This is where you'll find the hybrids—investments that aren't purely stocks or bonds but can still pay you cash. I think about this asset as your offbeat uncle at the Thanksgiving dinner table: somewhat unconventional and prone to odd opinions about the moon landing, but still part of the family.

Examples include REITs, typically commercial, publicly traded companies—think office buildings, apartment buildings, warehouses, and data centers that distribute their profits to you as a shareholder. As stated earlier, the legal structure of REITs requires roughly 90 percent of net profits to flow back out to shareholders, so you'll see REITs paying anywhere from 3 percent to 5 percent and above per year.

Other forms of alternative investments are energy pipeline companies structured as master limited partnerships, preferred stocks, and closed-end funds. These often deliver higher cash flow than traditional stocks and bonds while adding diversification to your portfolio, though they have unique risks and can be more unpredictable than their traditional counterparts.

You could place private investments in the "alt" club as well—private equity, private debt, and venture capital—though these typically require higher minimum investments and longer commitment periods. When we talk about these assets, I think of them as the "deep end of the pool" in the investing world. These are investments in private companies that don't trade on public markets or in private loans made directly to businesses. They can offer the potential for very high returns—sometimes multiples of what you'd expect from public stocks or bonds—but they also come with higher risks, very long lock-up periods, and far less liquidity. In other words, you can't just click a button and sell them like you can with a stock or mutual fund. Venture capital in particular is about betting on early-stage companies that might one day become the next Amazon or Google—or might just as easily fail completely.

For seasoned investors with significant wealth (qualified and accredited investors), these areas can be exciting and can diversify beyond the public markets. But for most retirees, I'd say they're more like specialty seasoning than the main course—you don't need a large percentage, and you want to be very thoughtful about how you use it.

The unifying theme is that these alternative investments provide the potential for appreciation while typically providing regular distributions, fitting perfectly into our TR = G + I framework.

Cash (and Cash Equivalents): So You Can Sleep Well at Night

This is your SWAN money. Your safety net. This is where you park six months or more of living expenses in things like CDs, money market funds, and high-yield savings accounts. **These funds are highly reliable and highly liquid, and you can access them immediately at any time.**

Crypto: The Weird Teenager Everyone's Talking About

You can't walk ten steps without someone talking about it, so I figure it's worth a mention. Unlike stocks or bonds, crypto doesn't generate earnings, dividends, or interest—it's purely driven by supply, demand, and sentiment. That doesn't mean it can't go up dramatically in price; we've all seen wild runs. But it can just as easily crash, sometimes overnight.

For that reason, I don't think of crypto as a reliable retirement asset. It's more like Vegas money. If you want to put a small slice of your portfolio there, knowing it could double or get cut in half, that's fine. But it shouldn't be confused with the steady compounding of businesses (stocks), bonds, or income-producing investments. In my mind, crypto can be interesting to dabble in, but it's not a foundation for building lasting retirement happiness. And I'll put my crypto where my mouth is: I own only a small holding in Bitcoin.

Commodities: The Silvered Old Grandfather

I tend to view commodities like gold and silver differently than stocks, bonds, or income-producing assets. Gold doesn't send you dividend checks, and silver won't pay you interest. They just sit there, in their own shiny way, relying entirely on what the next buyer is willing to pay. That makes them more of a psychological asset than a productive one, although they do have many consumer and industrial uses.

People often hold gold or silver as a hedge against inflation, geopolitical turmoil, or simply for peace of mind. And yes, there are times when they've surged in value during uncertain periods. But over the long run, they don't have the same track record of growth that comes from owning businesses or bonds. **To me, commodities can be a small satellite piece of a portfolio if they help you sleep better at night—but they shouldn't be mistaken for the engine that's going to fund your retirement.**

So now we've covered the asset classes. But before we get into what to DO, let's talk about DID.

The DID Principle: Dividends, Interest, Distributions

The cash flow you receive from all the categories we just discussed boils down to what we call the DID principle.

Note: Even though I may reference owning individual stocks, bonds, or REITs, you can also own all these in the form of mutual funds or exchange-traded funds (ETFs).

- **Dividends:** Companies sharing profits as cash with shareholders. When you own dividend-paying stocks, you get a periodic check that represents your slice of the company's success.
- **Interest:** The cash flow you earn for lending money (buying a bond) from the issuer, owning a CD, or keeping cash in high-yield accounts. This is your "reward" for essentially being the bank.

- **Distributions:** Payments from vehicles like REITs, pipeline companies, closed-end funds, private equity, and private debt. These often come monthly or quarterly and represent cash flow from the underlying assets.

When you put these all together, you get a multi-stream income engine—not just one faucet turned on but ten, twenty, thirty, or even a hundred different income sources. Each stream might be modest on its own, but collectively, they can form a powerful river strong enough to carry you through retirement.

One of the reasons I love multi-asset-class income investing is that it checks three important boxes, all at the same time: diversification, asset allocation, and balance. Let's break those down into plain English.

Diversification is the idea of not putting all your apples in one bushel. The strategy is to spread your money across a multitude of companies, bonds, REITs, etc., so you're not sunk if one of them hits a rough patch or an iceberg.

To me, diversification sounds so Investing 101 that sometimes I feel guilty even bringing it up. Everybody knows the concept, right? Don't put all your eggs in one basket, don't bet on one horse, and all the other idioms. We get it!

However, this seemingly fundamental rule gets violated all the time in the investment business. I saw it happen decades ago when I first started, and I still see it happening today. Here's how it shows up: Someone owns a company they believe in so much, they're sure nothing could ever derail it, or they have great loyalty to a company where they worked for a long time, or there are other financial reasons that make them not want to diversify, like wanting to avoid taxes. As time goes on and stock prices rise, selling stocks in order to diversify can create capital gains, which people try to avoid, which further boxes investors into a nondiversified corner.

A retiree from Memphis named Peggy recently emailed our podcast with a cautionary tale to share. She was a longtime UPS-er, a devoted employee of the United Parcel Service. So devoted she even loved the brown shirt and shorts. There are still companies where people work for decades and spend most of their careers. Employees often accumulate stock over long periods of time, and when a company has many years of strong, steady growth, investors get lulled into thinking nothing dramatic can ever happen to their beloved company's stock. Peggy, our listener, valued her former employer's long history and strong business model.

Peggy wore many hats at UPS, all in the spirit of delivering packages, for more than thirty years and had accrued $3.5 million in stock. Because she didn't want to sell and pay capital gains taxes, she'd slowly taken out money over time against her stock through a margin loan. The margin loan had helped pay off a home, fund her grandchildren's college tuition, and pay for both of her daughters' weddings. All worthy endeavors, which amounted to a seemingly manageable 20 percent of her stock's value.

However, things did go very wrong. What once was a $3.5 million position in 2022 had fallen to less than $1.4 million in 2025. A more than 60 percent drop in the price of the stock—a stock that most employees never thought would go down—created a harrowing situation of forced selling due to margin calls, where brokerage companies force investors to sell assets if their margin (loan) amount gets too high relative to the position's value.

This forced selling created a tax tsunami from the very stock Peggy was trying not to sell due to her low initial cost basis. She wanted the margin loan gone. After finally selling all of her stock—and paying the long-term capital gains the sale incurred—she was left with nearly nothing. She went from $3.5 million to virtually zero in the matter of a few years. She found herself in a waking nightmare, one she'd never even thought possible.

Since I don't want you to lose sleep tonight over Peggy's plight—you need those seven to eight hours—I'm happy to report that in addition to her paid-off home, she had an additional $1 million in real estate. So Peggy's going to be okay. My point is, she should never have been in this position, which caused her great stress and anxiety.

All that to say, every time I start thinking diversification is too obvious to mention, I hear another catastrophic story about someone who thought the rules about diversification didn't apply to them.

Asset allocation is the fancier-sounding cousin of diversification. It's not just spreading money among a bunch of different companies or bonds; it's spreading your investments intentionally across major asset classes like stocks, bonds, and alternatives in specific proportions. This is meant to heighten the overall stability of your portfolio with the understanding that these asset classes may move in slightly different directions—zigging when others are zagging. The goal is to structure your asset mix, so you can still aim for significant long-term returns but with less overall volatility. While diversification and asset allocation don't guarantee returns or eliminate the risk of loss, especially in a declining market, it can help cushion the blow if something goes wrong.

Balance is the sensible sibling in this family. It's the reminder not to go overboard in any direction. Balance keeps you from being 100 percent in the stock market at age seventy or sitting entirely in cash at age thirty-five. It's meant to keep the seesaw steady when markets get rocky.

Multi-asset-class income investing naturally forces you to practice all three: diversification, asset allocation, balance. By owning a variety of investments that create multiple streams of DID income—dividends, interest, distributions—you achieve diversification. By consciously placing money in the right places, you're executing asset allocation with intention. And by combining risk assets with stable assets, and short-term liquidity with long-term investments, you're attaining balance.

When you structure your investments this way, you don't have to panic every time the market sneezes. You've already built safeguards. You've got your taken-for-granted-uncle diversification, your smart-cousin asset allocation, and the steady-sibling balance, all working together to keep your financial picture in harmony. *Harmony.* Something I wish for on every family vacation we take—and usually don't get.

Now it's time to introduce you to my four favorite buckets.

The Retire Sooner Method Bucket System

Over the years, I've found that one of the most effective ways to explain income investing is through what's called the "bucket system." If you've heard of this before, great—but I'm going to put my own spin on it.

Here's the big picture: Think of your investment portfolio as four separate buckets, each holding a different type of investment. During your working years—what we call the "accumulation phase"—you're filling these buckets and letting the investments grow. Once you retire, you start drawing income from them in a strategic way, tapping some more heavily than others depending on market conditions and your specific needs.

This system applies to your liquid investment dollars: money inside your IRA, 401(k), Roths, and brokerage accounts. We're not including things like real estate or your primary residence here—those are valuable assets, but they're much less liquid and serve different purposes.

The Four Buckets

Let's dip into each of the four buckets and what goes in each one. Think of these as four different "jobs" your money needs to do.

CASH BUCKET (TYPICALLY 5–10 PERCENT OF PORTFOLIO)

Your emergency fund and short-term liquidity needs live here: six months or more of living expenses parked in CDs, money market funds, and high-yield savings accounts. This bucket represents complete control, safety, and immediate access. This isn't money you're hoping will grow dramatically; it's money you know will be there when you need it. Cash provides something invaluable in retirement: optionality and peace of mind.

INCOME BUCKET (TYPICALLY 20–50 PERCENT OF PORTFOLIO)

This is your bond headquarters—government bonds, municipal bonds, corporate bonds, and maybe a touch of high-yield. As we've established, bonds are basically IOUs: You lend money to a government or company by buying their bond, and they promise to pay you interest along the way and give you back your original amount at maturity. These maturities can range from thirty days to thirty years. This bucket isn't glamorous—you won't brag to your neighbor about your municipal bond ladder. But its role is stability and predictable interest income. Bonds are the anchor that keeps you steady when the waves start to swell.

> **INCOMING: A NOTE ABOUT INCOME**
>
> A quick clarification: Don't confuse the word *income* with just the income bucket. *All* of your buckets have the ability to generate income or cash flow. You may choose to have stocks in the growth bucket that pay *no* dividends, which is also fine.
>
> However, as an income-oriented investor, I'm a big believer that 90 percent or more of what you own should pay you some level of income, regardless of your age. This is how strongly I feel about income investing—it's a way to grow wealth without running out of capital over time.

Here's something crucial about bond investing that many people overlook: The interest rate environment when you buy matters enormously because your starting yield does much of the heavy lifting on long-run results. With an individual bond you hold to maturity, your total return tends to settle near today's yield to maturity, adjusted for any credit surprises. With bond funds and ETFs, prices bounce around as rates move, but as coupons get paid and reinvested, long-run returns usually gravitate toward the yield you locked in at purchase.

In other words, when yields are low, expect modest future returns; when yields are higher, the odds of better returns improve. This is why timing matters with bonds in a way that's different from stocks—you're essentially locking in your future return the day you buy. Bottom line: For bonds, yield is destiny.

ALTERNATIVE INCOME BUCKET (TYPICALLY 5–15 PERCENT OF PORTFOLIO)

Here's our eclectic team—the investments that don't fit neatly into traditional categories but still generate regular cash payments. REITs, energy pipeline companies, preferred stocks, and closed-end funds live here. These often deliver higher yields than traditional stocks and bonds, while adding diversification to your portfolio. As mentioned, we could throw PE, private debt, and venture capital in here, too.

GROWTH BUCKET (TYPICALLY 40–75 PERCENT OF PORTFOLIO)

This bucket is chock-full of stocks. Some are dividend-paying companies that send you a steady paycheck, while others are pure growth companies—think giant technology companies—that are there solely for appreciation over time. When it comes to dividends, the two acronyms I use most frequently with families are SHUT (staples, health care, utilities, telecom) for more defensive dividend-oriented companies and MEDFIT (materials, energy, discretionary, financials, industrials, technology) for more growth-oriented sectors. Between them, you get a broad cross section of the army of American productivity that powers our country's economy toward long-term growth.

Side note: If I were forced to put gold and silver (commodities) into a bucket, I'd have to put them in the growth bucket, since you're relying solely on appreciation.

How the Buckets Work: Accumulation vs. Retirement

During the accumulation phase, all four buckets are filling up and growing. Any dividends, interest, or distributions your investments generate gets reinvested right back into their respective buckets. You're not taking money out; you're letting the compounding machine do its work.

Figure 8.7 shows the four buckets during accumulation. These buckets aren't all the exact same size. They vary depending on importance

FIGURE 8.7. The Cash Flow Generating Bucket System at Work—Pre-Retirement/Accumulation Phase

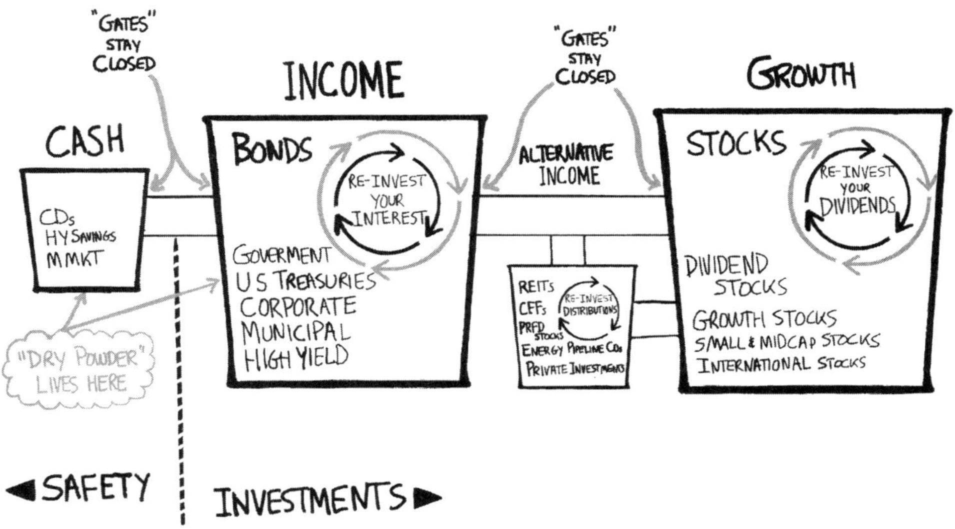

In the accumulation phase, income (cash flow) generated by each investment bucket is simply reinvested over and over again.

and timing. Some are bigger, more foundational buckets, and others are smaller—but still necessary. How much you allocate to each bucket is determined by your preferences and risk tolerance, which together will dictate how heavily you use each bucket and ultimately define your overall asset allocation.

Perhaps most importantly, you will see that there is "income" that's generated in each bucket. Income comes in the form of dividends from stocks, interest from bonds and cash, and distributions from the various investments in the alternative income bucket. **During the pre-retirement (accumulation phase), the income produced in each bucket should stay in that particular bucket and simply be reinvested and reinvested and reinvested.**

Here's where the magic happens. In your accumulation phase, you keep the tap closed and watch the four buckets fill up. But in retirement, it's time to twist the spigot and "open the gates." **This allows the interest from your income bucket, the distributions from your alternative income bucket, and the dividends from your growth bucket to flow back into your cash bucket, creating a steady stream of retirement income.**

See Figure 8.8 for the magic of income investing during retirement. That cash bucket is what you draw from for living expenses. And if you don't need all of your investment cash flow in a given year, you can reinvest the excess back into whichever bucket you choose.

This is what I love about the bucket system: It's visual, it's practical, and it makes the abstract concept of "portfolio management" into something concrete. You're not just "managing investments"—you're strategically filling and drawing from buckets based on your needs and market conditions.

One of my favorite investment books is *The Single Best Investment* by Lowell Miller. There's a great quote about how investing is much like a

FIGURE 8.8. The Cash Flow Generating Bucket System at Work—Retirement/Distribution Phase

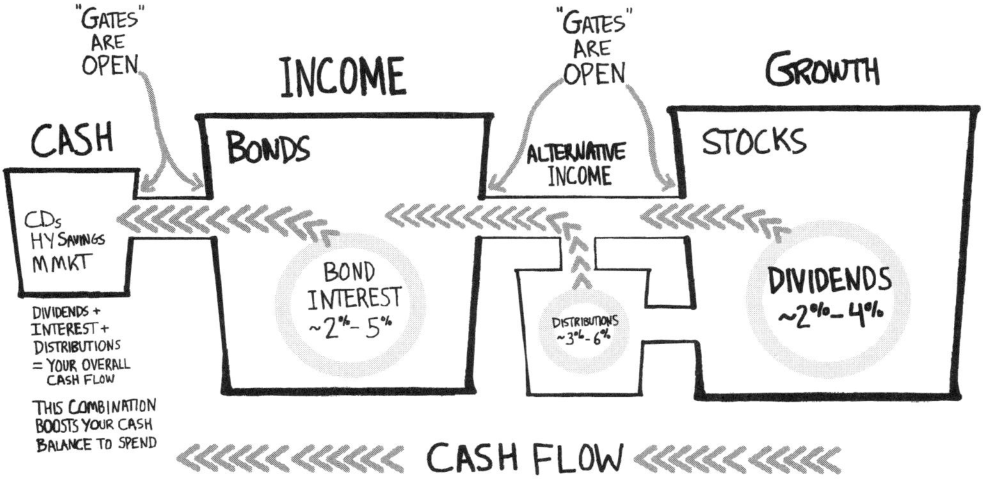

In the distribution phase, each of your investment buckets produces income (cash flow) that flows into your cash bucket—creating a steady stream of portfolio income you can actually spend in retirement.

"compounding machine that sits quietly off in the corner working for you while you go about your business . . . it's the money that money makes, added to the money that money has already made. And each time money makes money, it becomes capable of making even more money than it could before!"[6]

That's what makes this system so powerful. **With multi-asset-class income investing, you've created your own accumulation machine during your working years. Once you open the gates, it becomes your own retirement paycheck machine.**

The bucket system isn't the only way to approach retirement investing—but it's a great place to start. Over the years, I've found this to be the most effective way of explaining income investing to the families I work with every day.

PILLAR #2: DIVIDEND GROWTH

I like to think of dividends as the reliable paycheck of your portfolio. And dividend growth? That's your raise—not just this year but for the next ten, twenty, even thirty.[7]

This is why dividend growth investing is one of the most powerful tools available to retirees. It's not just about creating a stable income stream—it's about crafting an income stream that gets larger and more reliable the longer you stick with it. It's the ultimate antidote to the sneaky corrosion of inflation, which slowly but surely chips away at the value of the dollars sitting in your wallet. Dividend income, especially when it grows, acts as a built-in cost-of-living adjustment.

Let's look at the numbers. Although we can't predict the future, over the last 150+ years, S&P 500 dividends have grown at an average annual pace of roughly 3.7 percent—nearly twice the rate of inflation during those same periods, which averaged 2.1 percent.[8] As you can see in Figure 8.9, the trend holds even in recent years: In the twelve months ending June 2025, S&P dividends grew by 6.6 percent while inflation grew just 2.7 percent.[9] That kind of growth makes a massive difference because it's not just about a 6 percent raise one year—it's growth compounded over time.

Here's the mistake I see too many investors make: They look at the current dividend yield and think, *That's too low to matter*.

Maybe a stock is paying 2 percent, and they'd prefer something at 5 percent. But they're missing the bigger picture. They're judging a sixteen-year-old kid working part-time at a burger joint, without realizing he's going to become a partner in a thriving business one day. The real value is not the current yield—it's what that yield can become over time.

This is why I use a concept called Yield at Cost, or YAC. I'll say one thing for Chapter 8: If you owned stock in acronyms, this chapter alone could pay off your mortgage.

FIGURE 8.9. Annualized Dividend Growth of US Stocks vs. Inflation

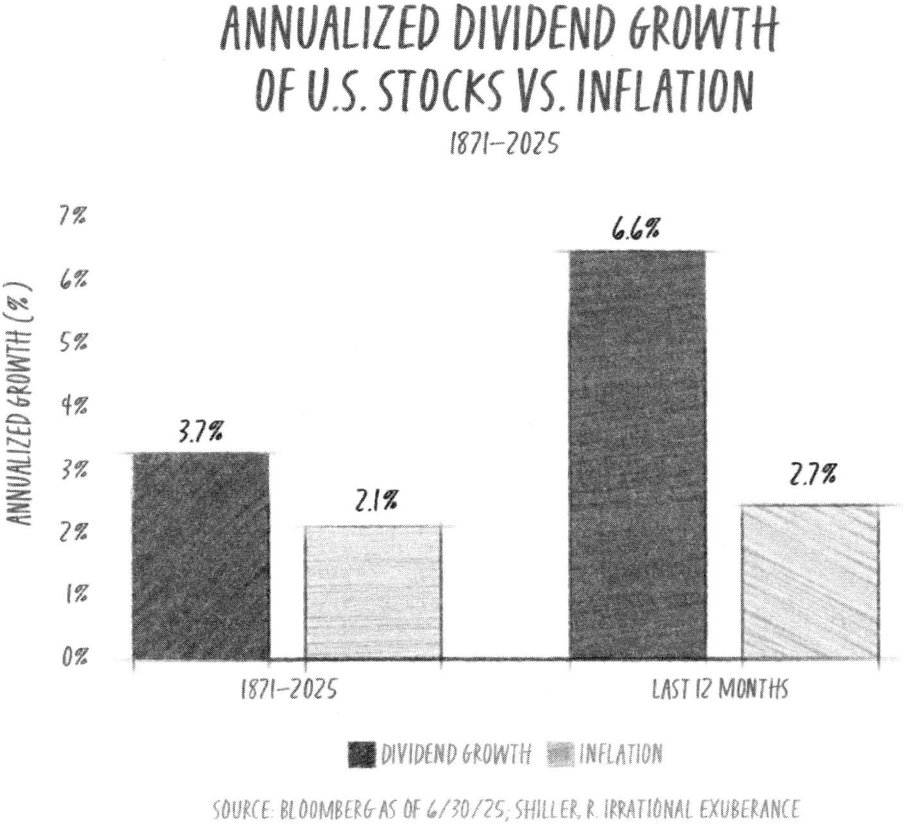

Source: Capital Investment Advisors investment research utilizing Bloomberg and Case-Shiller data

Current Yield is today's annual dividend divided by today's share price. **Yield at Cost** is today's annual dividend divided by the price you originally paid.

YAC reveals the "raise" that your dividend-paying stocks are giving you—even if the current yield looks unimpressive to new buyers.

Let me show you how this plays out with some concrete examples. (Data is from August 2013 through August 2025.)[10]

LOCKHEED MARTIN (LMT)[11]

- 2013: Price $122, dividend $5.32 (4.36% yield)
- 2025: Price $455, dividend $13.20 (2.9% current yield)
- **Yield at Cost = $13.20 ÷ $122 = 10.8%**
- Total return with dividends: approximately 410%

JOHNSON & JOHNSON (JNJ)[12]

- 2013: Price $89.55, dividend $2.80 (3.1% yield)
- 2025: Price $177, dividend $5.20 (2.9% current yield)
- **Yield at Cost = $5.20 ÷ $89.55 = 5.8%**
- Total return: approximately 186%

Dividend Growth in Practice: A Juicy Bite of the Apple

Whatever your feelings toward Steve Jobs—or how annoyed you are by the MacBook literati cluttering your local café—no one can deny Apple is a powerhouse. But it's not known as a dividend payer. Back in the aughts, if you mentioned Apple as an "income investment," people would have looked at you like you'd sprouted an iPod from your head. This was the growth darling; the maker of the iPhone, now permanently fused to hands around the world; the company that was supposed to be all about capital appreciation, not boring old dividends.

But here's what actually happened. In August 2013, Apple was trading at $17.79 per share and paying an annual dividend of just $.47—a modest 2.6 percent yield that barely registered on most income investors' radars.[13] Fast-forward to the summer of 2025, and Apple was trading at around $232 per share with an annual dividend of $1.04. The current yield? A measly 0.45 percent that would make any income seeker yawn and move on to something more exciting.

This is where Yield at Cost reveals the hidden story. If you bought Apple back in 2013 for that original price of $17.79, 2025's $1.04 dividend represents a 5.8 percent yield on your original investment. That's more than twelve times the current yield that ***new*** buyers saw in 2025.

The total returns tell an even more remarkable story. The stock price alone delivered over 1,200 percent gains, but when you factor in all those dividend payments over the years, your total return approaches 1,400 percent. Apple—the company nobody thought of as a dividend stock—became both a wonderful growth story and a surprisingly effective income generator for patient investors.

This illustrates why dividend growth investing can work so well, as long as you're patient. **You're not just buying today's yield—you're buying tomorrow's income stream from a company with growth prospects to keep raising that dividend year after year.** Sometimes dividend stocks are hiding in plain sight, masquerading as growth plays while quietly building an income engine that compounds over time.

The Mathematics of Patience

Individual stock picking isn't for everyone, which is why I also like to look at dividend growth ETFs like DGRO (iShares Core Dividend Growth ETF). This basket of stocks looks for companies with at least five consecutive years of dividend growth, excludes the highest yielders to avoid yield traps (dividends that are too high and at risk of being cut), and caps individual positions' weight to prevent concentration risk.

Check out Figure 8.10. From 2015 to 2025, a $1 million investment in DGRO would have grown to $2.4 million for an annualized return of 8.7 percent. More importantly for income seekers, the dividends

FIGURE 8.10. Power of Compounding Dividend Growth

Source: Capital Investment Advisors investment research as of June 2025

themselves more than doubled—growing from $24,217 in the first year to $53,405 by 2025, representing 7.7 percent annual dividend growth. The original yield of 2.4 percent became a yield at cost of 5.3 percent.

Sometimes it really is about sitting tight, whether or not you're sitting in front of a MacBook and an artisanal, fair trade, organic mocha chocolate pumpkin spice kale latte. Let's say you own a stock today that pays a 2 percent dividend. That might seem modest, especially when other options pay 5 percent or more. But if that company increases its dividend by 6 percent each year, in ten years your yield at cost will be over 5 percent. In fifteen to twenty years, it could be 7 percent, 8 percent, even 10 percent—all based on what you originally invested.

This is why we don't just chase the highest dividend today—we want the dividend that will grow. Today's 2–3 percent yielders are often tomorrow's 5–6 percenters. That's what YAC reminds us: When dividends grow, so does your income stream—if you give it time.

When you're building your retirement paycheck, you want it to be steady. But even better, you want it to grow. **Dividend growth investing is designed to transform your portfolio into a compounding machine—one that sits quietly in the corner, giving you a raise every year while you go about living your life.** Your money essentially asks itself for a raise and then tells itself yes.

PILLAR #3: DRY POWDER PRINCIPLE

One of the biggest risks for retirees isn't market volatility itself—it's how we react to it. Remember that loss aversion research we talked about earlier? The pain of losing money feels about 2.5 times stronger than the joy of gaining it. That's why bear markets, even though they're historically shorter and less frequent than bull markets, can feel absolutely overwhelming and drive us to make terrible decisions.

This is where the dry powder principle comes in: **having at least three years' worth of spending money above your guaranteed income streams, like Social Security and pension, in safety assets.** If you need $100,000 a year and you're getting $50,000 from guaranteed income streams like Social Security, your annual portfolio withdrawal need is $50,000. Multiply this by three, and you would want at least $150,000 in dry powder.

What makes up the dry powder is safe, liquid, high-quality bonds, but it could also include cash and money market funds. These bonds can be short- to intermediate-term US Treasuries, high-quality municipal bonds, or investment-grade corporate bonds. It's not there to dazzle you with growth or generate exciting returns. They are there to give you confidence and breathing room when the stock market inevitably takes a hit.

Here's how it works in practice. Imagine you're retired and living off your portfolio. You've got a cozy house with a paid-off mortgage, a great group of close friends, a solid financial plan, and a colorful retirement life map on the refrigerator beside your granddaughter's report card (straight A's). You also play golf and tennis, volunteer at the local cat café, make paper-mache sculptures, and sleep eight hours every night. You are, in other words, a very good student of the Retire Sooner Method, and a damn happy retiree.

Then, the market suddenly drops 20 percent or more—which happens roughly every four to five years, by the way. If you were invested purely in stocks, and you needed more than just your dividend income to cover your monthly spending, you'd face a tough choice: sell your shares at depressed prices to generate the cash you need for groceries and mortgage payments, or risk going *without* the cash flow that keeps your Alexa-activated lights on. Either way, the emotional strain becomes heavy.

But with dry powder, you have options. You can draw from the bond bucket while you patiently wait for the stock portion of your portfolio to recover. This keeps you from having to sell stocks at exactly the wrong time—which is what destroys most people's long-term returns.

In other words, bonds buy you patience. And patience might be the most powerful investment tool you can have.

Why This Makes You a Better Investor

You know I'm a numbers guy, so let's drill down. During major market downturns like 2000, 2008, and 2020, when stocks got hammered, high-quality bonds often provided stability or even positive returns. That stability is your dry powder at work.

When the stock market pulls back 20 percent or more, Figure 8.11 shows that it takes nearly twenty-four months for a 100 percent equity portfolio to recover. However, the light gray bar shows that a balanced

FIGURE 8.11. Diversification and Recovery Time During Equity Market Pullbacks

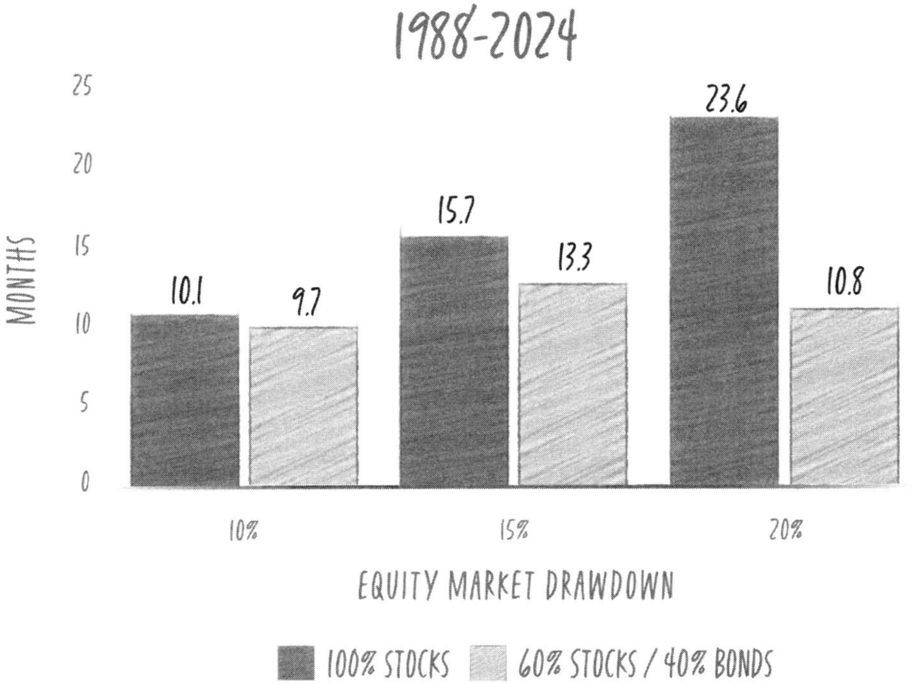

Source: Capital Investment Advisors investment research

60/40 percent stock–bond portfolio takes on average only 10.8 months to recover. This shortened recovery time is primarily due to a balanced portfolio having a much shallower pothole to climb out of.

Over the past forty-five years, bonds certainly haven't come close to matching stocks in total return. But they do accomplish something almost as valuable: steady, predictable income that often keeps pace with or exceeds inflation while providing a seat belt to allow you to be a more consistent, disciplined, and all-around better equity investor.

The families I work with who can calmly watch CNBC during market calamities without reaching for the panic button are the ones who have three years' worth of dry powder—and that's just the minimum. Many have five or even ten years' worth. They can sit tight during those inevitable red stretches on the bull and bear market chart we looked at earlier.

The dry powder pillar isn't about maximizing every single dollar—it's about maximizing your ability to stay the course. Bonds make the ride smoother and make you a steadier investor, and over a lifetime of investing, that steadiness can be worth just as much as the headline returns of a spicy-but-unpredictable all-stock portfolio.

Think of it this way: **Dry powder doesn't just protect your money during downturns—it protects you from yourself.** If stocks are the adrenaline rush, bonds are the safety harness. The harness doesn't make the ride less thrilling—it makes you brave enough to take the ride in the first place.

PILLAR #4: THE 4+ PERCENT RULE OF THUMB

We covered the mechanics of withdrawal rates in Chapter 2 with the classic 4+ percent rule. But we haven't discussed how withdrawal strategies interact with everything else in the multi-asset-class income investing approach.

Traditional withdrawal rate studies assume you're selling shares to generate the cash you need—a bit like chopping down trees to heat your house. But when you've built a portfolio using the first three pillars—multi-asset class, dividend growth, and dry powder in the form of bonds and/or cash—you're not just chopping wood anymore; you're running a sophisticated income engine with multiple fuel sources.

Think about it. If you've implemented pillar #1 (MACII), you're generating dividends, interest, and distributions from four different buckets. Pillar #2 (dividend growth) means your income stream from dividends should be growing over time, potentially reducing how much you need to withdraw from your principal. Pillar #3 (dry powder) gives you the flexibility to draw from bonds during stock market downturns instead of selling equities at depressed prices.

This changes the withdrawal game. Instead of robotically selling 4 percent of your portfolio every year regardless of market conditions, you can be strategic about where your income originates based on what's performing well and what might be lagging.

The original 4 percent rule from the 1990s was based on having between 50 and 75 percent in stocks and assumed you'd adjust withdrawals annually for inflation regardless of market performance. But William Bengen's 2025 book suggests that withdrawal rates could be based on 4.7 percent, which he calls the "universal safe max," as long as there's proper diversification.[14]

There are still few better guides than the 4+ percent rule of thumb when it comes to the safe utilization of your retirement savings. In a stretch of good stock market years, you might be able to take 5 percent. In a stretch of tough stock market years, you might need to tighten your belt, relying more heavily on your dry powder reserves, and take less than 4 percent. **The key is that the 4 percent range is your home base, and this rule of thumb provides retirees with flexibility in any given year.** Understanding and implementing the 4 percent guideline means you should not have to worry about running out of money, even accounting for inflation. The world changes, your circumstances change; your withdrawal rate likewise should be at least somewhat flexible. You're not locked into exactly 4 percent every year, come hell or high water. The rule allows you to adapt to market conditions while maintaining the income you need—an approach the happiest retirees have mastered.

Side note: There's one other component of income investing that doesn't get talked about all that much. A portfolio that is generating 2–3 percent a year just in income—dividends from stocks, interest from bonds, or distributions from other areas, like REITs or energy pipeline companies—by nature fulfills much of the portfolio work needed to get to the 4 percent range. I think of this cash flow as further mental cushion: Even without stellar stock market returns in any given year, your cash flow alone can get you very deep into the race when it comes to fulfilling your withdrawal needs.

PILLAR #5: TAX EFFICIENCY

Taxes don't always get their due weight in retirement planning, which is ironic because they can be one of the biggest drags on your wealth. Think about it: You can have the perfect asset allocation, growing dividends, and a rock-solid portfolio, but if you're handing over 20–30 percent of the income you need to Uncle Sam every year, you're essentially working for the government instead of yourself.

This is why tax efficiency is the fifth pillar of income investing. It's not just about what you own—it's about how you utilize it.

Tax Silos

Your investment accounts fall into three distinct tax categories, and understanding these silos can save you an enormous amount over your lifetime:

- **After-tax assets:** Your regular brokerage accounts, savings accounts, and money market funds. You've already paid taxes on this money, so you only owe taxes on any gains or income they generate.
- **Pre-tax assets:** Traditional IRAs, 401(k)s, pensions, and similar accounts. The amount you withdraw in any given year is a major determinant in your overall annual income and tax rate.
- **Tax-free assets:** Roth IRAs, Roth 401(k)s, and certain life insurance policies. As long as you are eligible and follow the rules, withdrawals should be completely tax-free.

Let me show you why this matters with a real-life example. Imagine a couple wanting to live on $100,000 per year in retirement.

Scenario One: Strategic Withdrawal

They withdraw $50,000 from pretax accounts and $50,000 from tax-free sources (Roth IRA or after-tax brokerage accounts). Because half comes in tax-free, only the $50,000 from pretax accounts is taxable. This keeps them in a low bracket—just a 10 percent marginal rate on that portion, resulting in approximately $1,850 in federal taxes (based on 2025 tax tables).

Scenario Two: All Pretax Withdrawal

They pull the entire $100,000 from pretax accounts (traditional IRAs or 401(k)s). Now their taxable income has doubled. They're pushed into a 12 percent marginal bracket with an 11.3 percent effective rate applying to more income than scenario one. Total federal taxes due: approximately $7,743. That's a $5,893 annual difference ($7,743 vs. $1,850). Compound that over a 25-year retirement at a 6 percent rate of return, and the inefficient withdrawal strategy could cost them roughly $320,000 in lost wealth. (See the full scenario analysis in Appendix B.)

Same portfolio, same investments, same returns—dramatically different outcomes based purely on tax planning.

This example uses 2025 federal tax brackets and assumes standard deductions for a married couple filing jointly. Your specific numbers will vary based on your state taxes, Social Security taxation, and other income sources—which is exactly why working with a qualified tax advisor or financial planner is so valuable. The principle remains the same regardless: Strategic withdrawal sequencing can save you hundreds of thousands of dollars over a retirement.

Beyond which accounts you use, tax efficiency also means putting the right investments in the right places:

- **Tax-efficient investments** (great for taxable accounts): Municipal bonds, index funds with low capital gain distributions, dividend-focused stocks that qualify for favorable tax treatment, and investments you plan to hold long-term
- **Tax-inefficient investments** (better in tax-sheltered accounts): REITs, high-yield bonds, actively managed funds with high turnover, and anything generating significant short-term capital gains

Once again, I'm bringing back the unsung hero—bonds—a recurring presence in this chapter. I'm finally taking these bad boys everyone thinks are boring out of the shadows and into the limelight.

And for good reason. **Municipal bonds** deserve special mention when talking about taxes. These local government-issued bonds typically offer interest that's exempt from federal taxes, and often state taxes too if you live in the issuing state. For investors in high tax brackets, a 4 percent tax-free municipal bond might be equivalent to a 6 percent taxable bond—sometimes making them the clear winner for the income portion of your portfolio.

What Is Tax Loss Harvesting?

Tax loss harvesting is the strategy of intentionally selling an investment in your brokerage (after-tax) account at a loss—not because you're panicking but because you're being *tax smart*.

When you sell an investment that's worth less than what you paid for it, you create a realized capital loss. That loss can then be used to offset gains from other investments you sold for a profit. If you still have leftover losses, you can deduct up to $3,000 against your regular income (like wages, pension, or Social Security). If there's still more loss left? It carries forward to future tax years.

This works with individual stocks, ETFs, and mutual funds—as long as they're held in a taxable brokerage account (and not in an IRA).

Let's say you bought $10,000 of XYZ stock and it's now worth $7,000. You sell it and lock in a $3,000 capital loss.

In the same year, you sell another ETF at a $3,000 gain.

Normally, you'd owe tax on that $3,000 gain—but now? *No tax owed.* Your harvested loss offsets your realized gain—dollar for dollar. Even better, if you want to stay invested, you can reinvest that money into a similar (but not identical) investment to keep your strategy intact without triggering the IRS's wash sale rule.

Tax loss harvesting is like financial judo—you take something that feels negative (a losing investment) and turn it into a tax-saving advantage. Used correctly, it can help smooth out your tax bill in volatile markets—and give you more control over when and how you realize gains.

What About "Direct Indexing" and How Does It Work?

Direct indexing is like building your own personal index fund, one stock at a time. Instead of buying a single ETF like the Russell 3000, which wraps all 3,000 stocks into one product, direct indexing actually buys the individual stocks inside the index, in your name, in a separately managed non-IRA account.

The upside? You get the same market exposure but with much more control—especially when it comes to tax management. Because you own the individual stocks, you (or your advisor or software) can *harvest* losses more precisely, take advantage of specific gains, or even remove companies that don't align with your goals, values, or tax situation.

Let's say you invest $100,000 into a Russell 3000 ETF. You get full market exposure, low fees, and a return very close to whatever the index does—but no real ability to harvest losses, as you own just this one single ETF.

Now let's say you invest that same $100,000 using a direct indexing strategy that mirrors the Russell 3000. You still get the broad market exposure, but if a hundred of the stocks go down while the rest go up (and you still get very close to the index return just like the ETF version), you can harvest losses from the individual losers while keeping the overall exposure. Those harvested losses can then offset capital gains or income in the future when you are ready to pull out some of the funds. The investment industry calls this "creating real tax alpha."

So instead of one fund that just goes up or down, you have thousands of dials you can turn throughout the year to stay tax efficient.

The Retirement Tax Advantage

Here's some encouraging news: Most retirees end up in a much lower tax bracket than they expect relative to their wage-earning, working years. When you stop working, FICA taxes disappear—that's about 7 percent savings right there on your first approximately $176,000 of income per person. Many states offer additional tax breaks for retirees, and you have much more control over your taxable income during this phase through strategic withdrawals.

The Roth Conversion Window

One of the most effective tax strategies used by successful retirees is taking advantage of the low-income years between leaving full-time work and the start of required minimum distributions at age seventy-three (or seventy-five for those born after 1960). This period often creates a valuable planning window, as household income may be temporarily lower than it will be later in retirement.

During these years, retirees may be able to convert portions of traditional retirement accounts into Roth accounts while remaining in relatively favorable tax brackets. By paying taxes intentionally at lower rates earlier, retirees can reduce future required withdrawals, limit lifetime tax exposure, and create greater flexibility in how retirement income is generated later on. Used thoughtfully, this window can help lower taxes over time and support a more efficient retirement income plan.

Tax efficiency integrates beautifully with the other four pillars. Your dividend income might qualify for favorable tax rates. Your municipal bond should provide tax-free income. Your dry powder reserves give you flexibility to withdraw from the most tax-advantaged accounts during different market cycles.

The goal isn't to eliminate taxes entirely. (Wouldn't that be nice?) The goal is to pay your fair share efficiently, keeping more of your hard-earned money working for you instead of working for the government. **When you combine smart tax planning with solid income investing, you're not just building wealth—you're keeping it.**

FINDING YOUR SWEET SPOT ON THE RISK CONTINUUM

Now you know all about the five pillars of income investing—and why I've built my whole investment philosophy on them. Have I convinced you yet?

Let's say, for the sake of this final chapter, that I have. You've had a "Eureka!" moment reading this book. You leaped up from your chair and said, "By Jove, I think he's got it!" You even ordered four buckets on Amazon to really bring the bucket system to life.

Clearly, you must be a smart person! (And according to the stats, a happy retiree.) So what's next?

You need to answer three crucial questions:

- How soon will you need to live off this money?

- What percentage should you allocate to each bucket?
- What's the risk associated with the balance you choose?

Benjamin Graham, the father of value investing, laid out a simple rule in his book *The Intelligent Investor*: Always keep some balance between stocks and bonds—never go below 25 percent or above 75 percent in either category.[15]

If you're forty years old, how much time do you have as an investor? Well, unless you've been a power saver since age twenty, you have roughly twenty to twenty-five years before you'll likely be in a position of complete financial freedom. Then you'll have another twenty to thirty years in retirement. That means you effectively have a half century of investing ahead of you.

A half century is a long time horizon. Remember this before you decide on your bucket balance. More years as an investor means more time to participate when our economy and stock market have good years. So unless you're completely afraid of taking any risk whatsoever, don't ignore the growth bucket, even if it's the most volatile of the four.

One of my favorite pieces of investment wisdom comes from John Bogle, legendary investor and founder of the eponymous Vanguard Group, who maintained anything less than a ten-year horizon was just speculation.[16] It might sound idealistic, but not when you consider the turbulent decade we suffered through from 2000 to 2010. If you flip back to Figure 8.11, you can see the resilience and recovery times during stock market downturns, proving that balance works.

If you don't like your risk level, you can modify it two ways:

1. **Shift your allocation:** Move a higher percentage from the income bucket to the growth or alternative income buckets. Less in bonds means less predictability but higher potential returns.

2. **Change the components:** Adjust the risk within each bucket by choosing more conservative or aggressive investments (i.e., small-cap growth stocks vs. dividends stocks, or high-yield bonds over US treasury bonds).

Target-date funds essentially put this process on autopilot, automatically becoming more conservative as you age, shifting from a high percentage of stocks when you are young to a high percentage of bonds once you are in retirement. Think of this as automatically adjusting the level of risk you're taking over time.

Now, I'm not a giant fan of target-date funds, as I think they often get too conservative too soon. But the concept of adjusting risk over time is important.

BRINGING IT ALL TOGETHER: YOUR PAYCHECK MACHINE

When everything's working properly, your portfolio can be a paycheck machine that generates predictable cash flow regardless of market volatility. Here's what you should expect from each bucket.

TARGET YIELDS BY BUCKET

- Income bucket: 2–5 percent (corporate bonds, government bonds, high-yield bonds, etc.) and will depend on prevailing interest rates
- Growth bucket: 2–4 percent (lower or no dividends from growth companies and higher payouts from dividend-paying stocks)
- Alternative bucket: 3–6 percent (REITs, energy pipeline companies, preferred stocks, and closed-end funds)

- Cash bucket: 0–4 percent (money market funds, CDs, etc.) depending on where the Fed is setting interest rates

THINKING THROUGH A GOOD AND BAD YEAR

Let's look at a hypothetical good and bad year.

In a good market year, your growth bucket might appreciate 15 percent while also paying 3 percent in dividends. Your income bucket could deliver a steady 4 percent in interest, alternatives could provide more distributions on top of this, and even cash should be earning you prevailing cash interest rates. Your portfolio value rises, but more importantly, your cash flow remains predictable.

In a bad market year, your growth bucket might drop 15 percent, but the dividend payouts should not stop, and if they paid you 3 percent last year, then there's little reason your stocks don't at least pay the same amount of cash flow again. Your income bucket continues delivering 4 percent, alternatives provide similar distributions on top of this, and cash continues to pay you as well. Your portfolio value declined, but your monthly income barely budged. This is why cash flow predictability matters so much for retirees.

The best part about this system is that your income doesn't disappear when markets get choppy—it just keeps flowing from multiple sources while you wait for values to recover. As we've seen from a historical perspective, the storm always quiets eventually.

To recap the five pillars of income investing:

1. **Stocks are the engine, bonds the seat belt, alternatives the boosters, cash the sleep aid to help you SWAN—sleep well at night.** Each bucket serves a specific purpose in your wealth-building machine.

2. **Dividend growth protects purchasing power.** Companies that consistently raise dividends typically outpace inflation by a wide margin, giving you built-in cost-of-living adjustments.
3. **Dry powder keeps you steady.** High-quality bonds provide the emotional cushion that helps prevent you from making terrible decisions during market downturns—and gives you a reservoir to pull from when stocks need time to recover.
4. **Strategic withdrawal rates maximize longevity.** The classic 4 percent rule provides a foundation, but modern research suggests more of a range starting at 4 percent (the 4+ percent rule of thumb), which is assisted when you're drawing from multiple income streams rather than just selling shares.
5. **Tax efficiency keeps more money in your pocket.** Smart asset location and withdrawal sequencing can save you a considerable amount of taxes over your lifetime, allowing more of your money to be working for you.

You did it. I know this chapter was longer than a CVS receipt, but you made it to the end. Now go drink some water—my wife insists.

All jokes aside, you don't have to be a numbers wonk who gets excited about compound-interest calculations to benefit from income investing. The concepts are straightforward. In honor of my office wall, we'll make it simple: **Stay invested, stay diversified, and stay disciplined.**

Market timing is a fool's errand; chasing the latest hot investment trend can be a wealth destroyer. But building a balanced, systematic approach to income investing—one that generates cash flow from multiple sources while providing reasonable growth potential—that's a strategy that can work for decades. I've seen it do exactly that.

Your portfolio should work as hard as you did to build it. Like Lowell Miller said, let your money "sit quietly off in the corner working for you while you go about your business." You've done your time in meetings, endured performance reviews, and smiled through retirement parties for people whose names you couldn't remember. Now it's your money's turn to work weekends and holidays—and you get to sleep in.

CONCLUSION

Time to Say Yes

I'm excited for you.

Regardless of where you are on this journey, whether you're in your thirties and you've got a long way to go, or you're in your sixties and you're seeking a guide to help you stay on track or maybe tweak how you think about a happy retirement, the Retire Sooner Method is for anyone who wants to use it. There's nothing like learning from a population of successful people—the happy retirees we've detailed and studied in this book.

I think the very act of getting this far in the Retire Sooner Method means you are well on the way to being one of America's happiest retirees. I also think the chances of you winding up as one of America's unhappiest retirees is slim to none. And Slim's out of town.

We started this journey with a simple premise: Happy retirees aren't just lucky—they're following a method. **After analyzing data from 1,200 Americans across all fifty states, we uncovered the five key secrets that unlock a 96 percent chance of retirement happiness.** Not 95 percent. Not 94 percent. Ninety-six percent.

Think about that for a moment. In a world where nothing seems certain—where the economy swings from boom to bust, where inflation eats away at purchasing power, where even the iPhone gets "upgraded" every year whether we want it or not—there's actually a formula that works. Not perfectly, but pretty darn close.

Remember the powerful finding from our research that launched a thousand ships (or at the very least 230 pages)? It was this: Simply getting to retirement—i.e., being in a financial position where you have the freedom to choose whether to work full-time—was a seismic inflection point. The participants who could confidently answer yes to that question showed happiness levels 21 percent higher than those who said no. That single word represents crossing the threshold from financial obligation to financial freedom.

Let's review the five fundamental secrets of the Retire Sooner Method:

- **Secret #1: Hit the Money Green Zones ($1 million or more in investable assets).** You discovered that reaching the financial Green Zone isn't about keeping up with the Joneses or hitting some arbitrary number you saw in a magazine; it's about having sufficient investable assets to generate the income you need with confidence and security.
- **Secret #2: Supercharge your super activities, aka, hobbies on steroids (280+ extra hours of core pursuits).** We learned that the happiest retirees invest 280+ *more* hours annually in activities that provide daily and yearly purpose, whether it's pickleball, volunteering at your church, or finally learning to paint those landscapes you've been threatening to create for decades.
- **Secret #3: Get a life! (i.e., a community).** In a world where 17 percent of Americans report having zero close friends, happy retirees buck the trend. They cultivate four or more meaningful relationships—not hundreds of social media connections but real people who know your story and your struggles.

- **Secret #4: Map out your future (a written financial plan and/or happy retiree life map).** Remember Charlotte and Ray, lying awake at three a.m. worrying about every headline? That's what happens without a plan. But when you map out both your financial future and your life vision, that buzzing mosquito of worry finally goes quiet.
- **Secret #5: Activate your Happy Retiree Superpower (a generous portion of quality sleep).** Lynne was right all along. Sleep isn't just rest—it's the foundation that makes everything else possible, and happy retirees inherently know this. When you're getting quality sleep, you make better decisions, maintain stronger relationships, enjoy your core pursuits more, and have more energy to live a joyous life.

Of course, making the right lifestyle choices isn't enough if your money can't keep up with inflation or provide the cash flow you need. The five pillars of income investing aren't a get-rich-quick scheme—they're a systematic approach to creating sustainable, worry-free income for decades.

Through multi-asset-class income investing, dividend growth, dry powder reserves, strategic withdrawals, and tax efficiency, you're not just preserving wealth—you're creating a paycheck machine that keeps running even while you're taking your daily walk to get in those steps. Your portfolio should work as hard as you did to build it.

WHAT'S NEXT?

You may have noticed that, even though we focused on five secrets, we managed to weave in many of the other twenty-five-plus findings that influence retirement satisfaction. The Retire Sooner Method is not static or rigid, something that can only be achieved by an immutable number of steps or strategies. I wouldn't doubt that you're nailing way more than five happy retiree traits anyway, including many of the ones we've outlined throughout the book.

Personally, I like visual guides, as you can probably tell from all the charts and drawings. As I mentioned earlier, beyond the straightforward appendix in this book, the QR code on this page will take you to a complete full-color guide to the research we've covered, with several additional charts as a bonus. This can be a great way to identify additional areas where small improvements might boost the probability of your retirement happiness. There's never a 100 percent guarantee, so the way you mix and match these habits, behaviors, and principles is entirely up to you.

WWW.YOURWEALTH.COM/RETIRESOONERMETHOD

GETTING INTO SHAPE

When I think about how to balance everything we've covered in this book, there's a lot to consider. We've talked about financial security—our means—and about building a rich set of core pursuits to create and maintain purpose—our meaning—and how to align those two complementary forces. To make this a repeatable process, my firm uses what we call the SHAPE Framework with families, which you can learn more about in Appendix B.

Here's the big takeaway: Retirement isn't a destination you arrive at and then coast. It's a twenty-, thirty-, even forty-year journey that requires the same intentionality you brought to building your career. As always, with work comes opportunity. You have the power to design a retirement that's uniquely yours. You're not stuck with your company's one-size-fits-all pension plan or limited to whatever Social Security provides. You can build something better, using a method that works.

You might start by taking an honest inventory. Maybe your finances are rock solid, but your social engagement could use a little work, and you know you need to get back out there, join some groups, and make some friends. Maybe you've got great friendships but no written plan. Maybe you've got everything except decent sleep because you're lying awake at night, worrying about rising costs and unrest in the world.

Whatever gaps you discover, tackle them systematically. Don't try to fix everything at once—pick one and make a plan for how you're going to address it. Then pick another one. And another. That's how to create the retirement you actually want instead of leaving it to chance or good intentions.

Because here's what I've learned after working with thousands of families: **A happy retirement is about having a plan that works, relationships that matter, core pursuits that fulfill you, rest that restores you, and enough financial security to support it all.**

You hold the secret in your hands. What happens next is up to you.

"Say Yes Cake"

(THE ULTIMATE RETIRE SOONER RECIPE)

mix together until happy

1. **$1.0 MILLION OR MORE OF INVESTABLE ASSETS.** *A solid financial base helps reduce stress and boost long-term fiscal confidence.*

2. **2½ HOURS (OR MORE) OF CORE PURSUITS.** *Daily hobbies and passions are the zest that brings your days to life.*

3. **SOCIAL SEASONING.** *You consistently nurture 4 or more close connections, also known as friends.*

4. **HAVE A FORMAL WRITTEN FINANCIAL PLAN.** *Your guide and reducer of financial anxiety for the future.*

5. **A GENEROUS PORTION OF QUALITY SLEEP.** *Great sleep quietly powers your energy, health, and happiness.*

THIS IS THE ULTIMATE HAPPY RETIREE RECIPE—*a powerful combination of five ingredients that, when mixed together, give you a very good chance of being a Happy Retiree. Can you be an HROB with just three or four of these? Sure. But when you've got all five in place, you're cooking up something truly special:*

A life recipe with a 96% success rate for happiness in retirement.

APPENDIX A

Research and Data Descriptions

If you liked all the charts, tables, graphs, and drawings in this book, that warms my math-loving heart. This appendix is meant to provide additional clarity and interpretation of what each visual in the book is really saying. You can also think of this section as a more comprehensive checklist for the Retire Sooner Method, an easy reference to becoming one of the happiest retirees in America—which I sincerely hope you will be.

Figure 1.1. Happiness Levels of Americans Who Are Retired vs. Non Retired. Eighty percent of retirees report being happy vs. only 66 percent of non-retirees. America is full of happy people; in fact, 74 percent of our research's total population falls into the somewhat happy or very happy group. The chart here shows that based on our research, there is a 21 percent jump in happiness levels for those who are retired compared to those who have yet to retire.

Figure 1.2. Happiness Levels by Investable Assets. Figure 1.2 shows a clear relationship between happiness and investable assets across three zones. Happiness levels are well below the baseline for those with under $100,000 in assets (Red Zone), stabilize near the baseline between \$100,000 and \$999,999 (Yellow Zone), and rise meaningfully once assets reach \$1 million or more (Green Zone). Above this level, happiness continues to increase but at a diminishing rate, illustrating a plateau effect where additional wealth produces smaller incremental gains in happiness.

Figure 1.3. Average Number of Core Pursuits. This chart shows that happy retirees average five or more core pursuits, while unhappy retirees have four or fewer, highlighting that engaging in a greater number of unique core pursuits (hobbies on steroids) is clearly associated with higher happiness. While an individual's mix of core pursuits may change over time, the key takeaway is to maintain at least five at any given time.

Figure 1.4. The Percentage of HROBs vs. UROBs Who Say Yes to "I Get Enough Sleep." This chart shows that happy retirees are nearly twice as likely to say they get "enough" sleep relative to unhappy retirees. In the data, 69 percent of happy retirees report getting sufficient sleep compared to just 38 percent of unhappy retirees.

Figure 2.1. Americans' Reported Biggest Challenges When Contemplating Retirement. This chart shows Americans' top reported challenges when contemplating retirement: Uncontrollable economic conditions (like inflation and an unpredictable stock market) ranked first, and declining physical and/or cognitive health ranked second. In addition, nearly half of Americans report worrying about running out of money, highlighting that financial anxiety remains a major concern independent of specific market or inflation risks.

Figure 2.2. Percentage of Americans (by Investable Assets) Who Rank Fear of Running Out of Money as a Top Financial Concern. Figure 2.2 shows that the fear of running out of money persists across all asset levels. In the data, 51 percent of Americans with $100,000–$499,999 in investable assets rank this as a top concern, followed by 45 percent of those with $500,000–$999,999, 39 percent with $1.0–$2.9 million, and even 24 percent of those with $3 million or more—demonstrating that financial anxiety does not disappear simply with higher wealth.

Figure 2.3. Happiness Levels by Investable Assets. This chart is the same as Figure 1.2.

Figure 2.4. Happiness Levels by Household Income. This chart shows a clear relationship between household income and happiness across three zones. Americans earning under $50,000 fall well below the happiness baseline (Red Zone), while those earning $50,000–$99,999 cluster near the baseline (Yellow Zone). Once household income reaches $100,000 or more, happiness levels rise meaningfully into the Green Zone, peaking in the $150,000–$199,999 range before leveling off. This pattern suggests a practical retirement income target of $100,000+ annually, where financial stress declines and happiness increases.

Figure 2.5. Happiness Levels Rise with Mortgage Payoff in Sight. There's a clear relationship when it comes to paying off our primary mortgage. This chart shows a strong relationship between mortgage payoff timing and happiness. Americans with more than thirty years remaining on their mortgage are 19 percent below the happiness baseline, while those with ten to twenty-nine years remaining cluster near the baseline. Once mortgage payoff is within nine years—or the home is fully paid off—happiness levels rise sharply, placing retirees into another financial Green Zone.

Figure 2.6. Effects of Withdrawal Rates and Likelihood of Success After Thirty Years in Retirement Relative to Various Portfolio Allocations. This table shows the probability of retirement savings lasting thirty years under different withdrawal rates and portfolio allocations, adjusted for inflation. Starting withdrawals around 4 percent combined with a moderately balanced portfolio produce very high success rates—between 98 percent and 100 percent. By contrast, higher starting withdrawal rates, such as 6 percent with a 60/40 stock–bond allocation, reduce the likelihood of success to roughly 67 percent.

Figure 3.1. Number of Unique Core Pursuits, Unhappy vs. Happy Retirees. This chart shows a clear inflection point in retirement happiness: Happy retirees have on average five or more core pursuits while unhappy retirees have four or fewer. Crossing the five-core-pursuit threshold creates a self-enforcing cascade where one meaningful activity naturally leads to another.

Figure 3.2. Core Pursuits—Time Spent Per Week, Unhappy vs. Happy Retirees. This chart shows that happy retirees spend significantly more time on core pursuits—about two hours and forty minutes a day versus one hour and fifty minutes for unhappy retirees. That's 280+ extra hours per year of purposeful activity. The data points to a clear sweet spot: Aim for at least 2.5 hours per day engaged in activities you love.

Figure 3.3. Top Categories of Core Pursuits That Bring Americans the Most Joy in Retirement. This chart summarizes the main themes that emerged from our open-ended question: *What brings you the most joy and purpose in retirement?* There's no wrong answer here—retirees find meaning in all kinds of core pursuits, but creativity, adventure, volunteering, and physical activity topped the list.

Figure 3.4. Number of Adventure-Related Core Pursuits. This chart shows that adventure plays a meaningful role in retirement happiness. Happy retirees average 1.9 adventure-related core pursuits compared to just 1.2 for unhappy retirees—and notably, 57 percent of unhappy retirees report having zero adventure-related core pursuits.

Figure 3.5. Top Core Pursuits By Activity That Bring Americans the Most Joy in Retirement. This wheel highlights a wide range of activities that bring joy in retirement, from group activities and travel to gardening, music, and dancing. While this fun list is diverse, one theme stands out: Most of these pursuits are done with other people, reinforcing that social connection is one of the most powerful drivers of retirement happiness.

Figure 3.6. Percentage of Americans Who Report Having a Strong Sense of Purpose. This chart shows that happy retirees are nearly three times more likely to report having a strong sense of purpose. The data suggests this purpose is not found, but created, built through sustained engagement in multiple core pursuits they enjoy and spend meaningful time doing.

Figure 4.1. Close Friendships Among Americans. This chart shows an overall long-term decline in close friendships among Americans from 1990 to 2024. The share of Americans with two or fewer close friends more than doubled, rising from 16 percent to 37 percent; those with three to four close friends remained relatively stable; while the percentage reporting five or more close friends declined sharply, from 64 percent to 42 percent.

Figure 4.2. Top Core Pursuits By Activity That Bring Americans the Most Joy in Retirement. This chart is the same as Figure 3.5.

Figure 4.3. Happiness Relative to Number of Close Connections/ Friendships. This chart reveals a strong relationship between the number of close friendships and happiness. Americans with one to two close friends fall well below the US happiness baseline, while those with four or more are above it. The data indicates a tipping point around 3.6 close connections, suggesting that four is a meaningful threshold, and five or more is even better for happiness levels.

Figure 4.4. I Have Enough Close Friends. This chart shows that happy retirees are about twice as likely relative to unhappy retirees to say they have enough close friends. In the data, 81 percent of happy retirees reported "enough" close connections, compared to 38 percent of unhappy retirees. Essentially, happy retirees are two times more likely to say they have enough close friends.

Figure 4.5. How Easy or Difficult Do You Think It Is to Make Close Personal Friends or Connections at Each Stage of Adult Life. This chart illustrates that making close friends becomes harder with age. Eighty-two percent of Americans in their thirties report it is extremely or somewhat easy versus just 34 percent in their sixties. However, happier older adults are significantly more likely than their neutral or unhappy peers to report that making friends remains relatively easy, even in later decades of life.

Figure 4.6. Marriage Matters. This chart shows that happy retirees are about 50 percent more likely than unhappy retirees to report being married or living with a spouse or partner, highlighting the strong relationship between marriage and retirement happiness.

Figure 4.7. Share of Retirement-Age Population Who Live Alone. This chart shows that unhappy retirees are about 60 percent more likely than happy retirees to report living alone. While living with a spouse or partner is associated with the highest levels of happiness, retirees living with anyone, such as friends, relatives, or in shared communities, consistently report higher happiness levels than those who live alone.

Figure 5.1. Confidence Around Financial Future. This chart shows that happy retirees are 2.25 times more likely than unhappy retirees to have a written financial plan. They are also roughly half as likely to report anxiety about their financial future.

Figure 5.2. Retirement Timeline: Step 1. This illustration shows how to begin mapping out your retirement by hand using a simple timeline that captures your current assets, age, planning horizon, and target retirement zone.

Figure 5.3. Retirement Timeline: Step 2. This illustration shows how to add key financial milestones and project future asset levels on your retirement timeline, helping translate today's savings and contributions into a clear view of what's possible by retirement.

Figure 5.4. Retirement Timeline: Step 3. This illustration shows how to layer in retirement income streams, investment withdrawals, Social Security, pension, and other sources to estimate total annual income once those streams all begin.

Figure 5.5. Retirement Timeline: Step 4. This illustration shows how the retirement timeline can be further customized to include multiple income sources, part-time work, and future financial goals, helping clarify how income builds over time as more streams come online.

Figure 5.6. Retirement Life Map. This illustration gives an example of a hand-drawn retirement life map illustrating how daily activities, core pursuits, relationships, and long-term goals can be visually integrated into a cohesive vision for retirement. Wendy's life map demonstrates how combining ongoing skills, new interests, health goals, community, and adventure can translate everyday purpose into meaningful yearly milestones.

Figure 6.1. I Get Enough Sleep. This chart is the same as Figure 1.4.

Figure 7.1. Americans' Reported Biggest Challenges When Contemplating Retirement. This chart is the same as Figure 2.1.

Figure 7.2. US Consumer Price Index. This chart illustrates the relentless long-term decline in the purchasing power of the US consumer dollar, which fell by approximately 48 percent from January 2000 to December 2025 due to inflation.

Figure 7.3. Consumer Price Index for All Urban Consumers: Used Cars and Trucks. This chart illustrates how inflation in a specific category, such as used cars and trucks, erodes purchasing power over time, showing how dollars left uninvested in your wallet or under the mattress lose value as prices rise. This chart shows how one "car dollar" in 2020 was only worth about $.75 by 2025.

Figure 8.1. Turning $10 into $20 Using Two Very Different Approaches. This table compares two hypothetical paths to turning $10 into $20: stock "ABC" driven purely by price appreciation and stock "XYZ" driven solely by the accumulation of income through dividends.

Figure 8.2. Impact of Inflation: US Consumer Dollar (Cash) Purchasing Power vs. Stocks. This chart compares the purchasing power of cash (the US consumer dollar) with stock market returns over time. Since 2005, cash purchasing power of the US dollar has declined by more than 40 percent, while the S&P has risen over 700 percent on a total return basis and nearly 300 percent after adjusting for inflation, highlighting the long-term advantage of investing in stocks over holding uninvested cash.

Figure 8.3. S&P 500: Maximum Intra-Year Drawdown vs. End of Year Total Returns. This chart shows that while the S&P 500 has delivered an average annualized return of roughly 12 percent since 1928, it has also experienced an average intra-year drawdown of about 16 percent. This highlights that long-term market gains have historically required staying invested through frequent and sometimes significant declines.

Figure 8.4. The Average Investor Underperforms Due to Market Timing. This chart is based on Bloomberg data and a DALBAR Inc. study titled *2025 Quantitative Analysis of Investor Behavior*, which examines annualized returns from 2005 to 2024. While stocks averaged 10.4 percent, a balanced 60/40 stock–bond portfolio returned 7.8 percent, and the average asset-allocation investor earned only about 3.8 percent. DALBAR's analysis—based on net mutual fund flows, including purchases, sales, and exchanges—shows that investor timing decisions significantly reduced returns, resulting in performance that was less than half of what a balanced stock–bond mix returned.

Figure 8.5. Missing the Best Days in the Market. This chart illustrates the impact of missing the market's best days on long-term returns. From 1995 to the present, staying fully invested in the S&P 500 produced roughly 8.8 percent annualized returns. Missing just the best ten days reduced returns to about 6 percent, while missing the best twenty days cut returns roughly in half—demonstrating how difficult and costly market timing can be.

Figure 8.6. Bull & Bear Markets. This chart illustrates the historical pattern of S&P 500 bull and bear markets. Bull markets have typically been longer, averaging 5.3 years; bear markets, while historically much shorter on average, are difficult for many investors to endure. Research shows that the pain investors feel during market declines is more than twice as strong as the joy felt during market advances. This underscores the importance of staying invested despite the pain of bear markets.

Figure 8.7. The Cash Flow Generating Bucket System at Work: Pre-Retirement/Accumulation Phase. This chart illustrates the four-bucket system during the pre-retirement (accumulation) phase. The buckets vary in size based on importance, stage of life, preferences, and risk tolerance, which together determine your overall asset allocation. Each bucket generates income through dividends, interest, or distributions. And during the accumulation phase, that income can be reinvested to support long-term compounding.

Figure 8.8. The Cash Flow Generating Bucket System at Work: Retirement/Distribution Phase. This chart illustrates the bucket system during the retirement (distribution) phase. In this phase, income generated from dividends, interest, and distributions can flow into the cash bucket, which is used for living expenses, giving you a steady paycheck in retirement. Any excess cash flow not needed for spending can be reinvested into the appropriate bucket, helping maintain balance and long-term sustainability.

Figure 8.9. Annualized Dividend Growth of US Stocks vs. Inflation. This chart compares dividend growth relative to inflation over time. Historically, S&P 500 dividends have grown at an average annual rate of about 3.7 percent, compared to inflation of roughly 2.1 percent. More recently, in the twelve months ending June 2025, dividends grew 6.6 percent versus inflation of 2.7 percent, illustrating how dividend growth can act as built-in cost-of-living adjustments over time.

Figure 8.10. Power of Compounding Dividend Growth. This chart illustrates the power of compounding dividend growth. From 2015 to 2025, a $1 million investment in DGRO grew to approximately $2.43 million, producing an annualized return of 8.7 percent. Over the same period, annual dividend income more than doubled—from $24,217 to $53,405—representing 7.7 percent annual dividend growth and increasing the original yield from 2.4 percent to a 5.3 percent yield at cost.

Figure 8.11. Diversification and Recovery Time During Equity Market Pullbacks. This chart shows that portfolio diversification can significantly shorten recovery times after stock market drawdowns. From 1988 through 2024, a 100 percent equity portfolio has historically taken nearly twenty-four months to recover from major pullbacks, while a balanced 60/40 percent stock–bond portfolio has recovered in an average of just 10.8 months.

Here's the QR code one more time, in case your phone is nearby and you'd like to see these charts in more vivid color. Plus, with this online version, you will find several bonus charts of happy retiree research, i.e., how happiness increases with age.

WWW.YOURWEALTH.COM/RETIRESOONERMETHOD

APPENDIX B

Planning Tools and Framework

This appendix features two tools that bring retirement planning to life: the SHAPE Framework and a Holistiplan tax scenario showing how smart tax planning lets you keep more of what you earn. Use these as starting points for conversations with your financial advisor.

The **SHAPE Framework** is a model developed by Capital Investment Advisors, LLC to help individuals think about the key ingredients of a happy, fulfilling retirement. It highlights the importance of balancing Means—the financial and physical foundations that support life (security and health)—with Meaning—the pursuits and relationships that give life purpose (pursuits and engagement). At the center is Alignment, representing the harmony between what you have and what matters most to you.

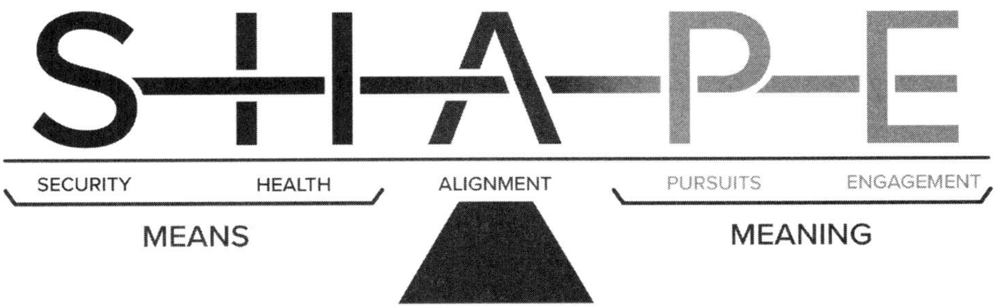

Holistiplan is a financial planning software platform designed to help advisors analyze a client's tax situation more efficiently and accurately. The system uses a client's tax return to automatically identify key planning opportunities and generate forward-looking tax projections.

In this book, the Holistiplan calculation included on the next page illustrates how tax planning can fit into a broader retirement strategy. The example is intended for educational purposes only—to show how integrated financial and tax planning tools can help retirees make more informed decisions about income, investments, and withdrawals.

DISCLAIMER

The concepts, findings, and opinions expressed herein are based in part on our Money and Happiness in America national survey conducted in 2025 of 1,200 US adults aged fifty and older. The survey was conducted by Capital Investment Advisors, LLC in partnership with The Center for Generational Kinetics. Participation in the survey was voluntary, and all responses were self-reported by the individuals surveyed. Only completed responses were included in the analysis. Accordingly, the survey results reflect the perspectives of those who participated and may not be representative of all US adults in this age group. References to specific financial figures, asset levels, or lifestyle outcomes are based on aggregate data and general trends observed among survey participants. Individual results will vary.

The views, thoughts, and opinions expressed in this book belong solely to the author, and not necessarily to the author's employer, Capital Investment Advisors, LLC ("CIA"). This publication is provided for informational and educational purposes only and should not be regarded as personalized investment advice or a reflection of the performance of CIA or its clients.

SCENARIO ANALYSIS | SAMPLE SCENARIO

Note: Calculations are not audited and should be reviewed with a tax professional.

	Scenario 1 $50K IRA withdraw	Scenario 2 $100K IRA withdraw
GENERAL INFORMATION		
Year	2025	2025
Calculation	Current Law	Current Law
Inflation Assumption	3.00%	3.00%
INCOME		
1040 INCOME		
IRA Distributions	$50,000	$100,000
SCHEDULED INCOME		
SCHEDULE 1 INCOME		
Total Income	$50,000	$100,000
Schedule 1 Deductions	$0	$0
Adjusted Gross Income	$50,000	$100,000
Standard/ Itemized Deductions	$31,500 (standard)	$31,500 (standard)
Taxable Income	$18,500	$68,500
Total Tax	$1,850	$7,743
Marginal Bracket	10.0%	12.0%
Effective Rate	10.0%	11.3%
Total Tax (Net of Refundable Credits)	$1,850	$7,743
FICA		
FICA	$0	$0
Tax Plus FICA	$1,850	$7,743
Effective Tax on Next $1,000 Ordinary Income	10.0%	12.0%
FEDERAL WITHHOLDING CALCULATOR		
Total Tax	$1,850	$7,743
Safe Harbor 90% of Total Tax	$1,665	$6,969
Difference	$1,850	$7,743

continued →

Holistiplan reports—Disclosures for Interactive Performance Tools
Information Provided by You Information that you provided about your assets, financial goals, and personal situation are key assumptions for the calculations and projections in this illustration. If any of the assumptions are incorrect, you should notify your Financial Advisor. Even small changes in assumptions can have a substantial impact on the results shown in this Report.
Inherent Limitations in Financial Model Results: Investment outcomes in the real world are the results of a near infinite set of variables, few of which can be accurately anticipated. Any financial model, such as the one used to obtain these results, can only consider a small subset of the factors that may affect investment outcomes and the ability to accurately anticipate those few factors is limited. As investment returns, inflation, taxes, and other economic conditions vary from the assumptions, your actual results will vary from those presented.
This report does not provide recommendations for any products or securities. Indices are unmanaged and do not include fees or operating expenses and are not available for investment. It is important to note that the broad categories that are used are not comprehensive and other investments that are not considered may have characteristics that are similar or superior to the categories that are used in this report.
Fees and Expenses: Fees and expenses are not included (i.e., fund fees, account fees, product fees, and advisory fees). Inclusion of those fees results in lower returns, which would affect the probability of achieving any particular outcome.
Taxes: This report includes limited accounting for taxes. We have estimated federal, state, and local taxes based on current laws with simplified deduction, exemption, and tax bracket parameters of the current year. In the projection, tax parameters are adjusted by an inflation assumption professional. Future tax laws may be significantly different than current tax laws and may result in higher or lower taxes due than what are reflected within this report.
General Disclosures The term "plan" or "planning," when used within a report, does not imply that a recommendation has been made to implement one or more financial plans or make a particular investment. Nor does the plan or report provide legal, accounting, financial, tax, or other advice. Rather, a report and the illustrations therein provide a summary of certain potential financial strategies. A report provides projections based on various assumptions and are therefore hypothetical in nature and does not guarantee investment returns or outcomes. You should consult your tax and/or legal advisors before implementing any transactions and/or strategies concerning your finances.
Any report generated by a third-party system or provided by us should in no way, and is not intended to, replace your receipt and review of account statements provided by your account custodian. It is important to compare the information in reports with the statements you receive from the custodian(s) for your account(s). Please note that there may be minor variations due to calculation methodologies.

The financial discussions, examples, and data presented throughout this book are illustrative in nature and are not intended as individualized financial, investment, tax, or legal advice. Readers should consult qualified professionals regarding their personal financial circumstances prior to implementing any investment strategy. The information provided is not an offer or solicitation of any product or service.

Current and future markets may differ significantly from those illustrated herein. Past performance is not a guarantee of future returns.

Any changes to assumptions that may have been made in preparing this material (e.g., the retiree surveys) could have a material impact on the information presented. There is no representation or warranty as to the current accuracy, reliability, or completeness of, nor liability for, decisions based on such information and it should not be relied on as such.

Investing in securities involves risk of loss. Equity investments are subject to market risk or the risk that stocks will decline in response to such factors as adverse company news or industry developments or a general economic decline. Dividend yield is one component of performance and should not be the only consideration for investment. Dividends are not guaranteed and will fluctuate. Among other things, fixed-income investments are subject to interest rate risk, reinvestment risk, and inflation risk. Real estate investment trusts (REITS) are subject to interest rate risks and changes in real estate values, property taxes, and occupancy rates. Master limited partnerships have risks associated with the specific industry or industries in which the partnership invests, such as the risks of investing in real estate, oil, and gas industries. Asset allocation and diversification are investment methods used to help manage risk. They do not guarantee investment returns or eliminate risk of loss, including in a declining market.

The Holistiplan tax calculation shown in this appendix is for illustrative purposes only. It does not represent personalized tax advice, nor does it reflect the circumstances of any specific individual or family. The example is based on hypothetical data and assumptions that may differ from actual results. Readers should consult a qualified tax professional or financial advisor regarding their own tax and financial situations. Holistiplan is a third-party software provider not affiliated with Capital Investment Advisors, LLC. Inclusion of this material does not constitute an endorsement or guarantee of any product, service, or outcome.

While every effort has been made to ensure accuracy, neither the author nor Capital Investment Advisors, LLC makes any representations or warranties regarding the completeness or reliability of the information provided.

Reader's comments about *The Retire Sooner Method* are those of the individuals providing them and pertain only to the author's book. The statements should not be interpreted as reflecting the experience of advisory clients or as a guarantee of retirement outcomes.

Acknowledgments

THE RETIRE SOONER METHOD is much more than a book. It has been a long-running research project, spanning more than fifteen years of working with, learning from, researching, and studying what really makes the happiest retirees tick. This book represents the culmination of that work. And because of that, there are a lot of people I'd like to thank.

First and foremost, I want to thank **happy retirees themselves**.

Over the past decade and a half, I've had countless conversations, meetings, emails, and chance interactions with retirees that, sometimes without me even realizing it at first, turned into mini–master classes on how to do retirement right—and occasionally, how to do it wrong. These real-world lessons have shaped my thinking more than any textbook ever could. They've influenced how I advise families, how I think about money and happiness, and ultimately how the Retire Sooner Method came to life.

Along the same lines, I owe a huge thank-you to our radio and podcast listeners and readers, who have taken the time to email me over the years to share their stories, lessons, struggles, and wins. Many of those notes have been priceless learning opportunities. Some challenged my assumptions. Others reinforced what I was already seeing in the data. And quite a few directly helped shape the ideas, examples, and frameworks that appear in this book.

A special thank-you goes to the people who were brave enough to share their real-life stories so others could learn from them. Joe and Cindy, Wendy, and others who appear in these pages opened up about their decisions, their habits, and their journeys. Their stories add real-world texture and humanity to the research, and I'm deeply grateful for their willingness to allow others to learn from their experiences.

Speaking of research, this project would not be what it is without it.

For this project, we were able to take our research and insights to an entirely new level thanks to Jason Dorsey and his team at the Center for Generational Kinetics (CGK). Without the depth, rigor, and discipline of the research we conducted together, much of this book would have remained opinion and educated guesswork. Instead, we were able to rely on real data—actual human financial and lifestyle behavior—to inform these pages.

I also want to thank my writing team, affectionately known as "The Avengers." Bree Barton, a very serious writer and the Tony Stark of the group, brought clarity, style, and heart to the process. Ryan Doolittle, a future SNL star, kept things human and occasionally hilarious. And the entire team at Greenleaf Book Group helped guide this project into a finished book with patience, professionalism, and genuine care for both the work and the message behind it.

I'm deeply grateful to my business partners at Capital Investment Advisors and to the entire CIA family. Your support, encouragement, and belief in this work made it possible to see this project through. This book reflects not just my ideas, but the culture, core values, and shared mission we've built together over the years.

Thank you as well to the amazing Porchlight Design Group for helping bring some of my favorite charts to life and to the Capital Investment Advisors research team, led by Connor Miller, whose work underpins so much of the data we explored. I'm also grateful to the

CIA marketing team, Mallory Boggs, and her associate, Baby Larry, who somehow managed to finesse the finest details of the Retire Sooner Method. Thank you to Andrea Rizk for helping make sure the world understands why this work matters, and to Jeff Lloyd, our lead brainstorm analyst, for his insight and creativity throughout the process.

Finally, to my wife and our four boys—thank you for your patience, your encouragement, and your perfectly timed "Are you done yet?" motivation. You've supported me through every stage of this long journey and are my most cherished core pursuit.

When you put it all together, this book—like most things that matter in life—exists because of a very real team of humans who care deeply about the work and the mission behind it. I'm incredibly thankful for everyone who has been part of this journey and who shares the same passion for helping Americans retire sooner, in the right way, and making it more possible.

Notes

CHAPTER 1

1. *2022 Survey of Consumer Finances* (Board of Governors of the Federal Reserve Board, 2023), https://doi.org/10.17016/8799.
2. Kelly Kenneally, *Retirement Insecurity 2024: Americans' View of Retirement* (National Institute on Retirement Security, 2024), https://www.nirsonline.org/research/retirementinsecurity2024/.
3. Paula Pant, host, *Afford Anything*, podcast, episode 153, "Why I Hate the FIRE Movement, Says Suze Orman," Cumulus Podcast Network, September 30, 2018, https://affordanything.com/153-hate-fire-movement-suze-orman/.

4. This graph and all others in the manuscript, unless noted otherwise, is derived from data collected in the 2025 Money and Happiness in America survey conducted by Capital Investment Advisors, LLC in partnership with The Center for Generational Kinetics.

CHAPTER 2

1. Throughout this book, names and identifying details of individuals have been changed to protect their privacy and confidentiality.

2. "The 4% Rule," Bill Bengen, https://www.bengenfs.com/the-4-percent-rule/.
3. Bill Bengen, *A Richer Retirement: Supercharging the 4% Rule to Spend More and Enjoy More* (Wiley, 2025).

CHAPTER 3

1. The experiences described are those of the individuals quoted. Their circumstances are unique and may not be representative of the experiences of others. No specific financial or retirement outcomes are guaranteed or implied.
2. Joe Saul-Sehy, host, *The Stacking Benjamins Show*, podcast, SB1638, "The Case Against Early Retirement," January 31, 2025, https://www.stackingbenjamins.com/the-case-against-early-retirement-1638/.

CHAPTER 4

1. Daniel A. Cox and Sam Pressler, "Disconnected: The Growing Class Divide in American Civic Life," Survey Center on American Life, August 22, 2024, https://www.americansurveycenter.org/research/disconnected-places-and-spaces.
2. All information in this section comes from the following podcast: Wes Moss, host, *Retire Sooner*, podcast, episode #162, "How Neuroscience Proves the Importance of Making & Maintaining Personal Connections with Michael Platt," June 28, 2023, https://www.wesmoss.com/podcasts/162-how-neuroscience-proves-the-importance-of-making-maintaining-personal-connections-with-michael-platt/.

CHAPTER 5

1. Teresa M. Amabile, Lotte Bailyn, Marcy Crary, Douglas T. Hall, and Kathy E. Kram, *Retiring: Creating a Life That Works for You* (Routledge, 2024).
2. Teresa M. Amabile, Lotte Bailyn, Marcy Crary, Douglas T. Hall, and Kathy E. Kram, "Retire Without Regrets," *Harvard Business Review* (November–December 2024), https://hbr.org/2024/11/retire-without-regrets.

CHAPTER 6

1. Shalini Paruthi, Lee J. Brooks, Carolyn D'Ambosio et al., "Recommended Amount of Sleep for Pediatric Populations: A Consensus Statement of the American Academy of Sleep Medicine," *Journal of Clinical Sleep Medicine* 12, no. 6 (2016), https://aasm.org/resources/pdf/pediatricsleepdurationconsensus.pdf.

2. American Academy of Sleep Medicine, "Seven or More Hours of Sleep Per Night: A Health Necessity for Adults," press release, June 1, 2025, https://aasm.org/seven-or-more-hours-of-sleep-per-night-a-health-necessity-for-adults/.

3. Julie Corliss, "Too Little Sleep May Be Hard on Your Heart," Harvard Health Publishing, Harvard Medical School, August 1, 2022, https://www.health.harvard.edu/heart-health/too-little-sleep-may-be-hard-on-your-heart.

4. Erin Bryant, "Lack of Sleep in Middle Age May Increase Dementia Risk," National Institutes of Health, April 27, 2021, https://www.nih.gov/news-events/nih-research-matters/lack-sleep-middle-age-may-increase-dementia-risk.

5. Katherine Bindley, Xavier Martinez, and Rebecca Picciotto, "AI Startup Founders Tout a Winning Formula—No Booze, No Sleep, No Fun," *The Wall Street Journal*, September 11, 2025, https://www.wsj.com/business/entrepreneurship/artificial-intelligence-startup-founders-bc730406.

6. Dan Buettner, *The Blue Zones: Lessons for Living Longer from the People Who've Lived the Longest* (National Geographic, 2010).

7. Allianz Life, "More Americans Are Worried About Running Out of Money Than Death," press release, April 22, 2025, https://www.allianzlife.com/about/newsroom/2025-Press-Releases/Americans-Are-More-Worried-About-Running-Out-of-Money-Than-Death.

8. American Academy of Sleep Medicine, "AASM Sleep Prioritization Survey," 2024 https://aasm.org/wp-content/uploads/2024/10/sleep-prioritization-survey-2024-financial-worries.pdf.

9. Tracey Sletten, Matthew Weaver, Russell Foster et al., "The Importance of Sleep Regularity: A Consensus Statement of the National Sleep Foundation Sleep Timing and Variability Panel," *Sleep Health: Journal of the National Sleep Foundation* 9, no. 6 (December 2023): 801–20, https://www.sleephealthjournal.org/article/S2352-7218(23)00166-3/.

10. James Clear, *Atomic Habits: An Easy & Proven Way to Build Good Habits & Break Bad Ones* (Avery, 2018), 32.

11. Anne-Marie Chang, Daniel Aeschbach, Jeanne Duffy, and Charles Czeisler, "Evening Use of Light-Emitting eReaders Negatively Affects Sleep, Circadian Timing, and Next-Morning Alertness," *Proceedings of the National Academy of Sciences* 112, no. 4 (December 22, 2014): 1232–37, https://doi.org/10.1073/pnas.1418490112.

12. "Blue Light Has a Dark Side," Harvard Health Publishing, Harvard Medical School, July 24, 2024, https://www.health.harvard.edu/staying-healthy/blue-light-has-a-dark-side.

CHAPTER 7

1. Jack Nicas and Ana Lankes, "Think 9% Inflation Is Bad? Try 90%," *The New York Times*, August 6, 2022, https://www.nytimes.com/2022/08/06/business/inflation-argentina.html.

2. "The Weimar Republic 1918–1929—Edexcel," BBC, https://www.bbc.co.uk/bitesize/guides/z9y64j6/revision/5.

3. "Consumer Price Index for All Urban Consumers: Used Cars and Trucks in U.S. City Average," Federal Reserve Bank of St. Louis, updated January 13, 2026, https://fred.stlouisfed.org/series/CUSR0000SETA02.

4. Capital Investment Advisors research using FRED data. "Consumer Price Index for All Urban Consumers: Food in U.S. City Average," Federal Reserve Bank of St. Louis, updated January 13, 2026, https://fred.stlouisfed.org/series/CPIUFDNS.

5. "Consumer Price Index, 1913–," Federal Reserve Bank of Minneapolis, https://www.minneapolisfed.org/about-us/monetary-policy/inflation-calculator/consumer-price-index-1913-.

6. Megan Henney, "US Home Prices Have Surged 47% Since the Start of 2020," Fox Business, May 13, 2024, https://www.foxbusiness.com/economy/us-home-prices-have-surged-47-since-start-2020.

CHAPTER 8

1. Marcus Lu, "Charted: The Declining Purchasing Power of the U.S. Dollar," Visual Capitalist, November 30, 2025, https://www.visualcapitalist.com/charted-the-declining-purchasing-power-of-the-u-s-dollar/.

2. Ben Carlson, "This Is Normal," *A Wealth of Common Sense*, January 25, 2022, https://awealthofcommonsense.com/2022/01/this-is-normal/.

3. Michelle Klotz, "Loss Aversion—Everything You Need to Know," InsideBE, https://insidebe.com/articles/loss-aversion/.

4. Stock Sharks (@stocksharks), "On average, bull markets run five times longer than bear markets. Bulls: +254% over 5 years Bears: –31% over 1 year," Twitter (now X), December 8, 2025, https://www.threads.com/@stocksharks/post/DSBVohXir5m/on-average-bull-markets-run-five-times-longer-than-bear-markets-bulls-over?hl=en.

5. Capital Investment Advisors investment research utilizing Bloomberg data.

6. Lowell Miller, *The Single Best Investment*, 2nd ed. (Print Project, 2006), 18.

7. While dividends are not guaranteed and can be cut or eliminated, they do provide investors with the opportunity for upside potential while providing some level of downside protection in negative markets.

8. Sean Ross, "Understanding S&P 500 Dividend Yield: Historical Trends and Insights," Investopedia, November 26, 2025, https://www.investopedia.com/articles/markets/071616/history-sp-500-dividend-yield.asp; "Historical Inflation Rates: 1914–2026," US Inflation Calculator, https://www.usinflationcalculator.com/inflation/historical-inflation-rates/.

9. PRNewswire, "S&P Dow Jones Indices Reports U.S. Common Indicated Dividend Payments Increase of $7.4 Billion in Q2 2025 as Dividend Growth Continues to Slow," S&P Global, press release, July 7, 2025, https://press.spglobal.com/2025-07-07-S-P-Dow-Jones-Indices-Reports-U-S-Common-Indicated-Dividend-Payments-Increase-of-7-4-Billion-in-Q2-2025-as-Dividend-Growth-Continues-to-Slow.

10. The mention of any company is provided to you for informational purposes and as an example only and is not to be considered investment advice or recommendation or an endorsement of any company. The reader should not assume that an investment in the securities identified was or will be profitable. Stock prices fluctuate, sometimes rapidly and dramatically, due to factors affecting individual companies, particular industries or sectors, or general market conditions. Dividends are not guaranteed and can increase, decrease, or be eliminated without notice.

11. "Lockheed Martin Corp. (LMT)," YCharts, https://ycharts.com/companies/LMT.

12. "Johnson & Johnson (JNJ)," YCharts, https://ycharts.com/companies/JNJ.

13. "Dividend History," Apple, https://investor.apple.com/dividend-history/default.aspx.

14. William P. Bengen, *A Richer Retirement: Supercharging the 4% Rule to Spend More and Enjoy More* (John Wiley & Sons, 2025); Lorie Konish, "He Invented the 4% Rule of Retirement Income—Why He Calls Inflation Retirees' 'Greatest Enemy,'" CNBC, September 3, 2025, https://www.cnbc.com/2025/09/03/4percent-rule-inflation-retirement.html.

15. Benjamin Graham, *The Intelligent Investor: The Definitive Book on Value Investing* (Harper Business, 2006).

16. Wes Moss, "The Legacy of Vanguard Founder John Bogle," *The Atlanta Journal-Constitution*, February 1, 2019, https://www.ajc.com/business/wes-moss-the-legacy-vanguard-founder-john-bogle/2PM3kFdUh-PW1sJpq4tWrtO/.

Index

A

AASM (American Academy of Sleep Medicine), 114, 116, 119–20
accumulation phase, in bucket system, 166, 169–70, 208–9
adaptability, 94
adult communities, 69–70, 86
adventure pursuits
  general discussion, 56–58
  and joy, 55
  number of, 57, 203
  overview, 20, 50
  and social connection, 72–74
Afford Anything (podcast), 12
after-tax assets, 182–83
"AI Startup Founders Tout a Winning Formula—No Booze, No Sleep, No Fun" (*Wall Street Journal*), 117
alternative income bucket, 168, 169–71, 189–90
alternative income investments, 160–61
American Academy of Sleep Medicine (AASM), 114, 116, 119–20
anticipatory happiness, 57
anxiety over economic future
  as challenge of retirement, 30, 133–34, 200
  general discussion, 29–31
  impact on sleep, 119–20, 122–26
Apple, 174–75
Aristotle, 4
asset allocation, 165
Atomic Habits (Clear), 127

B

balance, in investing, 165
bear markets, 158–59, 177, 208
Bengen, William, 41–42, 181
Bitcoin, 161
blue light, impact on sleep, 127–28
Blue Zones, 118
Bogle, John, 188
bonds
  in bucket system, 167–68, 169–71
  dry powder principle, 177–80
  income investing, 159
  inflation defense strategies, 144–45
  risk management, 187–88
  tax efficiency, 184
brain, social connections and, 74–78
bucket system
  accumulation vs. retirement phases, 169–71, 208–9
  alternative income bucket, 168
  cash bucket, 166–67
  in good and bad year scenarios, 190
  growth bucket, 168–69
  income bucket, 167–68
  overview, 166
  paycheck machine, 189–90
  risk management, 187–89
Buettner, Dan, 118
bull markets, 158–59, 177, 208

C

capital losses and gains, 184–85
car prices, impact of inflation on, 137–38, 139, 206

cash
  cash bucket, 166–67, 169–71, 190
  dry powder principle, 177–80
  flow of, in bucket system, 169–71, 208
  as safety net, 160–61
categories of core pursuits, right mix of, 50, 54–55
certificate of deposit (CD), 161, 166–67
challenges of retirement, 29–31, 200
charts
  descriptions of, 199–210
  overview, 15
  QR code for, 18, 33, 196, 210
children, 83, 113–14
Clear, James, 127
close friendships, decline in, 70–72, 203
commodities, investing in, 162, 169
community
  children, 83
  compound effect of social connection, 83–85
  and core pursuits, 72–74
  decline in close friendships, 70–72, 203
  enough philosophy, 129
  example of couple with, 69–70
  and happiness, 87–88
  living alone, 81–82, 204–5
  making new friends, 78–80, 204
  marriage, 81–82, 204
  neuroscience of connection, 74–78
  number of friendships, 76–78, 204
  overview, 10, 194
  socialization strategies, 86–87
  wealth and friendships, 80–81
Consumer Price Index (CPI), 135, 138, 139, 154–55, 206
consumer staples, investing in, 142
contributions, 98
core pursuit cascade, 52
Core Pursuit Finder, 48
core pursuits. *See also* adventure pursuits; life map
  community and, 72–74
  Core Pursuit Finder, 48
  creative pursuits, 55–56, 72–74, 106
  daily and yearly purpose, 65–66
  enough philosophy, 129
  example of couple with, 47–50
  general discussion, 18–20
  joy from, 61–63, 202, 203
  number of, 51–53, 200, 202
  overview, 10, 194
  physical activity, 60–61
  right mix of categories, 54–55
  sense of purpose, 64–65
  time spent on, 53–54
  top core pursuits by activity, 62
  volunteering, 59
  writing exercise for, 67–68
core values, identifying, 108, 109
CPI (Consumer Price Index), 135, 138, 139, 154–55, 206
creative pursuits, 55–56, 72–74, 106
crypto, investing in, 161
cultural confusion around sleep, 116–19

D

da Vinci, Leonardo, 21
daily purpose, 65–66, 108
data descriptions, 199–210
deflation, 135–36
DGRO (iShares Core Dividend Growth ETF), 175–76
DID principle, 162–66
diminishing marginal returns, 35
direct indexing, 185–86
disclaimer, 212–16
distributions, 163
diversification, 163–65, 178–79, 209
dividend growth
  inflation vs., 173, 209
  overview, 172–74, 191
  patience in, 175–77
  power of compounding, 176, 209
  in practice, 174–75
dividends, 153, 162
dragon of inflation, taming, 139–41
dry powder principle, 177–80, 191

E

economic future, anxiety over, 29–31, 133–34, 200
eMoney, 95–96
energy sector, investing in, 142

enough philosophy, 129
entrepreneurship, 145–47
equity market pullbacks, recovery from, 178–79, 209
eudaemonic happiness, 4
exercise
as core pursuit, 20, 50, 55, 60–61
in life map, 106
and social connection, 72–74

F

family
children and grandchildren, 83
core pursuits related to, 55
marriage, 81–82, 204
"Fast Friend" exercises, 87
fear of running out of money, 29–31, 201
Federal Reserve, 136
financial anxiety
as challenge of retirement, 30, 133–34, 200
general discussion, 29–31
impact on sleep, 119–20, 122–26
financial plan
assets tomorrow, adding, 98–99
creating at any age, 103–4
drawing basic, 97, 205
enough philosophy, 129
financial goals, adding in, 102–3, 205
and friendships, 80
general discussion, 89–91
and happiness, 205
Harvard retirement study, 91–95
income streams, adding up, 99–101, 205
key financial years/ages, adding, 98–99, 205
making, 95–96
overview, 10, 195
five pillars of income investing. *See also* multi-asset-class income investing
dividend growth, 172–77
dry powder principle, 177–80
4+ percent rule of thumb, 180–82
in good and bad year scenarios, 190
overview, 149–52, 190–92
paycheck machine, 189–90
risk management, 187–89
tax efficiency, 182–87
five secrets to happiness
overview of, 9–11, 194–96
recipe for happiness, 22–24
fixed-income securities, 145
4+ percent rule of thumb
general discussion, 41–45
in income investing approach, 180–82
overview, 191
401(k)s, 98, 99, 182–83
friendships
compound effect of social connection, 83–85
and core pursuits, 72–74
decline in, 70–72, 203
enough philosophy, 129
example of couple with, 69–70
and happiness, 87–88
living arrangements, 81–82, 204–5
making new friends, 78–80, 204
neuroscience of connection, 74–78
number of, 76–78, 204
overview, 10, 194
socialization strategies, 86–87
and wealth, 80–81

G

gig work, 55
gold, investing in, 162, 169
Graham, Benjamin, 188
grandchildren, 83
Green Zone
anxiety over economic future, 29–31
enough philosophy, 129
example of couple in, 25–29
4+ percent rule of thumb, 41–45
and friendships, 80
general discussion, 34–36
and happiness, 32–33
and household income, 36–38
how to get into, 31–32
mortgage payoff, 38–41
overview, 10, 194
plateau effect in, 35
where most Americans stand, 11–12
grocery prices, impact of inflation on, 138
growth bucket, 168–71, 189–90

H

happiest retiree on the block (HROB)
close friendships of, 77–78, 204
core pursuits of, 51, 53, 57, 202
living arrangements of, 81–82, 204–5
marriage of, 81, 204
overview, 4
sense of purpose of, 63, 203
sleep habits of, 21–22, 115, 200
Happy Gilmore 2 (film), 84
happy retirees
and community, 76, 87–88
defining happiness, 4
financial planning by, 21
five secrets of, 9–11, 22–24, 194–96
and investable assets, 199–200
lifestyle habits of, 18–20
money and happiness zones, 16–18
power of yes, 13–16
recipe for, 22–24
retired vs. non-retired happiness, 3, 13–15, 199
sleep habits of, 21–22
where most Americans stand, 11–12
Harvard retirement study, 91–95
health care, investing in, 142
hedonistic happiness, 4
high-yield savings accounts, 161, 166–67
hobbies. *See* core pursuits
Holistiplan, 212, 213–14
homes
location considerations, 86
mortgage payoff, 38–41, 145–47, 201
real estate investments, 143–44
household income, 36–38, 201
HROB. *See* happiest retiree on the block

I

ikigai, 14, 16
income bucket, 167–68, 169–71, 189–90
income during retirement, 36–38, 99–101, 201
income investing. *See also* multi-asset-class income investing
bull vs. bear markets, 158–59, 208
dividend growth, 172–77
dry powder principle, 177–80
4+ percent rule of thumb, 180–82
in good and bad year scenarios, 190
overview, 149–52, 190–92, 195
paycheck machine, 189–90
risk management, 187–89
tax efficiency, 182–87
inflation
bonds and conservative investments, fighting with, 144–45
dividend growth vs., 172–73, 209
fluctuation in, 139–41
general discussion, 133–37
and grocery prices, 138
private business investments, fighting with, 145–47
purchasing power, decline in, 154–55, 207
and real estate investments, 139
real estate investments, fighting with, 143–44
stock investments, fighting with, 141–43
and vehicle prices, 137–38, 139
intellectual challenges, in life map, 106
The Intelligent Investor (Graham), 188
interest, 162
investing. *See also* multi-asset-class income investing
bull vs. bear markets, 158–59, 208
dividend growth, 172–77
dry powder principle, 177–80
formula for, 150–51
4+ percent rule of thumb, 180–82
in good and bad year scenarios, 190
inflation defense strategies, 141–47
market-timing decisions, 156–58, 207–8
overview, 149–52, 190–92
paycheck machine, 189–90
recovery from market pullbacks, 178–79, 209
risk management, 187–89
tax efficiency, 182–87
investing in friendships, 87
investment income, 99, 101

J

Johnson & Johnson (JNJ), 174
joy, core pursuits linked to, 10, 55, 62, 202, 203

K

Kavanagh, Mike, 120

L

learning pursuits, 55, 106
life map
  creating, 107–11
  drawing, 109–10
  example of, 104–7, 206
  overview, 10, 195
  power of, 107, 111
  spotting alignment gaps, 109
  warm-up lists, 108–9
lifestyle habits, 18–20. *See also* community; core pursuits; sleep
liquid assets, desired amount of. *See* Green Zone
living alone, 81–82, 204–5
location of home, 86
Lockheed Martin (LMT), 174
loss aversion, 155–56, 177

M

making new friends, 78–80, 204
mapping future. *See also* financial plan; life map
  enough philosophy, 129
  general discussion, 89–91
  Harvard retirement study, 91–95
  overview, 10, 21, 195
  power of, 111
market-timing decisions, 156–58, 207–8
marriage, 81–82, 204
median net worth for Americans, 11–12
Miller, Lowell, 170–71, 192
Money and Happiness in America study, 3, 5, 9–11
Money Green Zone
  anxiety over economic future, 29–31
  enough philosophy, 129
  example of couple in, 25–29
  4+ percent rule of thumb, 41–45
  and friendships, 80
  general discussion, 34–36
  and happiness, 32–33
  and household income, 36–38
  how to get into, 31–32
  mortgage payoff, 38–41
  overview, 10, 194
  plateau effect in, 35
  where most Americans stand, 11–12
money market funds
  in cash bucket, 166–67
  dry powder principle, 177–80
  outpacing inflation with, 145
  as safety net, 161
  after-tax assets, 182–83
mortgage payoff, 38–41, 145–47, 201
Moss, John, 104, 118
multi-asset-class income investing
  alternative income bucket, 168
  alternative income in, 160–61
  bonds in, 159
  bucket system, 166–71
  bull vs. bear markets, 158–59, 208
  cash (and cash equivalents) in, 160–61
  cash bucket, 166–67
  commodities in, 162
  crypto in, 161
  DID principle, 162–66
  growth bucket, 168–69
  income bucket, 167–68
  market-timing decisions, 156–58, 207–8
  overview, 152–54
  stocks in, 154–59
  turning $10 into $20, 154, 206
municipal bonds, 184

N

National Sleep Foundation, 126
nest egg. *See* Green Zone
network effects, 83–84
neuroscience of social connection, 74–78

O

Orman, Suze, 12, 35

P

part-time work, 100
paycheck machine, 189–90
pension payments, 100
pharmaceutical companies, investing in, 142
physical activity
  as core pursuit, 20, 50, 55, 60–61
  in life map, 106
  and social connection, 72–74
pillars of income investing. *See also* multi-asset-class income investing
  dividend growth, 172–77
  dry powder principle, 177–80
  4+ percent rule of thumb, 180–82
  in good and bad year scenarios, 190
  overview, 149–52, 190–92
  paycheck machine, 189–90
  risk management, 187–89
  tax efficiency, 182–87
planning tools, 211–15
Platt, Michael L., 74–76, 78, 80, 86–87
pre-tax assets, 182–83
pretax withdrawal scenario, 183–84
price stability, 136
private business investments, 145–47, 160, 168
Proceedings of the National Academy of Sciences, 127–28
purchasing power, decline in, 134–37, 154–55, 207
"pure growth" vs. "pure income" investing, 154
purpose vacuum, 94

Q

quantity of sleep, recommendations for, 116

R

real estate investment trusts (REITs), 144, 160, 168
real estate investments, 139, 143–44
recipe for happiness, 22–24, 198
recovery from market pullbacks, 178–79, 209
Red Zone
  general discussion, 33–34
  and happiness, 17–18, 32–33
  income in, 36–37
  and years to mortgage payoff, 38–41
rental properties, 99, 144
research and data descriptions, 199–210
Retire Sooner Method
  five secrets of happiness, 9–11, 22–24, 194–96
  how it all began, 3–5
  QR code for resources, 18, 33, 196, 210
  "Say Yes Cake," 198
Retire Sooner podcast, 2–3, 74–76
"Retire Without Regrets" (*Harvard Business Review*), 91–95
retirement phase, in bucket system, 170–71, 208–9
retirement tax advantage, 186
retirement timeline. *See* timeline, retirement
Rich Ratio, 121–26
risk in investments, managing, 187–89
Roth conversion window, 186–87
Roth IRAs, 182–83
running out of money, fear of, 29–31, 201
Russell 3000 ETF, 185–86

S

S&P 500, 154–58, 172–73, 207–9
savings accounts, 161, 166–67, 182–83
"Say Yes Cake," 198
schedule for sleep, 126–27
secrets of happiness
  overview of, 9–11, 194–96
  recipe for happiness, 22–24
sense of purpose, 51, 63, 64–65, 203
SHAPE Framework, 196, 211
silver, investing in, 162, 169
The Single Best Investment (Miller), 170–71
sleep
  cultural confusion around, 116–19

enough philosophy, 129
example of couple with quality, 122–26
general discussion, 21–22, 113–16
and money worries, 119–21
overview, 10–11, 195
recommended quantity of, 116
and Rich Ratio, 121–22
structure and consistency of, 126–28
in unhappy vs. happy retirees, 200
Sleep Research Society, 116
social activities, 55
social connections
children, 83
compound effect of, 83–85
and core pursuits, 20, 72–74
decline in close friendships, 70–72, 203
enough philosophy, 129
example of couple with, 69–70
and happiness, 87–88
in life map, 106
living alone, 81–82, 204–5
making new friends, 78–80, 204
marriage, 81–82, 204
neuroscience of connection, 74–78
number of friendships, 76–78, 204
overview, 10
socialization strategies, 86–87
wealth and friendships, 80–81
Social Security income, 98, 99, 101
socialization strategies, 86–87
spiritual activities, 55
stocks
in bucket system, 168–71
bull and bear markets, 158–59, 208
direct indexing, 185–86
dividend growth, 172–77, 209
growth versus income investing, 152–54
inflation defense strategies, 141–43, 154–55
market-timing decisions, 156–58, 207–8
risk management, 187–88
tax loss harvesting, 184–85
strategic withdrawal scenario, 183
SWAN (Sleep Well at Night), 120, 124–25
synchrony, 75

T

target retirement zone, 97, 101
target-date funds, 189
tax efficiency
all pretax withdrawal scenario, 183–84
and direct indexing, 185–86
overview, 182, 191
retirement tax advantage, 186
and Roth conversion window, 186–87
strategic withdrawal scenario, 183
tax loss harvesting, 184–85
tax silos, 182–83
tax-efficient investments, 184
tax-free assets, 182–83
tax-inefficient investments, 184
time spent on core pursuits, 20, 50, 53–54, 60, 202
timeline, retirement
assets tomorrow, adding, 98–99, 205
drawing basic, 97, 205
financial goals, adding in, 102–4, 205
general discussion, 95–96
income streams, adding up, 99–101, 205
key financial years/ages, adding, 98–99, 205
overview, 97
to-do's, reframing, 67
traditional IRAs, 182–83
2025 Money and Happiness in America study, 3, 5, 9–11
20-percent increase in happiness after retirement, 3

U

uncontrollable economic conditions, concern over, 133–34, 200
unhappiest retiree on the block (UROB)
core pursuits of, 51, 53, 57, 202
friendships of, 77–78, 204
living alone, 81–82, 204–5
marriage, 81, 204
sense of purpose in, 63, 203
sleep habits of, 21–22, 115, 200
unpredictable economic conditions, anxiety over, 29–31, 133–34, 200

US Consumer Price Index, 135, 154–55, 206
utilities, investing in, 142

V

vehicle prices, impact of inflation on, 137–38, 139, 206
venture capital, 160, 168
volunteering, 55, 59, 72–74

W

wealth and friendships, 80–81
withdrawal rate, 41–45, 180–82, 191, 202
writing exercise for core pursuits, 67–68
written financial plan
  assets tomorrow, adding, 98–99
  creating at any age, 103–4
  drawing basic, 97, 205
  enough philosophy, 129
  financial goals, adding in, 102–3, 205
  and friendships, 80
  general discussion, 89–91
  and happiness, 205
  Harvard retirement study, 91–95
  income streams, adding up, 99–101, 205
  key financial years/ages, adding, 98–99, 205
  making, 95–96
  overview, 10, 195

Y

yearly purpose, 65–66, 108
Yellow Zone
  general discussion, 34
  and happiness, 17–18, 32–33
  income in, 36–37
  and years to mortgage payoff, 38–41
yes, power of, 13–16
Yield at Cost (YAC), 172–75, 176
You Can Retire Sooner Than You Think (Moss), 3, 9, 151

Author photograph by Ben Rollins

About the Author

WES MOSS, CERTIFIED FINANCIAL PLANNER™, is a managing partner and chief investment strategist at Capital Investment Advisors, a fee-only SEC registered investment advisory firm with over $8 billion* in assets under management. A dedicated financial educator, Moss has spent his career helping Americans retire sooner and happier through his research-driven Retire Sooner Method. Moss is the author of several books, including *What the Happiest Retirees Know*, and host of the long-running *Money Matters* radio show and the *Retire Sooner* podcast. A regular *Forbes* contributor and frequently quoted media source, Moss lives in Atlanta, where he leads a team committed to helping families find purpose and financial security in retirement.

* As of 12/31/2025